THE FILMS OF

JAMES WOODS

By Chris Wade

THE FILMS OF JAMES WOODS

by Chris Wade

Wisdom Twins Books, 2022

wisdomtwinsbooks.weebly.com

Text Copyright of Chris Wade, 2022

Cover image courtesy of Photofest

THE FILMS OF
JAMES WOODS

CONTENTS

"I never fought for green M & M's and a bigger trailer. I always fought for a better performance, a better approach to the scene, and a better interpretation of the script."

- James Woods to the author, 2021

INTRODUCTION

"I am proud of admitting that I am unequivocally an idiot savant when it comes to acting." - James Woods

James Woods has been entertaining and thrilling us on TV and the big screen for so long that it's hard to imagine a time when he wasn't around. It's as if he's always been there, on the hot lists of movie producers and directors, arriving boldly on a film set, keeping his co-stars on their toes. His name has been a permanent fixture on movie posters for decades, his face on VHS and DVD covers since they were first made available in stores. Woods is a film icon, but to me he's the kind of actor people might take for granted. "It's James Woods, he's always good!" It's true, of course, but I wonder if casual movie fans really grasp the level of work and dedication that goes into each of his performances. From Videodrome and Once Upon a Time in America to Salvador and Casino, from Ghosts of Mississippi and Nixon to The Virgin Suicides and TV's Ray Donovan, it's a varied and formidable body of work.

Woods has excelled in all manner of genres from the 1970s to recent times, but there are two particular roles that signalled his true arrival. All the great icons of film had to enter the movie pantheon at some point. With De Niro, people will say Taxi Driver; with Pacino, The Godfather; Hoffman, The Graduate. With James Woods though, he's been in so many great films down the years, and has always given his all in each one, that it seems hard to believe he suddenly shot into the public consciousness with his dual performances as Karl Weiss in the hit mini-series Holocaust (1978) and the psycho cop killer Greg Powell in The Onion Field (1979).

Of course, it isn't as simple as this, for no one is truly an overnight sensation. Prior to The Onion Field, Woods had been treading the boards to great acclaim and appearing on TV and in movies since the early 1970's. His current vitality and never-weakening spirit defy the fact he's been on our screens for fifty years. And his work really is the stuff of legend, even from the very start. The next time you watch The Way We Were (1973), for instance, remember he's Barbra Streisand's boyfriend before she is whisked away by Robert Redford. When you re-view such seminal 70's fare as The Gambler and Night Moves, you'll see the young Woods in minor roles. He was also in the likes of Kojak, The Streets of San Francisco, the first ever Rockford Files episode, as well as the first Welcome Back, Kotter - all this before he was a lead cast member of Holocaust (1979). His list of seventies credits alone, before his name was known to the public,

10

would make a career that most actors would look back on with pride. For Woods though, this was merely the opening chapter, and he was destined for a kind of cinematic immortality. The Onion Field, where he delivers one of the best performances of the 1970's, brought in one of the finest actors of our time.

It was in the 1980's then that Woods began to establish himself. From overlooked gems like Fast Walking and Split Image (both 1982), to David Cronenberg's nightmarish Videodrome (1983) and Sergio Leone's masterpiece, Once Upon a Time in America (1984), he was by far film's most intense, dangerous live wire. But he paralleled these harder edged parts with touching performances of more sensitive, often brittle men; especially in Promise (1986), where he won an Emmy and a Golden Globe for his work as D.J., the schizophrenic taken in by his brother (James Garner) after the death of their mother. Not only is it one of the finest pieces of acting in television history (it is still the most awarded TV film of all time), it's one of the best of the whole decade in any medium. Woods, that familiar face we all know, disappears behind the shell of that tormented, but vulnerable young man.

Remarkably in the same year he was Oscar nominated for his part in Oliver Stone's brilliant Salvador, where he played sleazy photographer Richard Boyle. The jagged tour de force was a sign that Woods' abilities had no bounds. After this he went on a remarkable run on TV and film, giving us some of the most memorable characters of the era; the enthralling Best Seller (1987) with Brian Dennehy; Cop (1988), which proved he could carry a more mainstream thriller (though his cop was very different from the usual ones of Hollywood movies); The Boost (1988), where he played a drug addicted yuppie crippled by a deep insecurity; True Believer (1989), as a committed ex-radical lawyer taking on a murder cas/

Immediate Family (1989), as an ordinary man adopting a child with his wife, played by Glenn Close; and at the end of that decade with My Name is Bill W. (1989), the seminal TV movie about the formation of the Alcoholics Anonymous, a performance which won garnered him another Best Actor Emmy. It plays regularly at AA meetings across the world to this day.

In the 1990's he seemed to stretch himself even further. At first there were more fun, mainstream pictures like The Hard Way (1991) with Michael J. Fox, Straight Talk (1992) with the great Dolly Parton, and the underrated Diggstown (1992) with Louis Gossett, Jr. There was also his hugely acclaimed turn as Roy Cohn in the brilliant TV film, Citizen Cohn (1992), widely regarded to be one of his most awe-inspiring performances. He also gave a remarkable run of supporting parts in such films as The Specialist (1994), Martin Scorsese's Casino (1995), in Oliver Stone's Nixon (also 1995), and as the sadistic, white supremacist in Rob Reiner's Ghosts of Mississippi (1996), a performance which earned him his second Oscar nomination.

The mid 90's were a particular high for Woods; he was fearless, diving into a part with all he had, no matter the size of the pay check was or the size of the role in question. The nineties also illustrated his knack of hopping from style to style, from genre to genre. This is best contrasted when you hold up key credits from the period; like Killer: A Journal of Murder (1995), where he plays America's first documented serial killer, Carl Panzram; the committed real life lawyer in Indictment: The McMartin Trial (1995); and Disney's Hercules (1997), where he voices the fire-headed lord of the underworld, Hades, a performance which for me and many others is one of the greatest in Disney history. The end of the decade saw more Woods gold, with his role as Jack Crow in John Carpenter's excellent Vampires (1998), the startling crime drama Another Day in Paradise

(1998), and the supporting parts in four true gems all released in 1999: The General's Daughter, Sofia Coppola's The Virgin Suicides, Oliver Stone's Any Given Sunday and Clint Eastwood's True Crime. It was a fitting end to one of the most fruitful decades for any film actor in history.

In the new millennium he continued to work in the highest quality TV and film, despite the fact he was often disillusioned with the industry and the roles he was getting offered. He began lending his talents to more light-hearted fare; like his hilarious cameo as an exorcist in Scary Movie 2 (2001), and the charming Stuart Little 2 (2002), voicing a sinister falcon. He was still taking risks, too; in the quirky, almost abstract Northfork (2003); as the father with Parkinson's Disease in This Girl's Life (2003); the foul-mouthed dad in the razor sharp Pretty Persuasion (2005); the frightening football coach in the remake of Straw Dogs (2011). There are also moments of pure joy in this period too, like his self referential cameos in Be Cool (2005), Entourage (2006), his ongoing part as himself in Family Guy, and his hilarious appearances in two episodes of the underrated Andrew Dice Clay series, Dice (2017). And let us not forget the string of meaty performances he has given on TV in the new millennium; like the brilliant TV film, Dirty Pictures (2000), which garnered more acclaim and award nominations for Woods; The Rudy Giuliani Story (2003), another critical hit for him; on ER (2006), giving a staggering performance as a sufferer of ALS; the often overlooked Too Big to Fail (2011); as the hot shot lawyer Sebastian Stark in the two excellent seasons of Shark (which ran from 2006 to 2008); and as the merciless hitman Sully in Season One of Ray Donovan (2013).

Listing such a body of work proves above all that Woods has consistently made good choices. But beyond recounting his filmography, the work needs to be seen, taken in, even studied to be fully appreciated as a complete contribution to the history of film and TV. Anyone who respects an artist's journey, someone who gives his craft his all, it's natural to be in awe of Woods' commitment to each role, to the sheer energy and dedication on display. Yes, he defines the part as written, often enhances what the screenwriter put on the page, and when playing a real person respects the being in question (if they are worthy of respect, of course), but Woods also expresses himself in the performances. He seems to look for answers, solutions, keys to human behaviour, explanations for psychological traits. Woods is clearly a man fascinated with what it is to be human, and he informs us on the human condition time and time again. It is this - along with many other things - which makes his performances so weirdly compulsive. His men are often flawed, unsavoury, even nightmarish, but they are all given multi-facets, enough contradictions and quirks to make them fully believable, rather than mere flat caricatures. We often understand his anti-heroes, even if we don't support what they do. And the excitement in watching Woods comes in the fact that one feels he is walking a tight rope at all times, that he is on the edge, unsure of where things are going, even if Woods the actor has much of it figured out before the word "action" gets called. It's this sense of danger, of wild spontaneity, which makes watching James Woods truly enthralling. I can count such actors on one hand, who are alive in the moment, and lend their creations (or the characters they are currently inhabiting at least) a real-life sense of vitality. That spontaneous magic is there in the finest jazz, in the spirited recordings of vintage Bob Dylan, in the early films of Marlon Brando. You get the feeling of magic happening, of something special being put down. Though unique in his own way this definitely applies to Woods' work.

Woods in 2006.

In one of our interviews for this book, James said something which jumped out at me. He seemed to define his craft and his whole career in one go: "If someone were to ask me to what I attribute my success as an actor, I would say, I never really knew my character until the last day of shooting, and then I finally had an idea of who he might be. And if I am involved in the making of the movie and the exploration of the character, as it is happening and captured on film, it becomes not so much a performance for the audience, but a conversation with the audience. And they get to participate. When people say they got very involved in my performances, I always felt I was sharing my performance with the viewer, not acting at them. It's almost like acting with them."

If we go back to his breakthrough film, The Onion Field may have been an unsavoury part, but Woods' vitality in the role opened up many doors for him, and he became a reliable, popular actor in Hollywood. While in some ways he was still an outsider, the studios welcomed him in the 80's and 90's, sure of the raw power he could lend their film. Yet even when he was firmly a part of the film industry, a box office draw, a "star" in the truest sense (meaning people recognised him, and came to see a film because he was in it), Woods still seemed to be on the outside looking in, often ironically and with a playful cynicism, the dangerous gambler who toyed with Hollywood, playfully mocked it even, but contradictorily loved aspects of it at the same time. It seems he kept his feet on the floor, continued taking roles that interested him, rather than making commercial choices for the sake of the pay.

His became the most ideal of careers. Woods had and still has influence, but because he is very much an actor in the real sense of the word, he is not fooled by the blockbuster mentality. Woods has been in some huge films, yes, but he somehow always seems more present, more real, more alive, and more dangerous than everyone else around him. Again, it feels like you are coming across a man who insists on being genuine. In interviews, on the screen - either way, you feel he represents a kind of truth. He isn't afraid to say certain things and does not shy away from what could be seen as a controversial role or viewpoint.

But he often had to fight for parts, and that idea of "never being the right guy" may have stung at times, but also undoubtedly inspired him to push more, to make sure we took notice of him. In a 1989 interview Woods joked, "I've always thought, if I were on a plane and there were an earthquake and all of California fell into the sea and there were no movie actors left, if I landed and called up the studios and said, 'Hey, fellas, I'm still here, there's one left,' some executive would say, 'Well, yeah, but I'm sure there's a football player in Kansas who would be better for the part. Just stay at the airport. We'll get back to you.'" Woods' success was a firm two fingers up to those who hadn't given him a chance, the fact that he was never "the right guy for the part". Yet through ambition and perseverance, he proved time and time again that he *was* the right guy for the part.

And the work speaks for itself. When you look at the filmography, that huge list of work, and also the vast amount of awards and acclaim, it's hard to find another actor to whom you can compare him. For as far back as I can recall, he was the guy whose appearance made you strangely comfortable (even if his character made you unsettled), mainly because you knew that what you were about to watch was going to be worth your time. There is not a single phony moment with Woods, and his sheer dedication to the craft, his devotion to each character, enriches whatever he is in. You can visibly see, also, that actors often have to step up to the mark when they are in a scene with him. Woods told me personally that this is

17

the way it is with Robert De Niro, that when you work with a master you have to be at your best. This undoubtedly applies to Woods too.

For him, it seems that doing the best he can is the top priority. In one interview he explained his process when approaching a role and a film: "I always have a rule that acting is acting and truth is truth and you just go out there and you do it. But what happens in each medium is that you have other responsibilities. The acting remains the same, but each medium has certain requitrments neccesary to make the acting work. When I'm working on a film, I just play the absolute purity of the moments. I don't worry about the pacing, because the pacing is going to be dictated by the director and the editor. On the stage I have to give pacing to the play. As an actor, you, in fact, become the editor of the piece, in terms of the timing. You are required to engineer the pace yourself. In television, everything is in so close, that you realize that most of what you do has to register in your thought process."

In another interview, he proudly called himself an "idiot savant." "I do it without any confusion," he said, "or restriction or ambivalence or hesitation, and it just flows, almost as naturally as anything in my life. So I don't have a big burden about it. I'm not one of those 'method' guys." He once also, hilariously I might add, joked that he didn't have to sit around pretending to be a turnip to prepare for a film.

The idea of this book, as with my others, came out of a genuine fondness for and fascination with Woods' work. In late 2020 I was working on a revised edition of my book about Once Upon a Time in America, and got in touch with James' representative to see if he might be interested in being interviewed for it. Expecting a no (come on, it's James Woods, I thought), I was stunned when the reply came back saying he'd love to chat about the film. The interview was set up that week, just before Christmas, and only a few seconds into our chat

I felt comfortable speaking to him. Before I had even asked him a question, the memories came flooding out, and he exuded warmth and generosity. I was also genuinely honoured that he shared his recollections of Robert De Niro, Sergio Leone, and life on the set of that amazing film.

In the New Year, I wrote a retrospective on his career, condensed as it was, for my cult film/movie geek publication, Scenes. Seeing as I had such fun writing about his work, it was then I thought about putting together a deeper study of it, and realised how much fun it would be. I think, in all honesty, he is one of the greatest film actors we have seen, so studying his body of work would be an honour and a privilege. I cautiously asked what he thought of the idea and was stunned when he was OK with it. Not only was he OK with it, he said he would be available as and when I needed information. I didn't expect to be able to interview him, but he kindly agreed to chat. Such generosity is rare in any walk of life.

We did our first lengthy interview for the book in early July of 2021, an amazing conversation which covered key moments of Woods' career. He was passionate, open, very funny and also fascinating to listen to and engage with. By the time we did the second and third interviews, his memories were flowing with even more ease. What was genuinely nice about it too, was the fact that James seemed to be enjoying it just as much as I was! As a man who simply worked and always tried to do his best in each role, Woods is not the kind of fellow who would usually stop and dissect his career, try to figure out why he took certain roles and played them the way he did. But in our discussions he found himself looking into his past, examining the twists and turns of his career, and it was amazing to hear him do so. By interview four, five, six and beyond, the insights only seemed to grow more profound. I felt lucky and honoured, but James didn't seem to want me to feel like the lucky one. His ego was non-existent. We were, in James' words, two film lovers having a nice long chat about movies. At one point he even said it felt like we were a pair of film critics talking about this guy called James Woods. Removing himself from his own career made it easier for him to assess the work.

Much of our chats are included in the following text, mixed in with my reviews of his movies and snippets of archive interviews from other sources. For the most part though, it is our recent conversations which offer the most in depth and illuminating details. He told me some amazing stories, made me laugh a great deal and gave me astounding insights into the world of film and the craft of acting.

This book covers the whole of Woods' on screen career, exploring all his work on film, TV, in cartoons and even video games. I had of course already seen many of them, but viewing them again (along with many more buried gems and underrated masterpieces) as a whole body of work was extremely rewarding. I certainly had fun, but for the most part I went away thinking just how brilliant an actor he is. I can think of very few who are as dynamic, who always know how to "do it right", never overdo or overplay, never to try and manipulate our emotions but at the same time make us feel strongly, to make us sit up and get involved. There is a sense of him being strangely feral, on the edge, as if he has dived right into the role and is constantly using his intuition, his natural abilities, to keep the part spontaneous. I think of Gerard Depardieu, a man so alive in each role that he seems able to play any type that comes his way. It's the same with Woods; villain, father, hero, monster, sleaze-ball, cop, cop killer, mobster, ordinary man... they are all here in this remarkable gallery of faces.

Woods always demands your attention in a film. He gives the script power, but he also enhances each movie because of his ability to improvise. "One of my better gifts," he said to me, "is the ability to ride with a scene. When someone changes something, it's like, you wanna get into ad-libs? You're bringing a knife to a gun fight, you know?

No matter what you say, I can dig my heels in and I can improvise for an hour. All because I have a sense of the character. And if I am not able to do that, I know there is something wrong with the script, the scene, or with the direction, or the other actor. Whenever I am stuck, there is usually a problem with the writing."

Another thing James said to me during the writing of this book stuck with me. It's something I feel defines what is so special about his work and the performances he commits himself to: "There may be better actors than me in the world; there may be more successful actors, those that have more Instagram followers or whatever... But the one thing I always took pride in was when I gave a performance, I hoped that people might say, You know, there may be better actors, there may be more famous actors, but no one could have given that performance in that way except for James Woods. The fact I put my stamp on it..."

This book, I believe, is like going on a journey through James Woods' career, but with the distinction of having James Woods himself as the tour guide. It was, in all honesty, an amazing journey for me, too, and a complete pleasure all the way. Looking into his career, and talking to the man himself all about it, has been a huge honour, and I cannot truly put into words how enjoyable, enriching and special the experience has been.

It was also great to speak with and hear recollections from those who've worked closely with James, like Oliver Stone, Jim Belushi, Sharon Stone, Debbie Harry, Harold Becker, Joe Wambaugh, Marc Frydman, Tim Metcalfe, and Dolly Parton. I hope you enjoy the book even a hundredth as much as I enjoyed writing it.

"I was overjoyed to say the least when I got the opportunity to work with James on Straight Talk back in the early 90's. I loved every day I spent on the set with him. He played my lover in the movie and I loved getting to live out a fantasy that I'd had for years. I always had a crush on him. I've always thought he was one of the greatest actors of all time... and even a greater kisser! You always have to pretend behind the scenes that you didn't enjoy the love scenes on screen. Well, I did. I will always treasure my time spent with him. He is a professional in every way and I'm sure that you will enjoy reading about his life in movies."

\- Dolly Parton, 2021

James Woods' high school yearbook photo.

THE FORMATIVE YEARS

You often read interviews with actors or see them on TV talking about how they always wanted to be a performer. They'd put on plays in front of their family, parade before the mirror in costume, re-enact scenes from their favourite movies. Yet with James Woods, a man who it seems was born to be an actor, this was not the case. Acting had never been a burning passion of his; he had other plans, but acting came out of nowhere and the bug bit him, keeping its teeth in his very flesh for decades. It became his primary outlet, his "work" as well as his passion. It drove him onwards, inspired him to succeed and go beyond his own expectations of himself. And he coupled this singular vision with a deep rooted loyalty to his family, the people he cherished in his life.

But his journey to becoming one of America's most acclaimed actors is a fascinating story. James Woods was born in April, 1947, in Vernal, Utah. His father was Gail Payton Woods, an army officer and heavily medalled World War 2 veteran. His mother was Martha, a remarkable lady who Woods adored, and he had a younger brother named Michael, with whom he was famously close. They were a happy, close knit, dedicated family. "My parents loved each other," Woods said during an interview with Cigar Aficionado. "I was raised in a house of total love and respect. My dad worked very hard and my mother was incredibly devoted to him. I can unequivocally, without any peradventure of doubt, tell you that I was raised with the kind of love that we only dream of. My mother and my father loved me and my brother like we love the air we breathe out of necessity. It was a necessity for them to love us in some deep inner genetic calling in their hearts and minds and souls. I have that as a standard."

James told me that his mother would read to him when he was a baby; and not children's books, but sophisticated literature. She was a very well-read lady who adored absorbing good literature, and she longed to share this passion with her son. "People would laugh at her," James said, "but she would say, 'You don't know if he can understand me or not.' And later they did a study and they found that children who were read to when they were babies often turned out more intelligent than other children. I said my first word when I was seven months old! And it wasn't 'momma' or 'daddy'. She used to give me a cookie I loved, and I reached out once and I said, 'Cookie!' I had heard her call these things cookies and I just wanted one! I don't know anyone else on the face of the earth who said 'Cookie!' when they were seven months old. My mom said to me, 'You could speak full sentences on your first birthday.' Hard to believe, but true. The joke in our family was I had been vaccinated with a phonograph needle, because I talked so much. I was a very loquacious kid, very much on top of my abilities."

Sadly, their lives were hit with tragedy when James' father died after an operation went horribly wrong. On his final day, from his hospital bed, Gail called Michael, who was only three years old at the time, up on the phone and told him he was speaking to him from heaven. He also wrote a long letter to James, one that he would cherish forever. "My father was my hero," Woods told Bobby Wygant in 1994. "He was a man who had two purple hearts in World War 2, he had been wounded terribly. He never talked about the war; he did his job because he had to. I knew he had suffered greatly during the war. I admired him. And I admired my mother. When my father died when I was 12 - God rest his soul - she carried on so admirably and filled the roles of two parents. My parents are truly my heroes."

After his father's death, and the devastating effect it had on the Woods family, he began taking on odd jobs to raise money for the household and help his mother. She in turn began to work at a nursery, and after a year or so, when the owner said she was moving on, Martha bought the business and began to run her own pre-school. She later re-married to Thomas E. Dixon, finding happiness again. Woods, raised in Warwick, Rhode Island, graduated from the strict Pilgrim High School in 1965, where he had been a high achieving, well-behaved student.

Considering his natural ability in front of the camera, it's odd that Woods genuinely didn't want to be an actor. He told Don Shewey: "I never even remotely thought of being an actor. Ever. I wasn't one of those kids who sat around singing There's No Business Like Show Business with a raccoon boa wrapped around his neck. There was a guy like that in my high school. I never wanted to do any of it."

Then came the turning point. When a regional drama competition came up, a friend of James' urged him to get involved in a play. "A play? What are you talking about? I can't act, I'm skinny, I have this weird voice." Eventually convinced, he played in the Little Foxes and enjoyed the experience. Acting was also encouraged by a lady called Joyce Donahue, who served double duty as girl's gym teacher and head of the theatre group. Woods fondly recalled her as one of the most perceptive directors he'd ever come across. He learned various lessons from Joyce, some of which would be valuable to him in his film years much later. Woods says he "learned at a very early age that the secret to playing villains is not to go around screaming and snarling... but to be a little more subtle and to think of yourself as being morally right. Anybody who thinks of himself as morally right is twice as chilling when he does something that is palpably and obviously morally wrong, because he does it with a kind of ease and grace."

Acting was still not on the cards as a career though. Offered his choice of scholarships in numerous colleges, Woods enrolled at Massachusetts Institute of Technology, the one his father had spoken about to him years earlier. Famously, as has often been reported, he blitzed his SAT test. Woods was a "homespun genius", and it's well known that his IQ was read as high as 184. Greatness was definitely in the cards, and he would be able to apply his intelligence to whatever field he took on. "One of my strengths in life was always my ability to communicate in a very clear way," Woods told me. "And it's because I love language." Communication, as it happens, would become his forte, both as a human being and as an artist.

At one point, as James told me, it looked like he might follow his father's footsteps into a military career: "I volunteered for the Air Force Academy and had been nominated by my United States Senator in Rhode Island, Senator Pastore. But then I had an accident where I severed the tendons in my right arm and I was medically disqualified."

He ended up studying Political Science, and was a member of the student theatre group Dramashop while still at MIT, which saw him perform in over 30 plays. He then became more interested in acting as an art form and craft. In 1969, Woods decided to drop out of MIT to become a professional actor. James had met Jon Voight, in his pre-fame days, and he had encouraged him to take it more seriously; as had Timothy Affleck, father of Ben Affleck, stage manager of a theatre company that Woods was an apprentice at. When he was offered a sizeable role on the stage, he asked for his mother's approval to drop out of MIT. She agreed he should follow his heart, and he went on to explore the craft that had become his passion.

Speaking later of this decision, it was clear he understood the weight of what he had done, and the possible consequences if it hadn't gone to plan. "It was a very wrenching and painful decision for me, in my senior year at MIT, on high dean's list and full scholarships, to decide that maybe I wanted to be an artist. I think it is actually something that my father would understand. Whether I'm making 30 grand a day or union scale, I have found something that I truly love, and that is something he would have admired."

"I just never anticipated it," James told me, when speaking about how he fell into acting. "It was really a kind of perfect storm. I had zero desire to act. When I was in college there was this great guy called Joseph Everingham, and he had been involved with the Bristol Old Vic in England for years. He retired and got this job at the Dramashop. We didn't have a theatre curriculum obviously at MIT, but we did have a beautiful extra-curricular programme. And there was this beautiful auditorium, and a theatre that had 204 seats. It was called the Little Theatre. They had a series of one-acts every semester, twice. So you'd rehearse for two weeks and do three or four days of performance. And then you'd do two more weeks and two more one-acts, and then you'd rehearse for five weeks for what we called the major play. And that would perform for two weeks straight at the end of the semester. So I could do, potentially, ten plays a year. And in fact I was the first freshman to be elected president of the Dramashop, because I did indeed do 39 plays while I was in college. Some were at Harvard, some were at Harvard Summer Theatre. And I actually did a play there once where they let you audition even if you didn't go to Harvard. They were open about that, which was nice. That was Harvard and Radcliffe - Radcliffe was the lady's side of Harvard, but of course it's all combined now. I did Peace by Aristophanes, which was with Terry Malick. Then we did the Trojan Women, and Stockard

Channing, whose name then was Susan Channing, played Cassandra in the play. So I got to work with a lot of people who later became famous, as I did. But we knew each other in college. It was kinda fun!"

A playbill from MIT Dramashop, for a production of Pinter's A Night Out. Woods is listed as playing Albert Stokes.

In that year he garnered extensive experience on the stage, appearing in all manner of roles and productions before his Broadway breakthrough at the Lyceum Theatre in a staging of Brendan Behan's Borstal Boy. Woods later revealed he got the role by perfecting an English accent, and actually convincing them he was a Brit. There is something of the young Orson Welles in this tale. In the 1930's the teenage Welles had travelled to Ireland and attempted to convince the theatre owners he was a well known American actor. Though they never really believed Orson's yarn, it seems that the producers of Borstal Boy were totally taken in by the English James Woods. The roles then got more prominent and in 1973 he was in the first run of Jean Kerr's Finishing Touches at the Plymouth Theatre.

30

For those who think Woods just appeared on screen as Greg Powell one day forget that he gained so much experience out on the boards learning how to interact with others, to act and react, to nail comedy, intimacy and high drama. He did it all on the stage before a crowd. He perfected his craft away from the camera, which is why even in his very earliest films he seems a total natural. Though Woods worked on his talent, he believes that such a skill is one you either have or not. You may be able to hone that talent, but you need to already possess it, to be born with that special something. It is most certainly not something that can just appear with teaching.

Musing on his decision to become an actor, this took James back to his childhood and the wonderful people who raised him. "I was just raised so well," Woods said to me. "I was raised by a war hero and a school teacher, who both loved children. I was raised by fantastic parents, a beautiful family. There is not a dud in my family, even my extended family. Everyone is just decent. I was raised and grew up surrounded by such decent and good people with the best of American values and the best of human ethics. So I found a great deal of joy in playing characters who were so completely different from me and my environment growing up. I played characters who were so different from me, and I am not sure that my struggle to become a successful actor would make such a great movie. Just a guy who worked hard, gave it his all, tried his best, behaved honourably, and those values were rewarded with success. That's not much of a formula for a screenplay. Most screenplays have this worthless son of a bitch who learns some value in life and does the right thing for once, and is heroic for a brief period of time. And we cheer him on. But me, a guy works hard and gets rewarded for hard work, gets some degree of acclaim and feels proud of the work he's done, and honours the values to which he was raised... there's no second act in that. There's no part where all is lost and the guy is trying to find his way home."

For the young Woods, it seemed that a long career on the stage would be his future. And he was happy with that. Movies were not on his mind, at least not yet. He was content doing Off-Broadway plays making 200 bucks a week, living, as he told me, in his "little artist's apartment. I was happy. I loved my little life in New York as an artist. We'd all hang out. And I literally worked on stage almost every single night for ten years. I was always in a play, always on stage. On Broadway I did several plays; Off-Broadway I can't even count how many I did. I won the Obie Award, the Theatre World Award, the Variety Critics Poll - over John Geilgud and Ralph Richardson one year, believe it or not, when they were doing Home (David Storey's play). So I had a good theatre career as an artist, and I was happy. Theatre was just the Holy Grail to me as far as acting was concerned. You know, that snobbery you have when you're in the theatre. 'We're theatre actors, we don't do movies, those are for movie stars who can't really act. The real acting is done on the stage.' All this kind of shit. But the badge of honour was that we were accomplished theatre actors, 'master thespians' (laughs), and of course I say that as a joke."

Woods recalled his early theatre days with much affection during our interviews. He also recalled to me a cherished memory of walking down the street one day and seeing a poster outside a cinema for Monty Python's Flying Circus: And Now For Something Completely Different. He and his friend tried their luck and went inside to view the film. "We were the only two people in the theatre, screaming laughing. I am proud to say that I was the first New Yorker to see Monty Python in New York. The first day it opened, the first showing. I thought it was the funniest thing I had ever seen and I never looked back."

In the early seventies, before the cinema was even a serious consideration for him, Woods had a chance meeting with a future co-star, Robert De Niro. James told me all about this encounter, as well as shedding some light on his theatrical roots and the relationships he had formed with other young actors.

"I was introduced to Bob De Niro by Barry Primus, who was one of his friends. Barry knew me from when I was an apprentice at the Theatre Company of Boston. That company had been in residence at the University of Rhode Island. J.T. Walsh and I were the two apprentices there, so we always played the spear carriers in these things. You know, we'd do a play with Blythe Danner, Barry Primus, all these wonderful actors. So Barry Primus called me in New York. I didn't have an agent, I didn't know anybody, it was horrible. So he called me and said, 'Hey, they're doing this movie.' I was like, 'Movie? Ah, I don't know, that sounds kinda weird. I'm a theatre actor!' And he said, 'No it'd be good. There's this guy, he's playing one of the lead roles, and the other lead role you would be perfect for.' And he said, 'This guy's name's Bob.' So I met Bob De Niro. He had broken his arm; he had his arm in a sling. I think it was by the subway right by St Vincent's Hospital. So Bob was saying, 'Yeah you'd be great for this part. The guy is kinda tortured about his religion, he doesn't want to be involved with crime but he is. It's called Mean Streets.' I said, 'Oh, sounds cool!' And he said, 'Yeah, you should come and meet the director, this guy Marty. Marty Scorsese.' I said, 'OK. So where's his office.' And he said, 'Oh, we're gonna meet him at his house, he doesn't have an office.' I was like, 'Right, this guy doesn't have an office? I'm gonna meet him at his apartment? Are you crazy? He doesn't have an office?' So I didn't go meet him. That might have been a mistake (laughs). But there you go. It wasn't an offer or anything, it was just a case of casting a part. And it was probably a long shot. But maybe they were thinking Marty might think I'd be able to play, if not Charlie, then one of the other parts. Anyway, it was nice of Barry to introduce me to Bob. You know, young actors helping each other out. But I don't know why I didn't go. Maybe I was doing a play on Broadway or something. I mean, I don't know why I would feel queasy about meeting someone for a part. I mean, I did think it was weird he didn't have an office (laughs). Like, is this a real movie? Why is there no office? Which was weird, because I didn't even have a job! It was some whimsical decision not to go meet him, and it was just insane that I didn't."

As well as pointing out a very real "could have" for Woods, the story also paints a picture of the bohemian excitement of New York in the 1970's, a place where future legends of cinema built up their reputations, looked out for each other and hustled for parts. It is also fascinating to hear that James, who would become such a natural before the camera, had serious doubts about his "movie star" credentials. "I was like, I can't be a movie star, I have bad skin, I'm skinny," James said to me. "I just didn't understand why and how I'd be in the movies. I never thought of myself as a movie actor, but a theatre actor who loved doing great classics and cutting edge, experimental theatre. I prided myself on those two things. I could have done that for a life time. I'd have been very happy doing it, actually."

Yet despite his hesitation about the movies, and his contentment on the stage, a film career was on the horizon. Given the strained experience of his first film, however, Woods would become sure that he was destined to remain a man of the theatre. Indeed, his film career could have been over as soon as it started.

NEW YORK
BEVERLY HILLS
CHICAGO
LONDON
ROME
PARIS
MADRID
MUNICH

ESTABLISHED 1898

news

WILLIAM MORRIS AGENCY. INC. XXXX
1350 AVENUE OF THE AMERICAS · NEW YORK. N.Y. 10019 · (212) 586-5100

JAMES WOODS

Height:	5' 11"	Hair:	Brown
Weight:	140 lbs.	Eyes:	Brown

EXPERIENCE:

Broadway - MOONCHILDREN, Bob, dir: Alan Schneider
THE TRIAL OF THE CATONSVILLE 9, David Darst,
   dir: Gordon Davidson
BORSTAL BOY, Tom Meadows, dir: Tomas MacAnna
CONDUCT UNBECOMING, Mess Headwaiter, dir: Val May
THE PENNY WARS, Tyler, Howie (u/s), dir: Barbara Harris

Off-Broadway - SAVED, Len, dir: Alan Schneider
   (received Obie for Distinguished Performance, 1971,
   and Clarence Derwent Award, 1971)

THE VISITORS
Films - ~~HOME FREE~~, Bill Schmidt, dir: Elia Kazan
   HICKEY AND BOGGS, Watt, dir. Robert Culp

Television - ALL THE WAY HOME, Andrew (NBC, Hallmark Hall of Fame)

Stock and Resident Theatres -

MOONCHILDREN, Bob, Arena Stage, Washington, D.C.
SOUTH PACIFIC, Professor, Jones Beach Theatre
ROSENCRANTZ AND GUILDENSTERN ARE DEAD, Mime (u/s
   Rosencrantz), Coconut Grove Playhouse
THERE'S A GIRL IN MY SOUP, Jimmy, Paramus Playhouse
THE HOMECOMING, Lenny, Provincetown Playhouse-on-the-
                                            Wharf
A TASTE OF HONEY, Geoffrey,   "   "   "   "
THE HOSTAGE, Mulleady,   "   "   "   "
LYSISTRATA, Commissioner,   "   "   "   "

FORMAL TRAINING: 1965-69, S.B. Massachusetts Institute of
                            Technology
                   1966, University of Rhode Island Summer
                            Theatre Festival

March, 1972

James Woods' 1972 Theatre World Bio, with hand written alterations.

Woods in his first film, Elia Kazan's The Visitors (1972).

THE VISITORS (1972)

James Woods made a decision to enter into the film world when he realised that, as a viewer at least, he just didn't go to the theatre all that much. The movies drew him in (he was a self confessed film snob/buff), but only because he could see that genuinely good work could be done on the screen if it was the right film. He was certainly enjoying his life as a theatre performer, but there was something about the movies - and the great actors one could see on the big screen, especially during the glory years of the 1970's - that appealed to Woods. And his first experience starring in a movie was not with some obscure art house newcomer, but with the legendary director Elia Kazan on The Visitors, released in 1972. Typically for Woods, he started his film career with one of the most acclaimed directors of all time, though it was not exactly a smooth sailing experience.

The film concerns a young Vietnam vet named Bill (played by Woods) who lives with his wife and son on her father's farm. One day, two of his supposed buddies arrive, unannounced and out of nowhere. It turns out they are old army friends from 'Nam, but the men harbour dark secrets from the past, which they are about to bring into Bill's supposedly idyllic family life.

Low budget, raw and gritty, The Visitors has a tension running through it which is at times suffocating; even from the opening scene with the baby crying and the young couple's early interactions, the unease bubbles and it's clear something unpleasant will occur down the line. When the two soldiers arrive, it's revealed that Bill is going to inform on his old allies, who raped and killed a girl in Vietnam, and the unease one feels at the very start is justified.

The Visitors was scripted by Elia's son Chris and was shot around the Kazan country house. Creaky in parts, its rough and readiness actually works in the film's favour. "This was done on 16mm film," Woods told me. "It was shot at his son's house in Connecticut. People don't realise that back then, it was the middle of nowhere. It was a farm basically; Elia had one house and Chris another. Nick Kazan later became a more famous screenwriter, but Chris wrote this one."

The film was inspired by true events, and written as a kind of sequel to Daniel Lang's article on the infamous Incident on Hill 192. Lang himself later expanded it into a book, Casualties of War, which was brought to the screen by Brian De Palma in 1988. Naturally, given its source material, The Visitors is engaging, but for me the main reason to watch it today is for Woods, for the first time the star of a film. As far as starring debuts go, it's remarkably assured. Woods has a total grasp of the character and it's clear his stage beginnings have influenced and aided his take on the part. From the first scene on he is in the skin of Bill, but there is a great shift in his mood when the friends arrive that Woods excellently puts across. In the first scene, he is awakened by the baby crying, gets up and heads off to work on the farm. When he arrives back and sees his past sitting right there on the sofa, he immediately changes. He is all nerves, jittery, unsure. But as an actor he has a quiet confidence here, a man who knows he has a long way to go in the film world but has the drive, the ambition and the skills to get there. He exudes raw talent and it's great to watch him now, all these years on, knowing what was to come.

It was a shame that very few people got to appreciate his assured performance in The Visitors at the time of release. Given the Vietnam War was still raging on in all its chaos, it was hardly a film the masses would rush to see at the theatres. A film that, in Woods' own words, was about "a guy testifying in an atrocity case in Vietnam", it was hardly box office fare. "Nobody wanted to hear about that," Woods said.

Speaking to me, James said that the angle the film took was totally at odds with the popular opinion of America's involvement with the war at the time. "People hated The Visitors," he said. "We screened it at the cinema next to Carnegie Hall. People yelled, they booed, and one literally threw his shoe at the screen. It was astonishing. There was such rage about that movie, because they felt that, here was Elia Kazan, who had his own troubled political history, having spoken and testified for the House Un-American Activities. And he basically was doing a movie about a guy who named names. And in fact Kazan and I ended up not getting along. He's a guy who likes to torture his actors basically. He was my hero before I worked with him. My favourite movie was On the Waterfront. I had seen the film twenty times. Working with Elia Kazan then was like working with Scorsese today. It was unimaginable, and here I was, working with Elia Kazan."

Unfortunately it was not the smoothest of collaborations. "One day," James continued, "we were driving out to Connecticut, it was a beautiful day. The countryside is like England out there, just beautiful. It was fall, the leaves were falling. We were in his little car, and he asked me about myself, looking for vulnerabilities, no doubt, so he could torture me. That was how he got performances out of people, the Method approach. I said to him, 'Listen, I have a question, maybe you can help me. How did it feel for you being called a rat by people who had once worshipped you in the industry?' He had hero worship status among actors, like the great Method director; after all, he had discovered Brando, James Dean - you name it. 'How did you feel about that?' I said. So, boy, let me tell you, that was the end of that relationship right then."

There was also a key moment when Woods and Kazan disagreed over a scene, which led to James standing up for what he felt was right. "He tortured the living shit out of me during that movie,"

James told me. "At one point he was being really rude to me. It was the first time I realised this, and I said to him, 'You know, you were once a hero of mine, but now you're acting like a raging fucking asshole. And to be honest with you, I'm right about how this scene is going to be played, and I don't give a shit if you're God, never mind Elia Kazan. I don't care what you've achieved, you're wrong, I'm right, I don't care if I ever work again; and I'm sure, after this little speech, I never will! But I am gonna tell you right now, this is the way we are gonna do the scene.' It was a scene where I basically explained my character's reason for doing something that would be unthinkable among comrades in arms, which was to testify against them for anything, even for something as horrendous as the rape and torture of this Vietnamese girl. And to his credit, Kazan sort of sat back and said, 'OK, let's do it again.' And I realised, Aha, I get it, this was just what he was looking for. He was trying to get me in a rage, he did get me in a rage, and that is what this character would do. And from that we re-wrote the ending of the picture. So in fairness to his memory, his technique, though miserable to experience, did often work very well. It was an ugly story but a fitting reflection of what was happening at the time. It was a kind of prescient movie. It was one of those movies that never had a chance, given its circumstance, but may some day be actually a kind of time capsule movie. It was a genuine representation of this emotional/moral time."

This was the first time Woods had stepped out in front of a camera (save for a student short film project at MIT he told me about, unofficially his on-camera debut), and he came out with a strong performance under his belt, having stood up for what he believed in against a well established, though polarising, figure of the film industry. The fact he was ready to risk it all so early on says a lot about James Woods' integrity and refusal to accept second best.

40

EARLY FILM AND TV ROLES: 1972 - 1979

Though he imagined that facing up to Elia Kazan might have damaged a potential career in the movies, Woods continued to land film parts as the seventies went on. Ambitious to do good work on the screen, he excelled in what came his way, and built up essential experience in front of the camera.

Though The Visitors had been a lead part (rare for a debut), Woods didn't go straight into another major role. In some ways his post-Visitors career was almost like a re-start, with Woods making his way up the ladder and working tirelessly. He was a reporter in Footsteps (1972), and also appeared in Robert Culp's private eye crime flick, Hickey and Boggs (1972), starring Bill Cosby and Culp himself, who had both starred in I Spy together. He played Lt. Wyatt, but it was a small part.

But the early to mid 1970's are interesting for Woods fans, because one can see his style maturing. This is evident in one obscure performance in particular. Although in the scheme of things it's another minor part, an often overlooked credit is the 1972 TV film, A Great American Tragedy. It was directed by J. Lee Thompson, and stars George Kennedy as an aerospace engineer who loses his job, struggles to get employment and sees his life fall apart. Thompson, an assured director if there ever was one, gives the film a cinematic touch while also keeping it personal. A man who could turn on tension in the likes of Cape Fear (1962), depict the turbulence of war in Guns of Navarone (1961) and direct on an epic scale in Taras Bulba (1962), Thompson always kept a human touch in his work, often without resorting to sentimentality. This is the case here too. He makes us care for the man and his plight but resists schmaltz. Because of this, it's engaging from start to finish, and reminds us of the fragility of our respective places in society. Woods plays Rick, the boyfriend of Kennedy's daughter. He is first seen cleaning the family boat, discussing the country cabin he's building. It's a small part, but already Woods has presence and individuality. One scene stuck out to me. While the family toast over a can of beer, Woods raises his can and says, "Yo ho ho!" The family all laugh, and the laughter seems real. The little outburst has the feel of an improvisation, and even if it isn't, it has that Woods spontaneity about it that makes such moments come to life.

More notable still was his role in Sydney Pollack's The Way We Were (1973), starring Barbra Streisand and Robert Redford. The reason his part in the film is more note worthy is not down to the script or what the director had in mind for James, but for Woods' ambition and determination to be seen and noticed. Playing the role of Streisand's boyfriend, Frankie, an intellectual contemporary at college, he is pushed aside early on in the film by her attraction to Hubbell, played by Redford. Frankie wasn't a major part of events in the screenplay, but Woods, adamant to get more work and screen time, told Pollack that he thought it would be important for him to be there present in the scene when Streisand can't take her eyes off Redford.

"I had five lines in the script," he said in a 1992 TV interview. "I was meant to work a day and ended up working ten days. Every time Streisand had a shot I'd wander in behind her. I was like the world's most assertive extra, basically. Sydney Pollack once said to me, 'I can't believe it, every time I look at dailies, you happen to be in the shot. How do you manage to be in every scene and I don't notice it?' There was a scene when Barbra and Robert Redford... she's trying to get his attention in a library. A silent scene essentially, beautifully structured. I said, 'Sydney I should be in this scene!' Sydney said to me, 'With all due respect Jimmy, you are a nobody with a capital N, and she is Barbra Streisand and he is Robert Redford, and they are falling in love in a falling in love story. You do not need to be in this scene, trust me.' So I go to Barbra and say, 'If you're like really nervous about looking at Redford and you have this crush on him, it'd be tougher if your boyfriend was right there. You're looking at him and then you're looking at your boyfriend. So maybe I should be in this scene.' So Barbra says, 'Sydney, the kid's in the scene!' It turned out to be a wonderful experience."

Pollack later acknowledged at an AFI seminar that, no matter how much Jimmy's antics bugged him (jokingly of course), he left him in the edit because he was right every time. Though it was primarily a method of getting more screen time, it just so happens that Woods was correct; his presence did heighten the tension for Streisand's character.

In this era, it has to be said that Woods was bringing more vitality to the small screen than he was the movies. In 1974 he was to be seen on the familiar set of Kojak, in the classic Death Is Not a Passing Grade episode, playing an on-the-edge criminal named Caz. By day, Woods' character is attending criminology classes run by Kojak, but by night he is performing robberies with his brother in law. One day while cracking a safe, things go awry and he ends up killing the owner of a store.

At first it seems that Caz might just be another cop show bad guy, but Woods' character, and his portrayal, is complex. He wants to prove he's smarter than Kojak by leaving clues for him so he'll know he's been there, but he also sees the veteran cop as a kind of father figure. Caz's own dad had been a cop but he'd never known the man. Undoubtedly, he sees something of his elusive old man in Kojak. And though he enjoys deceiving Kojak, he also wants him to know he's the man who's been outsmarting him all this time. It's a desperate bid for attention, approval even, while the finale is a rather moving conclusion to their strange father/son play off. And Woods plays it fabulously the whole way through. Even from his first appearance in the episode, he has an air of danger, a man compressing himself, a manipulator playing the long game. In the confines of an hour long TV episode, Woods delivers a powerhouse effort which bursts off the screen and brings the story into a higher level.

"Well that was interesting," James said when we came to the Kojak episode. "That was the episode they submitted for the Emmy, and it won it that year. I was happy about that. But it's funny how careers work. People come up in their careers all the time. The hot guy in episodic television at that time was Martin Sheen. He was gonna do the Kojak episode, but was unavailable. So they hired another fella who was up and coming named Richard Dreyfuss. But I think he got sick or something, so it was then offered to me. It was the first time I had been on a Hollywood set, and I remember I had been there about a half an hour. I walked into the bathroom, and I see that written on the back of the door of one of the stalls, etched into it were the words: 'Jim Woods sucks dick'. I mean, I'd only been there about twenty minutes or something. How can this be happening already? So I was a little depressed about it. So later on this guy was there on set and he called out, 'Jim Woods!' And I said, 'Yes?' And he said, 'No not you! Jim Woods the electrician,' who was standing behind me (laughs). I thought, Gee, that wasn't much fun."

On working with Telly Savalas, Woods had fond recollections. "But Telly Savalas was well into Kojak then, it was a monster hit, and everybody loved him with his lollipop and the whole 'who loves you baby?' thing. It's hard to imagine what TV was like before DVD and streaming services, all the evolution. There were like, three channels and it was like, 'Kojak's gonna be on!' And you'd wait to watch the episode. And in fact if you were gonna be on TV you'd get all your friends gathered round and you'd say, 'I'm gonna be on tonight! The episode's on tonight!' All your actor friends would come over and sit on your couch and you'd watch your episode. Telly was one of the big stars. There were a lot of those big cop shows - like Beretta, Kojak, Columbo, Rockford Files... But anyway, I did the Kojak episode. I have the scene where I'm dying and he cradles me. A lot of the big stars might do their side of the close up and then leave. The script supervisor would read his lines, because off screen he might not be there. So we did our scene, his close up first; and I'm dying, and I kind of started crying in the scene. And when they cut he said, 'Wow that was really great!' He was very complimentary to me. That made me feel wonderful. And the script supervisor said, 'Right Mr Woods, I'm gonna read Mr Savalas's lines now.' But Telly said, 'No I'm gonna do it. I wanna do the scene with this young man, he deserves it.' So it was like, Welcome to Hollywood! He was really a sweet guy. And he did do close ups with other actors by the way, but if he was busy he might have to go and do something else."

On the impact of the episode, James said: "But it was a nice introduction for me, because I got to work with a massive TV star. And the show was a huge audience favourite. So I'd say to people, 'Hey I'm on Kojak this week!' And they'd go, 'Oh my God, how did you manage to get on Kojak? Do you have a big part?' 'I'm the guest star!' 'You're kidding!' All the actors, we lived in this place called the Tennis Court apartments, all these little one-room apartments with a tennis court and a pool. And we'd all sit around the pool and an actor might be reading a script, and we'd say, 'What are you reading?' 'Nothing for you!' Because they didn't want you calling your agent and going for the part (laughs). Or they'd say, 'I'm doing this episode of Barnaby Jones' or whatever it was, and they'd say, 'There's this part, a bad guy, a drug smuggler, you'd be perfect! He's the killer!' Oh, a killer... thanks a lot (laughs). But the Kojak role, here was a part with an emotional evolution, a spiritual evolution, an intellectual evolution, a psychological evolution. It was very compact, but you could really do something with it. And you were interested in that character."

When the Kojak seasons were released in a DVD boxed set, the AV Club picked out the Woods episode as a highlight. Writing about the special features on the set and the retrospective interviews, they wrote: "It would've been particularly nice to hear from James Woods, who stars in one of the season's best episodes, Death Is Not A Passing Grade, as a sociopath who taunts Savalas by stealing the detective's personal effects and leaving them at crime scenes... Surely no other cop show that aired that week featured a pairing like the wiry Woods and the sullen Savalas, matching wits in the roach-infested spaces of rent-controlled New York."

He was also in the first ever episode of The Rockford Files, The Kirkoff Case (1974). "I did the very first episode by the way," James told me, "and the first words ever spoken on Rockford Files were by me to James Garner. So the character in the Rockford Files with Jim Garner, that was a guy who'd killed his own parents. I was drawn to these kinds of characters." It's another magnetic performance and is fascinating as a piece of proto-Woods magic.

Aside his television work, James also popped up in a number of motion pictures, some of which proved to be future classics. In Karel Reisz's The Gambler (1974) he was a bespectacled bank officer, sitting at his desk on the phone, being rather rude to James Caan's mother, an act he regrets rather quickly. It's a blink and you'll miss it appearance, but Woods even has this brief turn nailed to a tee. He is every bit the pencil pusher, the typical bank worker who goes by the book and is blind to human frailty, devoid of consideration for their potential woes, and totally committed to the almighty dollar.

He was put to more effective use though in Arthur Penn's seminal Night Moves (1975), starring Gene Hackman. Woods plays the small part of Quentin, a mechanic who gets entangled in a plot involving a private investigator, Harry Moseby (Hackman), who is looking for the missing daughter of an ageing veteran actress. Woods' screen time is limited, of course, but he dives into the part as if it were a starring role, lending his scenes an authenticity. A buttoned-up bank teller in his previous role, he now seems to have seamlessly become the seedy mechanic with ease, his face strewn with dirt and features harassed. He meets a nasty end in this one, and though his scenes are limited, he is effective. That said, the movie in itself is essential viewing, for it features Hackman in his prime and a brilliant and very young Melanie Griffith as the wild teenager who Moseby is searching for. Arthur Penn, the legendary director of Bonnie and Clyde (1967), had been off the radar for some time prior to the release of Night Moves, and his last film had been Little Big Man (1970), ill received at the time, but now something of a curious cult classic. Night Moves though, was something of a return to form, and remains one of his finest films.

James' memories of this film were vivid. "Well that was interesting," he told me, "and it was so thrilling to be in a real Hollywood movie. And here he was, Arthur Penn, who had not long done Bonnie and Clyde. He was a stunning, big director. I had this great part in this great screenplay. And Melanie was like a kid in it. I remember, she showed up one day with a box with two kittens in it, and they were actually baby lions, about two weeks old, because her mother was married to Noel Marshall, and they famously owned a big animal refuge. But Gene was in the movie, of course, and I really admired him. He'd just done The French Connection and The Conversation, and was like the biggest star in the world at that time. He was just a great guy. And my parents came out to visit the set. You have to remember, this was the first time I had a real part in a big Hollywood movie. It was a thriller, which I loved, with Gene Hackman, down in Georgia and Florida. I had the scene in Florida with the dolphins, when I'm found dead. I remember I was as sick as a dog. I had a temperature of 104."

The same year he was in an episode of the police drama, The Rookies (1975), A Time to Mourn, as well as the first ever edition of Welcome Back Kotter (1975). Titled The Great Debate, the episode opens up the massively popular Kotter series that starred a pre-fame John Travolta. The episode features Woods as a drama teacher named Alex, who pops up in tweed trousers, glasses and a cravat. The scene where he insists the head teacher deliver the line "Hello, Alex" again so it sounds more genuine, treating him like one of his students, is very funny. Woods plays it brilliantly, proving early on that comedy comes naturally to him. It's very seventies, extremely nostalgic, and good clean fun. The cravats get more garish as the episode goes on, too!

Woods showed more intensity in an episode of The Streets of San Francisco, Trail of Terror, which also aired in 1975. The highly popular series, starring Michael Douglas and Karl Malden as homicide detectives Keller and Stone, is always worth watching, and there are some genuine gems in the five seasons which aired between 1972 and 1977. Trail of Terror is a particular stand-out, with Woods stealing the show as a sailor with a short fuse. From his first appearance, storming off the boat, high wired and wound up, he spells trouble. He and his naval friends hit the town, looking for the owner of a jewellery store. When they find out the store is closed from a local bar owner (Woods gets nasty with him for no reason, illustrating his psychotic tendencies), they go looking for the jeweller at his home. Upon their arrival the man tries to escape, but the sailors pin him down. It's clear they want their share of the money that's owed them from certain sold stock. In a shocking moment Woods kills the man, hitting him over the head with a candlestick holder. The girlfriend (played by the great Meg Foster) flees the apartment, but the foursome pursue her with vigour, leading to more complications. This is mainstream American TV at its finest. The cast is fabulous, with Foster particularly effective; but Woods is above the material, giving a deep, exciting performance which hints at the future work to come in the 1980's and beyond. As far as his early to mid-seventies work goes, this episode is possibly the strongest example of what Woods was capable of as a fire brand, a scene stealer, and highlights his knack of dominating the screen.

"Here I was a theatre actor now doing TV," James said to me, "I think there was a little light that went off on a semi-conscious level that was like, 'Ah, you can do the same kind of work.' Remember I had that snob theatre thing going on. You know, 'Movies are for pretty boys, not for actors who develop character.' But you've got to remember, I was raised on these amazing American and British playwrights, who remain to this day the greatest in the history of theatre. So how was a TV episode going to compare with that? And then there's a part of you that sees how character development works regardless of the medium. I never thought TV was as fulfilling as the theatre, but once I started to have the power of being heard, the whole ball game changed. So I did a ton of this episodic TV; you know, Streets of San Francisco, Barnaby Jones, Rockford Files, Kojak etc. And it was all fun, I have to say, and they were great, great learning experiences, too. I mean, nobody tells you anything. I didn't know what a mark was. You know, like, 'Hit the mark? What?' And then you'd hit the mark and eureka, you kinda learn things as you went. I learned it all on the set. I learned all the technical things, so I could be free to be the actor I had been in the theatre. Truly, on the job training! So all in all right away I got to play complex psychological characters, because I did the guest star roles, almost invariably villains. All the guest stars were villains. Of course, the villains are the juiciest people to play."

He continued to work on film, too, and in 1975 was cast in the low-budget Distance, a movie about two army couples going through rocky patches in 1950's America. "We were filming it in rural Georgia," Woods told me, "and the story focused on the first year of racial integration in the army. It was a small independent, but a really cool movie way ahead of its time. Another cutting edge film. I did a lot like that. They may not have been widely seen, but they were always about something." Woods' performance in Distance was singled out in reviews, with the New York Times calling his acting "admirable".

He was cast as Walter the Addict in the TV movie, Foster and Laurie (1975), and also popped up in F. Scott Fitzgerald in Hollywood (1975), which featured his future Once Upon a Time in America co-star, Tuesday Weld. Bit parts in TV series like Bert D'Angelo/ Superstar were also decent credits for his CV, and gave him yet more experience of life on set.

He then found himself with Hollywood royalty in Alex and the Gypsy (1976). In this intriguing tale directed by John Korty, Jack Lemmon plays a bail bondsman who once lived with a gypsy, played by Genevieve Bujold, who in true gypsy fashion leaves after a matter of months. At the start of the film though, she is in jail and he is her bail bondsman. The picture then rewinds into flashback, and explores their unlikely relationship. Woods has a key part as Crainpool, Lemmon's office assistant, who gets dragged into the farce, despite his hapless qualities. Once again bespectacled, this was an era when Woods bounced between intense psychosis and clean cut characters with an air of academia. Though Alex and the Gypsy was overlooked, the film was no doubt a great experience for Woods, here playing a larger role and enjoying the company of the legendary Jack Lemmon.

He played the part of Danny Reeves in an episode of Barnaby Jones (1976), Sins of Thy Father, once again bespectacled in a part he gives his all. (A piece of trivia: Woods and Peter Ford were nearly killed during a scene involving a plane that went off when it wasn't supposed to.) The same year he also played a heavier part, that of a sniper in an episode of Police Story (1976), where he shoots a woman but also catches her child in the process. The episode was based on a true story, and once again Woods dives in head first. He is without redeeming qualities here, yet he chooses not to go for a cartoon villain approach. It's another early sign that his psychos were never going to be caricatures.

Even more a valuable experience for Woods was working on the TV movie, The Disappearance of Aimee (1976), which also starred Faye Dunaway and the legendary Bette Davis. The film, based on the true story of Aimee Semple McPherson who vanished in 1926, cast Dunaway as the title character and Davis as her mother, Minnie Kennedy. Woods has a supporting role as Assistant District Attorney Joseph Ryan. Working with Davis definitely left an impression on Woods. Having already been a fan of her all his life, he found his admiration only grew after meeting her. "Davis was the greatest actor in cinema bar none," he said. "There's Bette Davis and then there's everyone else." After filming, Davis and Woods became close friends, and remained so right up until her death in 1989. James even gave her eulogy at the Warner Bros. memorial. To this day he recalls his old friend with much warmth.

Woods continued to build his name on the screen. He had a role in the star-studded high profile TV movie Raid on Entebbe (1977), which explored the hostage crisis in Uganda in 1976. He was in fine company - the cast included Peter Finch, Charles Bronson, John Saxon and Yaphet Kotto, with whom he would be reunited in 1985's Badge of the Assassin - but it was a minor part as the bespectacled Captain Berg. Still, it was well received on American TV and was given a theatrical release in Europe.

One film Woods later expressed disappointment with was The Choirboys (1977), directed by Robert Aldrich, and adapted by Jennifer Miller from Joseph Wambaugh's popular book. Wambaugh, a police officer turned writer, enjoyed massive success in the seventies with his novels, especially his non fiction masterpiece, The Onion Field, which was also adapted into a feature in 1979 (more of this later on). He sold the Choirboys film rights to Aldrich for the then huge sum of 700,000 dollars, and perhaps naively expected more involvement with the adaptation. Focusing on a group of LA police officers, the stellar cast included Woods, Louis Gossett, Jr. and Charles Durning. But the film deviated too greatly from the original source. Wambaugh himself wrote a screenplay, said the first draft got good feedback, but never heard anything else from the producers. "There was total silence," he said. Aldrich then announced that he thought Wambaugh was not going to be happy with the film, because he had to alter certain aspects of the script and the tone in general. Aldrich's main gripe with Wambaugh's tale was that he didn't relate to the idea of "feeling sorry for a cop. You're not drafted to be a cop.

So you've got to take some of the heat if you don't like what people think about you. After all, that's an extraordinary pension you get in twenty years; nobody else gets it. In fact, I disagree with Wambaugh to such an extent that I don't think people really like cops." Wambaugh, rightfully betrayed by the shift in the script's moral conscience, said with justification: "They mutilated my work."

It was not well received. Vincent Canby called it "cheap and nasty", while Wambaugh himself, annoyed by the fact that Aldrich had corrupted his characters and made them immoral in certain ways, called it a "dreadful, sleazy, insidious film." He sued the film company and bought back the film rights to two more of his novels, The Black Marble and The Onion Field, so next time he could have more control when they made their way to the big screen.

In 2014, Woods said: "You know, the only one of all these films that I ever did that I didn't like, that I was really, really disappointed in, was The Choirboys. Because Robert Aldrich, you know, brought a sensibility that was all wrong to it. It was ridiculous, he just completely missed it. Completely missed it. It wasn't a fun experience, and it was a great book, a great character, but it was just turned into a silly TV sitcom. I just thought it was horrible. And Joe hated it, understandably. But then I got to work with Joe on The Onion Field, which was a completely different experience."

He had a bit part in an episode of TV's Family (1977), but it was the following year when things really began to change for him. In 1978 the TV film The Billion Dollar Bubble was aired in the US. Originally made in 1976 and screened as part of the BBC Horizon series, two years later it saw a stand alone release across the pond. Giving James the chance to be centre stage again, he played Art Lewis, a man involved in a two billion dollar embezzlement plot with the Equity Funding Corporation. Directed by Brian Gibson, it's a well made film and is consistently engaging, mostly due to the acting. Woods proved that all the working his way through TV and film bit parts had paid off. This is no flashy, showy guest spot, but a leading pillar part where he props up the picture. Not since The Visitors had he had such an opportunity to be the driver of the plot, not just the wham-bam firecracker or the psychotic villain. He takes this role and gives it depth, commanding the viewer's attention.

"Brian Gibson flew over," Woods told me, "he met me here, and I said, 'Look, I got a guy to play my henchman, he's great and his name is Christopher Guest.' They'd never heard of him. He was a complete unknown at the time. I was thrilled I got him the part. Chris and I had been room mates doing a play at Washington's Arena Stage and later on Broadway, called Moon Children. We stayed friends and ended up living on the same street in New York's Greenwich Village. We hung out together with a bunch of other young actors and writers. And I said, 'He'd be great for this.' We filmed it and had rooms next to each other in this little hotel. And we worked over there for the BBC. And what people never realise is that Chris is actually a member of the House of Lords, because his father was Lord Haden-Guest. So Chris had that status and we went to the House of Lords together. I said, 'What are we doing here? How did we get in?' And he told me, 'Oh, I'm a member of the House of Lords.' We had a great time doing that movie. And Brian became a big director here, and he was a good buddy of mine. And Chris became one of the truly unique directors of our time."

Though his big break was just around the corner, 78 and 79 saw him enjoy more challenging work on TV. He was part of a talented cast in the television picture, The Gift of Love (1978), with Timothy Bottoms and Marie Osmond. Adapted from O Henry's short story, the festive tale is a class drama about a wealthy woman in an arranged marriage to a man deemed suitable for her, but falling for a man from a lower class. Woods is Alfred, the wealthy suitor also unhappy with the impending marriage, given he has his own ornithological concerns to see to. Woods gives the character some depth, ensuring he isn't just a personified type, but a man who'd believably rather watch birds than walk down the aisle.

In The Incredible Journey of Doctor Meg Laurel (1979), a TV film starring Lindsay Wagner, he was the Sin Eater, an odd ball citizen of the remote town of Eagles Nest, where the Meg of the title (along with Granny) has ended up in hopes of becoming the doctor for the people of the land from whence she originally came. Proudly female orientated, the film does tend to go a little broad on the "redneck" front, but Woods does an excellent job as a more primitive example of man.

There is another buried gem here too. And Your Name is Jonah (1979), directed by Richard Michaels, is an intelligent, nicely acted drama about a boy deemed mentally disabled and then institutionalised. It is soon discovered, however, that he is not mentally challenged at all, but is actually deaf. The good thing about this film is that it doesn't resort to schmaltz outright. It is sensitively handled, yes, but it's also unflinching, getting to you in a more naturalistic way. It helps, of course, that the acting is so strong. Sally Struthers is good as the boy's mother, while Woods is excellent as the dad, struggling with the ramifications of this severe misdiagnosis. Dealing with such an important and little-explored dilemma, it's a minor lost treasure that deserves to be dusted off and released on a new DVD (out of print copies are costly), primarily as a reminder of the harsh consequences of a misdiagnosis, but also for the performances. Woods would dazzle many filmgoers that same year with his terrifying turn in The Onion Field, but here, in a lower key, less explosive movie, he quietly impresses as the everyday father. "He's not retarded, man, he's deaf!" he angrily tells a friend who doesn't quite get it. When asked how you talk to him, Woods yells, "I don't know how to talk to him!" He's a dad coming to terms with the fact his son is not "perfect", and Woods gives the part intensity and genuine frustration.

Woods also put in a couple of spots on the TV series, Young Maverick (1979), itself a follow up to the highly popular series that starred his friend and collaborator, the great James Garner. Woods played Lem Franker in Dead Man's Hand Part 1 and 2, perhaps the last time he would be seen on screen without people instantly recognising him as James Woods. His ensuing popularity would grow in the early part of the 1980's, but it could be said that his roles in Holocaust (1978) and The Onion Field (1979) launched him out of regular TV work and guest spots into a realm of his own. Young Maverick and much of the TV and film work covered in this section, are a brilliant collective document of proto-Woods, evidence that as each role went on he seemed to broaden his abilities, and deepen the part he was playing with subtleties and more concealed complexities. His vast experience on the stage did help immensely; indeed, one can see the command he has in every scene during the early TV and film years, and one can only imagine how powerful he was in the theatre during this period. But the work he had done on the boards ensured he was well prepared for the opportunities that awaited him - and the opportunities proved to be truly remarkable.

HOLOCAUST (1978)

For certain, Woods' first brush with serious and wide exposure came with his part in the major TV miniseries, Holocaust (1978), which was a massive success the world over. Running in four parts on NBC in the USA, before making its way out to Europe and beyond, this unflinching account of a Jewish family's suffering under the tyrannical ruling of Hitler and the Nazis is hard hitting, heartbreakingly tragic and beyond powerful. Though focusing on two fictional families whose fates personify the drastic differences in the treatment of the Jews and the "pure" race, Holocaust does not trivialise this awful period in time. By using real events and sticking to historical facts, some forty years later Holocaust remains a truthful, respectful reminder of what the Jewish people went through in that bleak, horrifying era.

Written by Gerald Green and directed by Marvin J. Chomsky, we follow the development of two German clans. The first are the Aryan family of the Dorfs. Erik (played by Michael Moriarty) is a lawyer with a wife and child, who joins the Nazi party and becomes the trusted accomplice of SS leader Heydrich (played by David Warner) on his rise within the Third Reich.

The other running thread is more harrowing and emotionally devastating, as we go along with the Weiss family, who struggle and crumble under the sickening Nazi regime. Dr. Josef Weiss (Fritz Weaver), the patriarch, and his wife Berta (Rosemary Harris), are German Jews who steadfastly believe their place in upper crust Berlin society makes them impervious to the forthcoming Nazi onslaught. They have three children, one of whom is Karl (James Woods), one of millions of helpless Jews swept up in Hitler's maniacal crusade for a "pure race", and is sent to a concentration camp where he meets his tragic fate.

Spanning the pre-war period up to its final days in 1945, Holocaust keeps us on the edge of our seats, as we genuinely prey for our heroes and damn the atrocities of the Nazis. The fact it begins at the joyous wedding of Karl and Inga (played by Meryl Streep)) makes what follows all the more harrowing. The writing, I genuinely believe, is totally respectful to this most delicate of subjects. If anything, I feel the series, if it were to be broadcast widely again, would bring attention back to a tragedy that over the years many have overlooked in their ignorance.

As it happens, Holocaust was watched by 120 million Americans when it first aired in 1978, a remarkable amount of people. In Germany too, a third of the population tuned in, and it caused a huge impact there. Many Germans expressed their shock and sadness, the whole country going into a national debate about the dark legacy of the war and Germany's part in it. Professor Frank Bosch saw the series as a landmark moment in the world's understanding of the Holocaust. "Survivors came to the Auschwitz trials and journalists didn't even interview them. No-one cared about the victims. That changed with the TV series Holocaust," he told the BBC.

It has to be said that Holocaust is brilliantly structured and directed as a piece of engaging drama, but it succeeds most because of the cast. They put faces to the tragedy and make you truly care. Documentaries may horrify and enlighten, but in making sure each victim is a fleshed out character you root, worry and weep for, the sick and brutal truth hurts all the more.

All the actors give their characters dignity, particularly Woods and Streep, who are phenomenal here. After playing psychos, gun men, outcasts and weirdos for a few years on TV and film, Woods is really given the opportunity to display the wide breadth of his abilities. He soars as the ill-fated Karl in what was surely his strongest performance up to that date. He had, of course, been highly effective in everything he had done previously, but Holocaust marked a true turning point for him as an actor, and only led him to more greatness. He becomes Karl Weiss in a totally committed performance that is a complete tour de force.

That said, this was not merely an opportunity for someone to show their acting chops with some heavy material. Woods stated that he genuinely wanted to pay his respects to the victims of the Holocaust, to do an honourable job in immortalising both their pain and the nightmares that ensue when innocents get caught up in a megalomaniac's vision. His character goes through a complete journey, has an arc which ends in tragedy. Woods begins portraying the character as a bright young man with a bright future. He is marrying the girl he loves, hopes for a fruitful life ahead within his close knit, affluent family. In no time at all though, he is clad in striped grey, holed up like a rat in a prison, starved and beaten, all because of his ethnicity. The way Woods transforms before our eyes from hopeful to hopeless is staggering. The most upsetting scene for me, and the real line in the sand moment, is when he is interrogated by the SS. When they ask him "the name of the whore who gave birth to you", you can see his heart tear in two. Slapped roughly around the face, he must answer the question their way. When they press him on "the name of the pimp who raped her", he must answer with his father's name. It's a heartbreaking scene, and the look on Woods' face - disbelief mixed with genuine upset - makes your heart ache. Then he is dragged away for a beating, and we hear his yells of pain. It is then that Karl, and indeed we the viewer, know the tide has turned. It's utterly gut-wrenching and played with masterful skill.

Woods was conscious of the fact that they had to get this right, that such a subject could not be trivialised and that authenticity has vital. "It was an amazing experience," Woods said. "I remember I was standing in the gas chamber at Mauthausen with Meryl Streep. The effect those places have on you.... words can not adequately describe of course. One man who was in the show with us had in fact been in Dachau, and he had escaped. He was still getting a disabled pension from the West German government... He had been beaten by the Gestapo and he had to undergo a series of operations on his back... And I said to him, 'What's it like coming back here and putting on these striped pyjamas and everything?' And I remember Meryl saying to me, 'If this thing isn't as good as we think it's gonna be, we're going to hell. This thing has to be brilliant, or they just can't air it.' The impact it had! It was a great lesson."

Speaking to me about working on the epic drama, Woods said: "That was a huge experience. It was the second highest rated mini series on television at the time. You know, I was playing the lead with Meryl Streep. We were both new and unknown. We filmed in Austria for months on end, seven months we were there. I was there the whole seven months. And this role started with my wedding and ended with my death. It was huge. And I played a virtual victim. A heroic victim, but a victim. But it was a monumental production with such monumental actors. I mean, I just could not believe the people I was working with."

James then told me a story from during the promotion of the series. All the actors were giving interviews, and one day he found himself in front of a young reporter from a small newspaper. She asked Woods how the writers had come up with "all this stuff." Woods explained that the Weiss family were fictional but based on real people and accounts, an amalgamation of well educated, well-to-do

Jews living in Berlin. "No," she pressed, "I mean all this Holocaust stuff. The gas chambers and the concentration camps. How did they come up with all that stuff?" Understandably, James was stunned. "I stopped for a moment," James told me, "and I said, 'I don't understand what you're asking me. What do you mean? You're aware this is based on history aren't you?' And to be fair, she was young. But she went kind of white, very pale, and said, 'What do you mean?' I told her it had really happened. And she got really shaky. She was so stunned. To her credit I ended up explaining it all to her. I never forgot that. But when we were shooting Holocaust, they did a poll in West Germany and 85 percent of the Junior High School students were not familiar with who Hitler was. Maybe they suppressed that part of their history, but it was still shocking."

James also told me a very moving and upsetting story from the shoot. They were filming in a concentration camp and there was a scene where Woods had to be hoisted up and tortured. One of the Holocaust survivors, who was working on the series as an adviser, made some comments on accuracy. Then he explained to James that this very thing had happened to him when he was a young man imprisoned in a camp. Woods was moved beyond belief. Even when recalling this to me in 2021, 40 plus years later, he was verging on tears.

One thing I noticed whenever we spoke about Holocaust was the weight that James' voice took on. He knew what a responsibility it was to fill such a role, but he was also aware that he owed it to the brave people, both the survivors and those who died at the hands of the Nazis, to give the work all he had. And he certainly did that, for it remains a brave, dedicated and very moving characterisation. Mr Weiss could not have been more different from the role that made Woods an acclaimed star, The Onion Field's sociopathic killer Greg

Powell, but the important thing is that Woods is equally effective in both guises. The fact he could convince so thoroughly as such opposed men, a killer and a victim, was a credit to his abilities to be truthful and real in whatever role he had been given.

THE ONION FIELD (1979)

There are moments in film history where it's clear that something unexplainable is happening, often when a new star comes to the fore and captures the world's imagination. It isn't because they are about to be famous, because fame itself has little to do with the work; it's down to the person having that certain special quality, the fact that they are in the right moment at the right time, that all the planets have aligned and they are so at their peak that wide recognition is inevitable. One thinks of Dustin Hoffman in the opening airport scene of The Graduate (1967); Jack Nicholson doing his "to old DH Lawrence" shtick in Easy Rider (1969); Robert De Niro blowing up a postbox in Mean Streets (1973). They are landmark moments that introduced us to the actors we love the most. And I would add to that list the first time James Woods comes into The Onion Field (1979), during the shoe shine scene, and says, without a hint of friendliness, "Hi, I'm Greg Powell." It's clear that a true great has arrived, and it seems that it definitely felt like that at the time; after all, many critics and filmgoers who saw the film upon its release have said so. With The Onion Field came a true original, a new force who would explode into 80s cinema and introduce a whole new way of acting, a totally fresh sense of urgency and vitality. In many ways, Woods was to personify the whole decade that lie ahead, a period of excess and go-getting, where millions had a sudden urge to succeed and get to the top. Woods' characters have this all the way through the 80's, only the manner in which they strove for success was varied, and often rather questionable. Still, it felt like a shift in the way a leading movie actor took on a role and grabbed the attention of moviegoers.

The Onion Field is a powerful and often very moving drama based on a true story, originally adapted into a book by LAPD sergeant and author, Joseph Wambaugh. It concerns the infamous murder of LAPD police detective Ian Campbell, and the escape of Officer Karl Hettinger from the scene of the crime. The two officers had pulled over a car with suspicious drivers, Greg Powell and Jimmy Smith, the latter just out of prison, the former a crazed sociopath without a care in the world. Greg pulled a gun on the cops and forced them into their car, where they drove out to the outskirts of town. Pulled out of the vehicle, Powell murdered Campbell in cold blood, and Hettinger fled into the night. The subsequent farce of a trial to lock up the killers - among the most dragged out in US history - highlights the painfully fatal flaws in the legal system. It also begs the question, what is justice? And sadly, it seems vitally important that the true tragedy of Ian Campbell's fate got lost in the mix. Indeed, in both the film and the book, it becomes clear that the two men responsible for the death of one man and the mental scarring of another had far more rights than they deserved. Hettinger never recovered from the horror, and he suffered from mental problems for the rest of his life.

The Onion Field had been a best seller on the book shelves and Wambaugh was hoping to see the story, one he felt was a very important one that had to be told, come to the big screen. I asked Joe how he first became interested in the case. "It wasn't the unique and terrible incident itself that fascinated and finally obsessed me; it was the aftermath, when Karl Hettinger resigned from the LAPD for the crime of petty shoplifting. I had been assigned to Parker Center, the main headquarters of LAPD during the same time that he was working there following the kidnap and murder. During those months he had been forced to attend numerous roll calls where he was compelled to recount the events. By then, Monday-morning-quarterbacks had decided that he should never have 'given up his gun', even if it had resulted in him and Ian Campbell being shot to death on the street in Hollywood. Whenever I saw him, the pain in his face was haunting. Yes, he was already turning into a ghost."

Wambaugh was so committed to the project that he famously self-financed the film with director Harold Becker. Wambaugh told me: "The self-financing has been pointed out to me many times as being one of the dumbest movie-making decisions of that era. After seeing what a terrible movie was made from The Choirboys, I decided that self-financing was the only sure and certain way to attain complete control in the movie world. In addition to a big chunk of our own money, my wife raised funds from friends and other ordinary people, money that could have easily been lost despite our good intentions. Investors were reassured because Dee and I proposed that all investors would be paid back every dollar before any of our own investment was returned to us. I am happy to say that all investors were repaid and we neophytes actually made a small profit on the movie."

On getting Harold for the film, and knowing he was the right man for the job, Wambaugh told me: "I saw Harold Becker's first and only movie effort, an obscure British film called The Ragman's Daughter, and I liked everything about it. It was made on a shoestring, which is what we were trying to do. His first little UK movie proved that Harold could do a lot with a small amount of money, and that with his photography background it was sure to be beautifully shot."

Given it was their own money they had riding on the picture, Becker and Wambaugh had firm control, and both men could ensure (despite their own financial risks) that no Hollywood producer or chancing hack disrespected the truth for the sake of a proposed profit. After all, Wambaugh did once say that he felt he had been put on this earth to write The Onion Field. It was a story he believed in, and given he had been greeted with approval for the book (by the public and other police officers alike), he had to ensure the movie adaptation was respectful to Campbell and Hettinger.

The finished film is a rare gem. Becker directs beautifully, a true actor's director who lets the players get to grips with the material. He establishes a mood of unrest from the start, but it is only that fateful night when Campbell is killed that the atmosphere shifts into truly dark territory. That scene, as Ian watches the moon and hears the beloved bagpipes in his ears, brings forth a feeling of pure dread. The blast of the killer's gun rings in our ears, as does Jimmy's animalistic howl of a scream. It's a heartbreaking scene, with Ian wiping the tears from his eyes brought on by the onions around them in the field, and then rubbing his partner's hand before taking the bullet. From here on, everything changes. The script is faultless of course, and together Becker and Wambaugh helped craft one of the most honest and compelling films of the era.

Becker and Wambaugh were aided by a terrific cast; Franklin Seales is brilliant as Jimmy Smith, while Ted Danson and John Savage are also very convincing as the two cops, the one sadly murdered, and the one that escaped with his body, but not all of his mind. But the most striking and indeed disturbing performance comes from James Woods as Greg, a sociopathic narcissist who can turn the charm on just as quickly as he can draw a gun. This star making turn, which earned Woods rave reviews and a Golden Globe nomination, is a breathtaking, terrifyingly convincing piece of work which is right up there to this day as one of the finest acting feats of 70's American cinema.

Becker and Wambaugh had a disagreement over the casting of Woods. The real Greg had blue eyes, while Woods' are brown, and Wambaugh strictly saw Powell as a cold eyed killer. "I was dead set against the actor Joe wanted," Becker said. "I saw Greg Powell in Woods. It wasn't that he physically looked like him. The lookalike was in the persona."

In his taped audition, Woods knows that he was electrifying. "I uncorked the rage of 10 years on them all," Woods said in a 1980 interview. "It was a scene where I pull a gun on another petty crook. I did the scene, dropped the gun, said, 'Thank you,' and drove away." Woods told me that if that audition didn't convince them he was right for the part, then nothing would, and he wished them luck with their picture. He had uttered these words in the spur of the moment, and there was no calculated motive behind this seemingly hedonistic exit.

Speaking to me at length about this landmark film and his own breakthrough performance within it, I felt honoured to get such a detailed insight. "I wasn't the original person cast," James told me. "Joe wanted all lookalikes exactly. There was a fine actor named Stephen McHattie who Harold and Joe were gonna use. My agent Todd Smith actually convinced them to do a screen test. Joe was against it. I went in for the screen test and I did one scene, the one when I threaten the guy with the gun. After, I walked out. And I found out later that Joe's wife Dee turned round and said, 'There's no question, he's the guy. That's him.' And Joe very much trusted Dee, and I ended up getting the part. And honestly, I feel that if there was a part I was destined to play, it was that part."

Wambaugh himself told me of the casting of Woods: "Jimmy Woods never let me forget that I had my eye on a different actor, because the actor had a physical resemblance to the killer, Gregory Powell. That is until my wife, Dee, came to auditions and saw Jimmy reading for the part and said, 'He's the one.' Jimmy always praised Dee's perspicacity after that and wondered how she ever married a dumb shit like me. Harold instantly recognized Jimmy's profound intensity."

On the film itself, James said to me, "We all felt like we were doing something that was a mission. I'm very pro-law enforcement, and I think cops have a tough job. And I love history, and this was a historical story. There are six different levels of reality when telling a story in Hollywood, legal levels. You can say something is A True Story, Based On A True Story, Inspired By A True Story, Inspired by True Events... It goes on and on, right? We went for This Is A True Story, meaning legally you can't say anything or show anything that isn't actually the truth. It was even down to the colour of the socks we wore during the trial. Everything was so unbelievably accurate."

Franklyn Seales and James Woods in The Onion Field (1979).

In keeping the film accurate, Woods ensured his portrayal was as authentic as possible and not merely a pantomime villain. Though a sociopath, Woods gives the man a multitude of dimensions, and he is no straight-forward bad guy. In Woods' hands, there is something rather uniquely unusual about the man, even though he is still completely dangerous and best behind bars. Woods puts in little touches no other actor could have, simply because he approached him as a man who killed one fateful night, but wasn't going around killing all day everyday.

Wambaugh explained to me how authenticity was key in the making of the picture: "The title sequence is unique and says what it means. Not the cop-outs we always see, like, this is based on a true story or suggested by a true story, etc. Our movie opens with five words: This is a true story. And yes, Harold kept that in mind from beginning to end. There was nothing added or deleted for Hollywood enhancement. I can't think of another movie as true as this one. I observed every foot of film that was shot on location or on set. I was the guy, bundled up and freezing at night, sitting far enough away from the director so as not to distract. Jimmy's scene where he holds a gun in the face of a crime partner, hand trembling with rage, was an attention-getter. When we started this movie I told Harold that he would never again have such autonomy and utter authority over a film as he would with The Onion Field. I think he will attest that I was right. This is Harold Becker's movie."

When I think of Woods as Powell, a number of moments enter my head. There is one scene which I find particularly disturbing. In the middle of the night, Jimmy is laid awake listening to Greg and his partner performing loud sex. Having enough, he goes outside and gets into the car, ready to drive away. Already he is unsure about spending much more time with Powell and his "family". Just as he starts the car, Greg appears out of nowhere in the darkness, naked, almost snarling, looking down at Jimmy in the car. It's the first time

Powell comes across as genuinely frightening, and it is from here on we sense the shift in mood.

A hint of misplaced arrogance is also revealed in a key scene. Early in the picture, Greg boasts to Jimmy that he is a sexual maestro, and basically that his girl would never need to go to bed with another man because she is so spoilt with his love making skills. As he says this, with a certain amount of misguided pride, he is unaware of the fact that Jimmy and Greg's "oh-so satisfied" girlfriend have actually just had sex, albeit on the couch, and rather messily. A small detail, it's another example of Greg's delusion.

Another scene in particular stands out, and it's darkly funny, strangely enough. It comes in the opening 20 or so minutes. Greg, Jimmy and another petty crook are out in their car, looking to rob a store or two. Woods' character is rather proud of his "disguise" as he puts it, applied carefully so that the authorities will not be able to identify him. This disguise, in actual fact, consists of a fake mole and two dyed eyebrows. It's a brief moment of humour in a very dark film, but this little touch (which happened in real life) is what makes Woods' performance so believable. "By the way," Woods told me, "when he (Greg) was arrested, on the arrest warrant, he was described as a white male with a mole on his left ear. His so called disguise worked against him!"

There were other subtle touches too, as James informed me: "I did that hop skip jump step when I go across the street to disguise my walk. Harold was laughing so much he had to put a cloth in his mouth. We were afraid his laugh would be on the soundtrack. It was funny, I had to admit. We had so much fun making that movie."

In true form, Woods gives Greg certain elements which are oddly funny, and at times, rather pathetic. And of course, such details make the murder of the innocent officer all the more powerful and devastating, given that we really don't expect it from this rather inept criminal.

"I suppose existentially a man who pulls the trigger is a killer," Woods told the New York Times, "but I never saw Powell as such. Killers, like other people, live their lives from moment to moment. The chilling thing about the murder is that I was as surprised as anyone in the audience when I pulled the trigger."

"That character was fascinating to me," Woods told Fresh Air in 1999, "because he would put on a fake Southern accent. He would always try to be other than he was. With true stories there are always things that in real life you cannot imagine. And we meticulously researched the film. It was difficult 'cos I was playing a cop killer, but... killers aren't killing every minute of the day. They still have to buy groceries and get their laundry done. I try to give a character like that a life, an entire life and how he would think about the everyday boring details about living his life. Then along the way, unexpectedly, this capacity to destroy in a horrific way just erupts. That's how it is with sociopaths. You have to think about the objectives and goals people have... And the super objective of any sociopath is, How can I get what I want all the time and still appear to be a normal citizen when I have to, to get other people to do it for me?"

James told me that the odd little bolo tie Greg wears, with the scorpion embedded into the plastic, was something that he himself brought along to the set. It seems like a tiny detail, but such details are the making of a classic performance. "For me," he said, "that was the image of that character. But it was very skeletal, that role, I wanted to look skeletal. I lost some weight for the part, and I actually had my dentist build a gold tooth around my real tooth. I thought it would be cool for him to have a gold tooth. I nearly lost a real tooth doing that movie."

About his experiences during the filming, Woods told me: "I think some of the scenes Jimmy and I did are among the most authentic of my career. And we were surrounded by real cops, some of whom had been part of the task group that went through all the legal machinations of this incredibly long case. And they (the cops) said, 'It's like the real guys. You *are* those people.' And that is not what Franklin was like off set, but man, he got into that character and I believe I did too. And we were there! And just look at the cast; Ted Danson, what a performance; John Savage, what a performance. One after another after another in that movie."

As a history buff interested in law, Woods was also intrigued by the crucial mistake Powell makes which changes the course of the lives of all four men involved in the shooting. He told me: "I was fascinated by the fact that this all hinged on one person's misunderstanding of the Little Lindbergh Law (a law inspired by the kidnapping of the Lindbergh baby). Greg Powell thought that once they kidnapped the cops they were gonna go to the gas chamber if they were caught, because they've already kidnapped somebody. But it's actually kidnapping somebody for ransom or for kidnapping with grievous bodily harm. Neither of these had taken place until he shot Ian Campbell. And it was never determined who fired the final shot. Hettinger looked back and saw the two men who were dressed exactly alike - and they did that on purpose that night. And it was dark. Even though one man was white and one was black, at night and in the light of the moon on the onion field it was hard to tell who was who. So he never knew for sure who had fired the fatal gun shot into Ian Campbell's chest when he was lying on the ground, the shot that killed him."

I asked James if he ever met the real Greg Powell. "You know," he said, "it's interesting. I had a chance to meet him, as I had a chance to meet Byron De La Beckwith (who James played in 1996's Ghosts of Mississippi), and I always felt that I didn't wanna meet real killers, because as an actor I wanted to do, but as a moral man I don't want to inflate the ego of people who are really vile, worthless... I mean, I will begrudgingly call them human beings. So my attitude was that I knew enough of the story from what I could get out of Joe and so on. And they were willing for me to meet him, but I said, 'No, I don't wanna meet him.' I had no desire to meet him."

Given that as a committed actor Woods is fascinated by the human condition, playing Greg Powell offered him an insight into that most curious of beasts - the sociopath. "For me," he said, "it was an opportunity to learn about the differences between sociopathic behaviour and psychopathic behaviour. Sociopaths have no regard for human life. And what happens is, a sociopath kills someone and is having lunch ten minutes later, and they could be talking about a baseball score. It was believed that Greg Powell had some brain damage from abuse as a child. He had shrinkage of the brain which had never been diagnosed. So he may have actually had real physical evidence of being a brain-damaged sociopath."

Woods became very passionate when we spoke about The Onion Field, and I could have listened to his thoughts and memories of this one film alone for hours. "The Onion Field is very important for me," Woods told me. "It was the moment I went from being an actor to being a - and I put this in quotes, because I am not being arrogant - a 'movie star' or whatever I was after that. I became a significant player in the movie industry. It was my launch pad into my career as a movie actor."

For James, Holocaust and The Onion Field are interconnected in his mind, and one story he told me explained why. He said that no one really knew about The Onion Field until Harold Becker and Joe Wambaugh decided to take it to Cannes to try and sell it to a distributor. Woods, naturally, was excited, and asked if he could tag along. When he was told they couldn't afford to take him, Woods saved up all the money he had, and got a plane ticket to the Cannes Film Festival. He didn't even have enough money to get a hotel room.

"Holocaust had just played in Europe," James told me, "and you have to remember this is before the internet, before videotape - anything. And it was huge, a huge hit in Europe and America. So I didn't know this. I didn't even have a publicist. And they were there in Cannes, Joe and the producers. And they said, 'Wow, you're here?' And I said, 'Yeah, on my own money though.' And they said, 'Well, you're on your own.' And all of a sudden the paparazzi come over and they're taking pictures, and I'm turning round to see who they're taking pictures of, and it's me. They go, 'Mr Woods, Mr Woods!' And everyone's going, 'What the fuck?' I was as dazed as they were. And they were going 'Karl!' Karl was the character I played in Holocaust, and they were taking tons of pictures. And they asked, 'What are you here for?' And I said I had a great new film out called The Onion Field. So the press said, 'Wow, tell us about it.' So I said, 'Hang on, I want a first class ticket back, and you got to put me up at the Carlton. Otherwise I'm not saying anything (laughs). I don't even have a bed tonight guys!' So they said, 'OK you got it.' I got my ticket and got my room."

James told me that Dennis Davidson Associates were publicising the film and had a female agent out there pressing for screenings. "But basically they didn't think anyone wanted to see it. Nobody gave a shit. And they arranged a screening of The Onion Field for, like, one buyer. There was this one guy there with his assistant, and she was translating the movie for him. There was no one else there. I said, 'This is ridiculous!'"

Francis Ford Coppola's Apocalypse Now was showing at Cannes the same year, and James managed to wangle himself a ticket inside. At the Majestic the next day, all the critics were gathered together. One of the head critics of a certain paper was pontificating before his colleagues over the apparent meaning of the film, and about how Coppola had gotten Joseph Conrad's original source novel, Heart of Darkness, totally wrong. James, a big fan of Conrad's work, corrected him and basically massacred the guy, bringing him down a peg or two. Rex Reed, the famous film critic, happened to be there, and thanked James for his stellar work in shooting down this pompous ass. Reed then introduced himself to Woods and said he was aware of his work in the theatre. Thinking on his feet, James asked Rex what he was doing the next day. He told him he was solidly booked up with screenings, but that he was free between 10 a.m. and 12 p.m. Excited, Woods insisted he would get a print of The Onion Field, meet him at a small venue and screen the movie for him. Reed agreed to be there. Sure enough, at 10, Reed turned up "slightly hung over" but ready to watch The Onion Field. "And there he was," Woods said,recalling the incident. "I got to give him credit. But the girl with the print didn't show up for twenty minutes. She was out partying or something. Finally, she turns up and I begged Rex to stay." Seated and ready, somewhat typically, the projector bulb blew out, which they speedily replaced. Then, finally, the film started rolling.

Once it was over, the lights came back on. James apologised for the mishaps and awaited Rex's appraisal of the film. Reed did not comment right away, but he did invite James to an afternoon critic's luncheon. Artists didn't usually go to such events, and though Woods thought it an odd idea, he went along. "I'd never been to anything like this," he told me. "I'm just a kid from Rhode Island. It was a big deal! Rex Reed was very flamboyant, and very self assured to say the least. But very sweet. And I'm there, and he hasn't said anything about the movie. In the middle of the lunch he stands up and taps his glass. 'To our lovely hosts... and to my friend James Woods!' And they all clapped and were like, 'Who is this young man?' And Rex said, 'He happens to be one of the leads in the best film at Cannes this year. And if you haven't seen it, see it, because it's the best film I have seen this year. It's a great movie. You'd better call Dennis Davidson Associates and take a peak.'"

More critics saw the film, and when James and the team behind The Onion Field returned to the United States, it had received a two page review in Newsweek, being declared one of the best films of the decade. "It was phenomenal," James said. "My whole life turned around. I got nominated for a Golden Globe for Best Actor. That was fun, and that was the turning point in my whole life."

Woods, of course, is tremendous in The Onion Field, but the film excels in every area. It remains a very disturbing and thought provoking classic of independent film, and is viable proof that if you hang on to your integrity, you will be rewarded and the film will endure. It also catapulted Woods into the film industry's major league.

HAROLD BECKER ON
THE ONION FIELD

The acclaimed director of The Onion Field, and other gems such as
The Boost, City Hall and Sea Of Love, spoke to me about meeting
James Woods for the first time, casting him as Greg Powell, and the
making of The Onion Field.

Do you remember how Jimmy got the part?

Yes. I even remember the first time I met Jimmy Woods. He came to
see me and he was a relatively unknown actor. The part had been
written - and remember this was based on a true story. The actual
character he was going to play, the actual killer, was residing at San
Quentin. We were going to tell a true story, to bring the reality of the
character to the screen. So we needed a very special actor for that.
And Jimmy, who did not look anything like Greg Powell, I knew he
had it in him to be Greg Powell. The picture hung on that whole
portrayal; the energy and the drive of the picture, the reality of the
movie, is tested by that performance. And it was to me and the world
at large an amazing performance. It literally drove the movie. We've
seen a lot of killers on the screen and everything, but he gave it such
an intensity that you felt more in the moment. We were really
watching this cold-blooded cop killer. He sort of left the artifice
behind.

It's fascinating hearing your views, because I love that film so much.

I mean, I can remember vividly - and this is over 40 years ago, we're
talking 1978 - I can remember the first time I met him. I remember

our first meeting. The script describes him as having icy blue eyes and blond hair. Nothing like Jimmy, but before the audition was over I knew that Jimmy was the character. That the inner character was there and the rest would take care of itself. It was a big moment in my life, and in Jimmy's.

Is it true that Joe Wambaugh was set on the other actor, and you had to persuade him that Jimmy Woods was the right guy?

That's right. Joe, who wrote the book, a brilliant writer, but being a writer and knowing the actual people, when he saw Jimmy he did not strike him, and to him that was not Greg Powell. He thought of a blond with icy blue eyes. And Jimmy said he'd do a screen test for us, and of course that screen test proved to me, and Joe, that we had the right actor for the part.

When you come across a special actor like James Woods, is it a stand out moment for you?

Oh yeah, it always is. When you find the real thing it's always a moment, you know? And I can't imagine the film without Jimmy. He lent such credibility to that character. This is a cold-blooded killer who kidnaps a cop, takes him to the onion field, and shoots him point blank in the face. To do it with conviction, that's what goes through you.

Greg Powell is such a weird character. I mean, I know he was a real guy, but in the film you can immediately tell he's a sociopath, yet he also has this strange little way about him. Like the mole and the little

skip over the road. And then all of a sudden, even he seems surprised when he blows Ian Campbell away.

Well, the interesting thing is that first half of it is a crime melodrama, and the second half is a series of trials in which time the character is fleshed out and you get the depth of him, and it takes the second part to really inform you who this Greg Powell was. It was not just a two dimensional character who puled the trigger.

Yes, and that's what is so interesting about the film. It is a film in two halves, but it doesn't feel jarring.

Exactly, and that was the challenge of the movie. You see the other dimensions of the character when Jimmy Woods as Greg Powell is brought in for questioning. You are already beginning to see the other dimensions of him; the bravado falls away and you get into the depths of the person who was behind that gun. That is what made it, to me, a memorable performance and a memorable movie.

Well I think the scene in the onion field is one of the most disturbing and haunting scenes I have ever seen.

Oh, it felt so real. And Franklyn Seales, as we were shooing it, when Jimmy pulls the trigger... it's hard to describe it even now, but Franklyn Seales started screaming! That was not in the script. It was not rehearsed. It's in the film. He started to scream. That is how affected he was, that is how affected everyone was, it was that real, and that is what I wanted to create. I wanted to create that kind of depth, because we have seen plenty of shootings and mayhem on screen, but this just had to be real. Joe Wambaugh said to me that the most important words in the script were, This Is A True Story, and that was my responsibility. I found Jimmy, I met James Woods, and I knew I had the character who could carry this movie.

If you watch key films from that era, when a key actor first arrives, like Robert De Niro in Mean Streets, you know something is happening. I think when James Woods comes into The Onion Field, you feel that same level of magnitude.

Exactly! It's something that goes beyond. You experience something that goes beyond what you normally get from a film, beyond entertainment, that you are watching something real. And that is the hardest thing to get, to go beyond the cliché.

What kind of direction did you have to give in that film?

The important thing is to create an environment in which the actor can express the character. You don't direct actors in terms of the acting, but in terms of the direction you go in. You create an environment. Like with Franklyn screaming there, he forgot he was in a movie. He was living it! And that's what you wanna feel like when you are watching it. All I had to do was set the stage for the performance, and that performance has to reach beyond. There are a million adjectives for it, but the final thing is to just do it. It's like catching lightning in a bottle. You know when you have it. That was the heart of that film. I think it's one of Jimmy's most indelible performances. He never met Greg Powell - he didn't have to. He had to bring his own inner self to it.

WOODS ON SCREEN: 1980 - 1982

In the wake of his acclaim for The Onion Field, Woods enjoyed a run of interesting roles on the big screen. After such a critical success, it was understandable that he was offered a rush of scripts. But he had to make the right choice, not merely the easiest. Even though the frightening Greg Powell cast a formidable shadow over the whole film, thankfully Woods' performance did not see him typecast as an all-out sociopath. Granted, he did go on to perfect a certain type of unhinged, intense man, but his parts were infinitely more varied. And when he did play a sociopath, it was never a caricature; Woods ensured each one had humanity, albeit often in a warped sense.

But James never set out to be a "success" in the sense that a movie star is a success. He wanted to act, to be good at that craft. "It's funny," Woods told me during one of our chats. "My movie career was never supposed to be a commercial star career. I liked to think of myself more as - at my height - deeply appreciative that people saw me as one of the most pre-eminent independent artists in the film community. If I could be regarded in any way it would be that, that I was a part of the independent film industry. All these independent movies that had something to say..."

Given he had found his initial run of acclaim with director Harold Becker and Joe Wambaugh, it seemed only right that he should team up with them again, even if this time it was more of a favour and he did not have a prominent part. In 1980's The Black Marble, adapted from Wambaugh's novel, Paula Prentiss plays an LAPD sergeant who, with Valnikov (played by Robert Foxworth), is investigating the kidnapping of a wealthy woman's dog. The scheme, as it turns out, is run by Philo Skinner (Harry Dean Stanton), the owner of a dog grooming parlour. Though the film develops into a love story between the two stars, like many of Wambaugh's stories it focuses on the psychological and emotional stress that police officers endure in their work. The Black Marble is a fine character study, and to top it all off, it features a marvellous cameo from Woods as a street fiddler. It's a strange and beautiful scene, and Woods, whose arrival is unexpected (even when you first watch the film awaiting his appearance), gives the moment a certain tenderness which few would usually associate with him. It's a hidden bit of gold in his rich filmography. It should also be noted that Woods did the cameo for free. He told the New York Times in 1979 while promoting The Onion Field, "I owe it to Joe Warnbaugh. He and Harold Becker gave me five minutes to prove myself. They let me test for the part of Greg Powell in The Onion Field even though Joe didn't think I was right for it. He's the only one in 10 years in this town who was willing to give me five minutes to prove myself." He returned the kindness with a highly memorable cameo. Harold Becker told me had Jimmy in as his "lucky penny".

In 1981 he had a supporting part alongside three established stars, Sigourney Weaver, Christopher Plummer and William Hurt, in Peter Yates' Eyewitness. Scripted by Steve Teisch, it tells the story of a New York caretaker, Daryll (Hurt), who is a huge admirer of TV reporter Tony Sokolow (Weaver). When a wealthy Asian with links to the underworld is murdered in the building where Daryl works, Tony feels the janitor may have some information. Though actually unaware of any real details, he entertains the reporter's intuitive nature because, essentially, he is besotted. Perversely, the real killers begin to suspect that Daryll does know more than he is letting on, and then the real trouble starts. Meanwhile, Tony's husband to-be, played by Christopher Plummer, is up to no good, and may be a much shadier character than people assume.

Brilliantly written and directed, Eyewitness is a solid thriller which benefits from just the right amount of tension. Noting is overcooked for the sake of sensationalism, and there is genuine intrigue in the predicament the two leads find themselves in. Weaver and Hurt are brilliant here, but one cannot ignore Woods' part as Aldo, a manic friend of Daryll's who winds up getting himself in a spot of bother, despite the fact he has nothing to do with the murder at all. Woods puts in a splendid turn, raising thought provoking questions about the fascination of crime, and the bizarre wish of some to be a part of that world, in any way possible. One of the funniest lines in the film comes when the two cops, played by Steven Hill and a young Morgan Freeman, are talking of Woods: "When Aldo was a little boy he must have wanted to grow up a suspect."

But there is much more to Aldo than a young guy wanting in on the world of seamy crime. A Vietnam veteran who served alongside Daryll, Aldo is open about the fact he believes he was a coward in the war, while his good friend Daryll was a decorated hero. Aldo is also keen on his sister marrying Daryll, because he wants to be part of a big family. This man, pathetic in some ways but also likeable in others, was fired from his job with Daryll, and is desperate to be accepted. He attempts to manufacture a place where he can be welcomed, accepted and embraced. He rather movingly speaks of a fantastical family get-together when everyone is happy to see Aldo when he arrives. A coward born to fail (at least in his own eyes), he attaches himself to the murder in a bid to feel a part of the action, to be in the thick of things for once, rather than just the guy on the side-lines looking in.

Though Aldo is referred to as a coward in the script, when I put this point to James himself he had a different view on the character and his time in Vietnam. "Well you know, what is interesting about it is that when you look at that war, and this is my view on it, anyone who set foot in that country was a hero as far as I'm concerned. It was such a mosh pit of violence. Oliver Stone told me he was terrified in Vietnam all the time. A lot of my friends who were Vietnam veterans said it was terrifying. It was a jungle. They had no control over their environment. It was just this horror show. So, Aldo's character, I lamented that about him. Being in terror in the middle of battle, you're a hero just for being there, dude."

I brought up the fact that, though shady, Aldo was a sympathetic character, and Woods played him so that you really did feel for the guy. And the more we spoke about Eyewitness, a forty year old film at the time, the more Woods recalled of the filming. "I saw him as a guy who could have had his own little movie. And one thing I loved about shooting it was when I got to sit on the back of the motorcycle with the TV set (laughs). Another thing I loved was Peter Yates. I remember we were doing a scene once, and Yates was standing with the script supervisor, who usually take notes on the set. So it came to Take Six and he said to the script supervisor, 'Write B.A.' And I was like, 'Wait a minute, does B.A. stand for bad acting?' And he said, 'Quite frankly, yes.' He put down a note that I had given bad acting (laughs). He said, 'Well it wasn't what I wanted for the scene.' I said, 'It's fine, you don't have to back-pedal, I'll do it again!' We became friends after. I had a great time. Bill Hurt and I became great friends too after we did that movie."

When we came to Bill Hurt's performance, James mused on the talents of his contemporary. "Bill and I had a great time. He's a very unique actor. He's kind of a master of spare acting. He is a master of minimalism of acting. Every actor of a generation admires the great actors of his own generation, but they are also in a robust way competitors. So it was often a case of, 'I hope I get that part. Oh, Bill

Hurt got it!' Or, 'Oh, Jimmy Woods got the part!' So Bill and I grew up in the same class if you will. We were always competing for the same roles, even though we were different types. And I greatly admire him. I thought he was one of the great actors of my generation; and he still is! We even ended up against each other at the Oscars (in 1987). I am proud to say he was one of my fellow actors and friends."

On the subject of William Hurt, Woods continued: "What is remarkable about Bill as an actor, is his great ability is the spare invitation into the character's soul. In many ways he is the opposite of what I do as an actor. My characters are often very flamboyant, and they reach for the stars. My characters are always reaching for the stars hoping to get over the fence. But he would not move and just let the heavens sort of reach him. So it was interesting to work together because we worked in very different ways. And I think that worked for the characters being so different in Eyewitness too."

This got James on to the subject of playing men who are outsiders, and who are not often the central focal point but someone on the sidelines who piques the filmgoer's interest. "I love playing these marginal characters - and I say marginal as in their place in society or their world or whatever. I think these characters who are marginalised but are also in the structure of the piece, rich, vibrant, supporting characters - which is a category I embrace by the way... I don't think you have to be the star of the movie. I made a career of playing supporting characters who kind of steal the attention of the moviegoer. I think those characters come to life when the lead character embraces them and respects them. It comes with the generosity of spirit of great leading actors who embrace an actor who has some degree of talent, and certainly emotional and spiritual investment in the character."

In 1982, Woods appeared in two films which were among the most interesting of his career, roles which were full, meaty, and gave him space to stretch himself. The first was in Fast-Walking, the first of two collaborations with director-producer James B. Harris. This gritty, often plain seedy drama is set in a prison in Oregon. Woods plays Frank Miniver, nicknamed Fast-Walking, a well-liked but totally corrupt jail guard who runs prostitutes for Mexicans. What makes this act particularly sleazy is the fact he runs his "operation" out of his cousin's local convenience store. At one point he "tries out" a sexy woman named Moke (Kay Lenz), who robs him at gun point. But we haven't seen the last of her. She happens to be an accomplice and some-time girlfriend of tough prisoner Wasco (Tim McIntire), who aids Frank on his less-than-savoury shenanigans. There is also the arrival of Galliot (Robert Hooks), a black political prisoner who comes under the radar of Wasco, who wants him killed, while Frank is offered a large sum of money to help him escape.

Harris first came up with the idea for Fast-Walking when he read a book by Ernest Brawley called The Rap. He wrote the script in 1980 and filming began in July of that year on a budget of 4 million dollars, with Montana State Prison as the primary location. Though the shoot ended in August, it wasn't released until two years later.

This murky, often grubby film is as engaging as it is unexpected. With its questionable characters, and their equally questionable motives, no one could win an award for citizen of the year, but the script ensures we do not judge or condemn. We accept, at times reluctantly, the truth of these people's lives. Frank himself, for instance, is presented to us as-is from the word go. The very first shot of the film, for example, is a close up of him driving with a fellow guard while smoking a huge joint, clearly stoned and rambling gibberish. Right away, we accept that Frank/Fast-Walking is no ordinary, law-abiding guard. Woods plays him with such charm that we don't even mind the fact he is basically a pimp, and might even justify it with the fact he's low paid at the jail. But Woods pulls it off by somehow not making Frank loathsome. Indeed, he is both liked and likeable, and though his actions are often vile, Woods relents from resorting to fiendish characteristics. He lacks the high nervous energy of some other early characters of his, being more laid back and generally sure of himself. The supporting cast are great too, especially M. Emmet Walsh as the mouthy sergeant (who has a very memorable moment when Fast-Walking catches him in bed with a lady), and Robert Hooks as Galliot. It's most notable though for Woods, here taking a much-welcomed lead central part; though of course, it's more anti-hero than straight hero. He excels all the way through this brilliant, sadly overlooked gem.

The other film from 1982 was Split Image. The picture stars Michael O'Keefe as Joshua, a college gymnast, supposedly clean cut, who is lured into a youth religious cult by Rebecca (Karen Allen), which is led by Kirklander, played by Peter Fonda. At first he is sceptical, but soon learns to see things Kirklander's way. Troubled, his parents (Brian Dennehy and Elizabeth Ashley) hire a bounty hunter named Charles Pratt (played by Woods) to take him out of the cult by force and reverse the brainwashing he has been subjected to.

Split Image is very entertaining in its own right, but also raises genuine concerns over organised religious cultism, and the danger of following a supposed guru. Directed by Ted Kotcheff, it avoids melodrama and predictability, and benefits from a group of very strong performances. The best, for me at least, come from Dennehy and Woods; Dennehy the stressed, well-meaning father, Woods the ballsy live-wire hired to exorcise the young man's mind. In the deprogramming sequence, he tries to degrade the image of

Kirklander by spitting on his picture, then setting fire to it. In the end, Woods comes up with a better method; brutalising the boy's father in front of him, even spitting on him too, in a bid to bring back to the surface the undying love he has for him. It is this paternal link that revives Joshua.

Sporting a thin moustache, Woods puts in a brilliant, high-wired effort and inserts healthy doses of darkly comic relief. The brain washing scene, as disturbing as it is (the psychedelic tinge to the screen; the moment Joshua sees Woods as a weird creature harassing him through his fish-lens vision) is tinged with black humour. The way he gets up as much phlegm as possible before hocking on Kirklander's glossy image, and then tauntingly puts a flame to it, is genuinely funny. There is also the scene when Dennehy and his wife first hire him, and he admires their home. "I live in a real piss hole," he adds with a smile. One doesn't see Woods here, but the wily, wiry bounty hunter adamant on bringing the boy back to his home and restoring his mind.

I singled this film out in one of my interviews with Woods and he told me all about it: "Now Split Image was interesting. I ended up meeting Ted Kotcheff, who became one of my best friends; like Harold Becker, like Oliver Stone, the people I have worked with several times, and we became great friends. So, Ted hired me for that part in Split Image. We had about twenty pages of script for the de-programming scene. And I improvised a lot. Ted always loved me because there was a famous line in the film, about the kid snacking on dog shit. I had told them that in cults they make them eat dog shit. I was encouraging them to understand how serious these cults were. Actually, our technical advisers on that were two real de-programmers, who de-programmed Scientologists. The stuff they told us about those guys, that's another story. I mean, I won't go there.

Anyway, the film ran out of money. Ted said, 'We have all this filming to do, I don't know what we're gonna do.' So, what happened was, Ted actually paid the crew, I worked for free. You know, I said, 'I'll work for free, don't worry about it.' We improvised for three days, non-stop, we never stopped. We just took an hour break, slept, and then improvised that entire twenty-page sequence in three days. And we held on to the film. We worked for free. You don't see a lot of that now. You know, it was like, We're doing an independent film, come on, let's get this movie made and stop us getting ripped off by someone. Ted put his own money on the line and we said, 'We're gonna help you out. We're gonna get this move made!' I mean, it's frustrating that the company wouldn't pay for it, but they paid for it once we gave them the footage, and they said, 'OK, we'll reimburse you.' And it was like, 'Why didn't you do that in the first place?' But we got the movie made and that was that. It's something I'm proud of. And I made a lot of friends on that movie; Michael O'Keefe of course, and Brian Dennehy, who I made Best Seller with. I just loved Brian. And Peter Fonda, he was a sweet guy. I remember him as a sweet man that I liked very much, an underrated actor. I liked all the people I worked with on that movie. Just wonderful, a wonderful group."

These films, all released in the glow of his acclaim for The Onion Field, took Woods out of his psycho mould, his Greg Powell darkness, and expanded his screen image. He was now the intelligent, street wise, often rather sleazy, but ultimately likeable and charismatic modern man. And he was on the cusp of a greater recognition which would come his way in the next few years.

Images from the original trailer of Videodrome (1983).

VIDEODROME (1983)

"A Clockwork Orange of the 80's."
- Andy Warhol

*"Do I want to do a weird film with David Cronenberg? Of course I do!
And it turned out to be very prescient. I see people walking down the
streets with the cell phones glued to their hands. It may as well be a
flesh gun. We are in the Videodrome!"*
- James Woods to the author

Among James Woods' most celebrated films, David Cronenberg's
disturbing sci-fi thriller Videodrome can turn even the most open
minded art film fanatic's brain to mush. The man who had directed
such terrifying body horror flicks as Scanners and Rabid hit an early
peak here with his darkly allegorical attack on outside influence and
its ability to control the freewill of the viewer turned receptacle. But
the film is also about the merging of tech and flesh, the idea that
technology is merely an extension of what it is to be human.

Woods is Max Renn, the owner of CIVIC TV in Toronto, who
stumbles upon a mysterious show called Videodrome, which
reportedly depicts real life violence. When he meets disc jockey Nikki
(Debbie Harry), Max is lured into the weird and not so wonderful
world of the drome. Sucked within its paradoxical, mind bending
weirdness, Max loses track of what is real and what is imaginary,
what he is seeing and feeling himself and what is being presented to
him by the Videodrome. The whole thing, a kind of psychedelic/
psychological odyssey, culminates in one of the most unforgettable
finales in horror history.

The idea of Videodrome came to Cronenberg in his early years, in his childhood in fact, when he became paranoid that one day he would tune his TV into something very weird indeed. Speaking later, he expressed his fascination with the dark side, and the idea of "people locking themselves in a room and turning a key on a television set so that they can watch something extremely dark, and by doing that, allowing themselves to explore their fascinations."

He finished his first draft of the script in early 1981, though he did scrap some scenes before filming commenced. (One scene in particular, where Max chops off his leg and develops a grenade as a hand, would have been particularly interesting.) Once Cronenberg scored a financial hit with Scanners, he was able to raise the budget for Videodrome. David and his two producers, Claude Heroux and Victor Solnicki, thought of Woods for the role of Max early on. He too was keen on being involved, having expressed his fondness for Cronenberg's The Brood. Once they met in Beverly Hills the pair got on well, and James was on board. Then pop icon Debbie Harry was picked by Cronenberg after being impressed by her work in 1980's Union City. With the cast signed up, filming began in October of 1981.

One thing that people always talk about when it comes to Videodrome is the special effects. Nearly forty years on, Rick Baker's work is as impressive as ever. At times painfully realistic, not once do we feel we are looking at a latex trick. The abdominal slit that Woods wears is a particular stand out, though it wasn't exactly welcomed with joy by the actor himself. Fitted inside the sofa, with the fake stomach glued on to him, he found it extremely uncomfortable, at one point announcing, "I am no longer an actor. I'm just the bearer of the slit."

Appearing on Johnny Carson in August of 1981, while filming Videodrome, Woods was jovial about his suffering on set: "I spent the day yesterday in a body cast for this movie. They were doing special effects. Rick Baker said he wanted to do some casts of my body. Why would you wanna challenge that? So I went over. And I was sat there with plaster up to my waist. They said, 'OK it's lunch, we're gonna come back in a couple of hours. Take it easy.'"

For the scene on the couch, Woods told me that he was bound inside it on his knees for 14 hours! "I could not move," he said, recalling it with a certain horror. "I was literally locked into it like a prisoner. It was very hard on me. People laugh, like, How hard can it be? But it was tough. *You* try to be motionless on your knees, taped into a device like that for 14 hours. It's panicky. Make sure you don't drink a lot of water before hand!"

Speaking to me about the film, one that has been a favourite of mine for many years, I took the opportunity to really probe Woods about every aspect of this curious masterpiece. "David was not sure what the story finally was," James told me. "I love David, he is a very interesting man. He said to me, 'Look I am offering you a movie, there are only 70 pages of it, there isn't a third act. Are you willing to go to work and hope that we have it done by the time we start shooting?' I said, 'Sure.' I had seen Scanners and The Brood and thought, Wow this guy is creative! So I went up to Toronto and we started working. I was in every single scene for the movie. I never got a break. They were really long hours. The make up was just unbearable, it took hours to put on. Rick Baker was fantastic. And for its time it was astonishing make up. But the story, I remember thinking, Oh this is about a snuff film, that's creepy. And then it goes immediately way beyond all that. And I just thought, Shit! And we'd be shooting a scene where I'd wake up and Masha (played by Lynne

Gorman) would be in bed next to me and I was expecting it to be Nikki (Debbie Harry), and then it'd be Masha and she'd be dead. I was like, 'What the fuck?' I said, 'David, is this in Videodrome here or is this in real life?' He goes, 'I'm not sure.' So I said, 'OK, I guess I'm not sure either, then.' And we'd talk about it a lot. And it put us in a frame of mind of the evolution of this character, as a human being going into a video world that connected everybody somehow, that was now going to become flesh. These things are in chunks, in events, and you understand some of it and you don't understand other parts of it. There are people who you trust and people you don't trust. There's a logic that has its own cosmology. It's impossible to predict it or understand it. I thought it was all really creepy and really intriguing."

Then when the film came out... "Nobody saw the movie," James remembered. "I went to see it at a movie theatre on a Saturday morning, and literally I think it was me and like four other guys. Nobody got it, nobody understood it. It got some interesting reviews, however. But then I spent the next thirty years having people come up and say, 'God, I love Videodrome, it's one of my favourite movies', and it started to get a life of its own. And in the process Videodrome backed into a status that went beyond a cult status. It became one of the most prescient movies ever made. I watched a girl the other day crossing the street in Beverly Hills and she was almost hit by a car. She was crossing the street looking at her cell phone, she did not look up at the lights, just literally stepped off the curb and straight into traffic. I just thought, Videodrome! In the film it was a gun he pulls out of his stomach, this girl pulled a phone out of her bag. She probably doesn't know what the American Revolution was about. Like, who did we fight with in the revolution, was it Lithuania? No idea about history. She only cares about something that someone has texted her or is tweeting at her. So the bottom line is, this movie told us that the world was gonna change, we were gonna become cogs in a matrix where we no longer have any independent capacity to think or grasp our environment or our place in that environment, neither geographically or intellectually. We are now literally blobs in a matrix. We have lost ourselves. It won't be long until they put chips in us. People laugh about that, but I guarantee it will happen. Maybe not in our lifetime, but it will happen."

Woods fans may know that the ending of the movie was something he worked out himself with Cronenberg, insisting they go and shoot some more footage to round off the finale. David hadn't written an end chapter that Woods was truly happy with; after all, Cronenberg's original ending involved mutated, deformed sexual organs and Max being reunited with Nikki, after death, on the set of the Videodrome. David later said the idea clashed with his own atheist beliefs.

Woods recalled to me how the ending came about. "David called me up after we'd finished it and said, 'Do you like the ending?' I said, 'No, I'm not sure about the ending.' He said, 'Me neither. How would you feel about coming up and talking about it?' I said, 'Sure.' He said, 'Great, I'll call your agent.' I said, 'No I'll just come up, don't worry about it.' I think I drove up actually, I think I drove up from New York to Toronto. So we did two more endings, we did three endings in all. And we were never happy about the ending completely. We could not figure out the ending, and that's the truth. And here's why..." Woods' voice then took on a kind of secrecy, and he began to whisper. "No one can figure out the ending of Videodrome because it never ends. It completely absorbs you until you no longer exist. That's what is happening now in the world of the internet, of iPads and cell phones. We are completely dissolving, and that's what Cronenberg saw. But I think Videodrome was the most prescient and insightful and disturbing of all those kinds of movies. I asked David,

'Where do you come up with these ideas? You look like an insurance salesman.' He said, 'I know. I don't think about it, I have dreams. These are all from dreams I have.' So I said, 'Well, that's amazing.' But he is a wonderful guy, a wonderful director. He offered me The Fly but I couldn't do that make up again. It was a pity, I'd have loved to have done more with David, but there we are!"

James then pondered on the imaginative casting. "To have me do it, who was seen as this kind of intellectual guy who was also a bit of a renegade, meaning that was my image as an actor. A kind of cutting edge, intellectual, rebellious guy, and that's what Max Renn is. And casting Debbie Harry was interesting. She is this huge star who has no sense of being a star, like zero sense. She is this innocent, sweet girl. We were doing a sex scene once when she's on top of me moving around. And David said, 'You know, you guys don't look like you're having sex.' And she said, 'Oh are we supposed to be having sex? I thought I was just kinda moving around.' She was totally in love with her boyfriend, Chris Stein, and she was just incredibly sweet. Maybe people think that's foolish, but in my experience she was one of the most innocent people I've worked with. She was perfect for the part. She was a great piece of casting. I don't think anybody else could have played that part. I just loved working with her. "

On working with Woods, Debbie Harry told Prevue in 1983: "Yes, I was excited about working with him. He's a very energetic, thoughtful actor who would make suggestions, and talk scenes over with me. When there were games played or tempers on the set, he was really helpful. I couldn't have been luckier. Well, at the end of every take, he would make a really funny remark..."

When I asked Debbie Harry about her memories of the film in 2021, she told me: " I was both nervous and excited when I got the part. At that point, I had been a big fan of Cronenberg's earlier more cult films. Maybe it didn't seem as weird to me as it might have to others. And James Woods was always charming and professional."

I asked Debbie if James' past experience on film and TV sets helped ease her nervousness at all. "Yes, Jimmy was intense and helpful at the same time. You are right, he knew what he was doing and he very often would end a scene with something unexpected or a joke which made everyone relax after some sort of intensity."

I asked Debbie what her favourite scenes in the film are: "The intimate scene in the apartment with the cigarette burning, the dreamlike scene in the red clay cell with all the water. Also the one at the end when Nicki appears on TV - long live the new flesh."

I also asked Debbie how she looks back on her role in the movie and dealing with such a mysterious, complex subject: "I feel like this opportunity was a very fortunate break in every way. I think I was approaching the business of making a film in an extremely naive way and did not know many of the threads of interaction going on around me. In a sense this was good for both me and my character. For me to keep out of the twists and turns of the work environment and for my part as a character who was never really identified as being real or something only on TV. At that time, there was not the term 'virtual' which would have made Nicki not only better understood, but also would have taken away some of her mystery."

As this book studies the performances of Woods within the films, I must add that he gives a brilliant effort. Carrying the film, and often being our eyes, our guide if you like, in this strange and mysterious, often very dangerous world, he grounds the film, though naturally he can only do this for so long. Though Max begins to lose control of his own reality, Woods does keep control of his performance, never overdoing things as other actors often have in the horror field. He takes it on like any other character, someone in a predicament, a man looking for answers and hoping to find them, even if his quest might be hopeless. He self destructs, but it is a destruction of his own choice, if not his own making. Max is a man unafraid to head into the unknown, but in doing so, by submitting to his curiosity, he sacrifices himself.

Is Cronenberg's film a warning against the darkness that exists out there in the world? A meditation on the relativity of reality? A straight forward warning against the inevitable onslaught of dangerous outside influences? Whichever it may be, Videodrome is shamelessly good entertainment. It's a wild, exciting picture, and various moments from it have haunted me since my childhood; most of all, the image of Woods putting the gun into his stomach, which he produces later on when he most needs it; his head going into the TV presenting Harry's gigantic pout; the pulsating video tapes; and the ironically self destructive finale. Cronenberg's film is as vital as ever before, and it holds up well despite the subsequent advances in technology. In an age where tapes and clunky equipment are a thing of the past, making way for the condensed and digitalized world of today, Videodrome is still relevant, for though the gadgetry has evolved, the message is as relevant as ever. In fact, it's even more so. We are more controlled than ever before by the media, by so called entertainment, by our fancy little devices and gadgets. Perhaps the modern reality we find ourselves in is even more terrifying than Cronenberg's nightmare vision...

ONCE UPON A TIME IN AMERICA (1984)

"Not only is Sergio Leone in that pantheon of great directors, he deserves his own pantheon."

- James Woods to the author

All cinematic masterpieces start their life somewhere, and for Sergio Leone, the adventure began with a book he had read and fallen in love with in the 1960's, Hoods by Harry Grey. Leone loved Grey's inside take on the life of the Jewish mob, and was desperate to meet him. But Grey, real name Harry Goldberg, proved elusive for some time. Sergio knew he was the only man who could bring his story to life on the screen, and use Grey's tale as an allegory for the rise and fall of America; its prospering in the post-depression/pre-war period, then what some see as its moral and aesthetic decay in the 1960's.

For years the picture was an obsession to Leone, the "dream project" as others have referred to it. For a long time the film seemed an impossibility. In time though, once he began committing all of his energy and passion into bringing Hoods to the big screen, things he could never have imagined began to come to fruition.

Leone had gone through a huge list of possible actors to play the lead part of Jewish gangster David "Noodles" Aaronson. The casting was vital, perhaps the most important decision to be made in the movie. In the early days of development, rather ironically, the role was sitting firmly in the lap of acclaimed French actor Gerard Depardieu. This was in 1975, around the time the film's eventual star, Robert De Niro, was filming with Depardieu in Italy for Bernardo Bertolucci's controversial epic, 1900. Gerard spoke little English at the time, and wanted the role so badly that he promised to learn English and attempt to perfect a convincing Brooklyn accent.

However, for better or worse, this was not to be. (Other reports say he was set to play Max.) At the turn of the 1980's, Leone envisioned Paul Newman as the older Noodles and Tom Berenger as the younger man, and other names included James Cagney and Richard Dreyfus. For the role of Max, Noodles' best friend turned nemesis, Harvey Keitel and Dustin Hoffman were considered. In the end, it was James Woods who filled in the role of Max, Noodles' best friend. Here, he was given one of the most important film roles of the period. Naturally, Woods gave it his all.

The script was finalised in October of 1981, and in the end it was credited to six men - Leone, Piero De Bernardi, Enrico Medioli, Franco Arcalli, Leonardo Benvenuti and Franco Ferrini. Anyone interested in the idea of a screenplay as a stand alone piece of work, rather than just a bare-boned blueprint for a film, should read the script to Once Upon A Time in America from front to back. Filming began in 1982 and lasted over a year, going from New York to Italy, Rome's Cinecitta Studios, and many places in between.

We start our journey of Noodles' life in the thirties, in an opium den in fact, where Noodles (De Niro) is flaked out. He envisions a flashback, a recent event in fact, of the police taking three bullet riddled bodies away from a crime scene in the pouring rain, as a phone rings and rings for what seems like an eternity on the soundtrack (all is revealed later of course). Meanwhile (the film's first sequence in fact), a group of gangsters go to his house and kill his moll. Searching for Noodles, they arrive at the opium den, but Noodles is ushered out the back door and flees into the night. The young Fat Moe (Harry Knapp), friend to Noodles and his gang, is receiving a vicious beating by the gangsters, but he refuses to reveal Noodles' whereabouts. Later, while most of the gang go off in search of the "rat", Noodles arrives and blows one of the gangsters away,

James Woods and Robert De Niro, Cannes 2012.

Woods and De Niro, Cannes, 2012.

saving Moe's life. Noodles then retrieves a key from the grandfather clock in Moe's domicile and departs, leaving his bruised friend on the ground. When he learns that a large amount of money he expected to be located in a railway locker has gone, seemingly vanished, Noodles flees for Buffalo, buying a one way ticket with no plans to return.

We next find ourselves in 1968, when Noodles returns to Manhattan after years in hiding, old, droopy eyed and one-note. He returns to Fat Moe's restaurant with the news that someone has sent him a letter regarding arrangements for a "friend's" burial. Reuniting with Moe, we see how time has aged them. Later, Noodles gets the key to the railway locker (it is later revealed that Noodles and his gang set the locker up as kids to stash away their savings), opens it and finds a suitcase stuffed full of money. Apparently it's an advance on his next "job".

Between this, we are cast back to 1920, in Brooklyn, where Noodles and his gang are introduced as children. We meet the young Max, Cockeye and Patsy, plus other extended members of their circle, like Deborah, the object of Noodles' affection (played in the younger scenes by Jennifer Connelly, and by Elizabeth McGovern in the rest). Leone captures this era wonderfully. In with the beauty though are ugly truths. Theirs is a rough and ready world of crooked cops, rival gangs and sordidness. Getting their acts together, Max, Noodles and the boys quickly rise in the underworld, building up their reputations to take over their local area. Though there is affection between Noodles and Max, there is also a strange tension which often borders on hostility. After stabbing a rival gang member to death for killing the youngest member of their group, Noodles is sent to prison.

He is released in 1932, where he meets back up with his old pals, while Max (James Woods) has clearly become the leader in getting the boys established as serious criminals, not just petty crooks. They run a bar in the prohibition era, bootlegging and being the "muscle" for union man Jimmy O' Donnell (Treat Williams).

In the adult scenes, there is even more of that tense rivalry between Noodles and Max, and though friendly, their respect for one another warps into competitiveness. Yet there is a strange brotherly love beneath the surface. The two differ drastically; Max wants the gang to be bigger, better and richer, while Noodles is happy for it to stay small time. He enjoys the life of crime; this is proven during a bank robbery where he viciously rapes a clerk, Carol (Tuesday Weld), who later becomes a high class hooker and then joins their extended gang, funnily enough as Max's lover.

As time goes on, Noodles' personality becomes more detached and wistful, and he starts to drift away from the others. There is one key event that changes it all. Still infatuated with Deborah, Noodles takes her out on a romantic date, hiring the whole restaurant for the night - an example of both his power and the fear he instils in people. They enjoy a perfect evening, but Deborah, now an aspiring actress, informs Noodles she is leaving for Hollywood the next day. Saddened, the date is over, and the pair end up in Noodles' chauffeur driven car. As the driver takes them homeward, Deborah tries to softly kiss Noodles, but he reacts by viciously raping her. In the near four hour cut, he actually rapes her twice, violently, with no regard for the pain he will be causing her. For him, this is a reckless act. She is leaving, and will be out of his life forever. He's asked her to stay and be his woman, but she knows life with him would be no fun, that he would lock her up and possess her as his toy. The rape then, is a destructive act, though in the long run the ordeal destroys him more than it does her. She experiences pain and horror at that moment, but his viciousness spurs her on in her career, and she later becomes

104

successful, with Noodles just a face from the past. For him, the rape is a landmark moment, the point where it all goes wrong. It's a sickening display of carelessness which even Noodles himself appears to instantly regret upon finishing.

As she leaves to pursue her dreams the next day, Noodles watches her train depart the station. Haunted by his arrival, she glances at him blankly and simply pulls down the blind as the train chugs away, smoke permeating in the air. It's one of the most gut wrenching scenes in cinema history.

It is here when things really shift. Eventually Noodles returns to the gang. He has been away, drugging himself up in the opium den while Max and the gang are formulating their next plans, one of which is to rob the Reserve Bank, something which Noodles sees as certain suicide. Carol and Noodles plot to get the gang busted, seeing a small sentence for incited robbery preferable to death. Noodles rings the police and his friends, apparently, end up getting shot dead by the cops. He glumly watches as their bodies are taken away in bags. It is then we learn why Noodles left for Buffalo, not to return for thirty six years.

In the latter day scenes, the haunted Noodles hears repeatedly of a Secretary Bailey, a name mentioned in a news report of the murder of the District Attorney. When Noodles visits the Bailey foundation, he is faced with an aged Carol, who tells him that the police tip-off that she and Noodles supposedly concocted was an idea instigated by Max all along. While there, Noodles spots a picture of Deborah on the wall, taken when the foundation first opened (Carol tells him she's a famous actress). He tracks her down and visits her in her dressing room, backstage, while she is appearing in a play. Done up in white face paint, which she gradually rubs off as the scene goes on, she appears to have not aged a day. This, of course, is how Noodles sees her, as the same beauty he let down all those years ago. She has aged of course, but we see her youthful looks through the eyes of a regretful old man still hopelessly in love.

When Noodles enquires about the identity of Bailey, Deborah is vague and becomes flustered when asked for information. He asks her whether he should take up the invite to visit the mysterious Secretary's house for a party. Deborah becomes increasingly edgy and nervous. Noodles now has an inkling that she and Bailey have lived together for years, but she cooks up a story of Bailey being an immigrant who got with a woman who died in childbirth. Becoming increasingly frantic, she advises Noodles not to go. As he leaves her dressing room, Noodles comes face to face with Bailey's son, who is the exact spitting image of a young Max (both parts are played by Rusty Jacobs). It's another heart stopping moment in the film, handled beautifully by Leone in his slow zoom.

In the end, Noodles goes to the party, and though he never says it, he knows Bailey is the elderly Max. Max tells him the tale; that he faked his death and married Deborah, taking away from Noodles the one thing he always wanted. But Noodles doesn't rise to it. Given that he knows he is about to be assassinated, Max/Bailey urges Noodles to kill him. Asking his old friend to do the deed is his final offering to Noodles. But in Noodles' eyes, Max is already a dead man; after all, Max "died" all those years ago. He will not take up Bailey's offer and slowly leaves the mansion.

Noodles exits the mansion's grounds and heads up the dark, quiet street. Behind him, he hears a rubbish truck starting up. As it comes down the road towards him, Max (or someone resembling Max) appears from the gates of the mansion. Max marches towards Noodles, then the truck obscures him. When it drives onwards, Max is gone and nowhere to be seen. Noodles observes the truck as it passes him by, and it is clear that something freshly inserted in the mincer is now being crushed into tiny bits. Is it Max? Or has he faked his death once again? Deliciously, we never learn the truth. That's up to us.

The very last scene is a flashback to 1933, where Noodles is entering the opium den, removing his coat and getting comfortable as his drug is being neatly set up in a pipe for him. He begins to puff away, and float off to his happy place. The film ends with a close up of Noodles' grinning face, a strange, contorted grin that shows us the tortured man at his most content. The credits roll over his goonish smile, eyes crinkled in glee.

As a meditation on loss and regret, no film can measure up to the towering stature of Once Upon A Time in America. A devastating, painful and at times extremely sad document of one man's attachment to his past, it's a film that - if we are talking about the full Leone cut of course - becomes soothing in a perverted fashion; the more melancholy and morose Noodles and his life becomes, the sweeter the film seems to be. It is beautifully filmed, wonderfully acted and is a treat from start to finish, a feast for the eyes and senses. It is, in short, a masterpiece, and I have rarely if ever come across another film which matches its power and poignancy. It is haunting, enthralling, brutal and bitter-sweet.

At the core of the film are those two performances from Woods and De Niro, almost a dual effort, with the two men playing off each other, complimenting each other with contrasting moods and movements. As James Woods told me, he likened their face off to that of a cobra and a mongoose, Max the coiled up snake ready to attack at any minute. There is indeed a feral quality to Woods here, but he keeps himself in check. It's there in the eyes, a man who is so clearly close to the edge at all times, ready to crack, but too

107

narcissistic and egotistical to let go. He must, at all times, remain the manipulative controller, the puppet master who, when all is said and done, steers things exactly the way he wishes them to go. Woods does not play Max as an outright villain; indeed, we often like him, and he is at times very funny. But he is at heart a cruel man, always out to do one over on his supposed friend.

To say Leone slaved over the edit would be a massive understatement. At first, he chopped it down to six hours, but the studio was adamant it should be shorter. In the end, he came to a 3 hour 40 minute cut, which was widely released in Europe. In the US however it was chopped down to over 2 hours and the back-and-forth structure, which makes the film so unique, was scrapped. Critics hated it, and perversely the same writers who saw the full cut thought it one of the greatest mob films ever made.

Speaking to me for my book on the film in December of 2020, Woods looked back on this most special of films: "I loved the movie; I loved all the people on it. I mean, it was a great personal experience. Some things you've done you're very proud of them, great movies, but they may have been difficult to do. Not that this (Once Upon a Time in America) wasn't difficult to do, it was definitely a challenge, but on others you just might not have had a personal best experience. You know, this was just a particularly joyous experience. All the people who were in it stayed friends for life, and we look back on it as a great moment in our lives. When I was at the anniversary screening of it at Cannes, I was with Bob and Jennifer Connolly and Elizabeth McGovern, and we were all on the red carpet... Gucci had spent over six million dollars on restoring the picture, Ennio Morricone was there, and I was with Bob and the reporters kind of noticed that De Niro was crying, he had tears in his eyes. I said, 'Bob are you okay?' You know, I never really knew if Bob had liked the film a lot, because it was a little less realistic and a lot more operatic than the other stuff he had done on organised crime figures in the past; such legendary movies as Godfather Part II. And he said to me, 'You know, this is the last time we'll ever do something like this.' I said 'What do you mean?' And he said, 'Well...' I mean Bob is not a big publicity guy, he's very shy. He said, 'You know, the red carpet for a film that's really great.' I asked him if he was going to watch the movie. He said, 'Yeah, let's stay and watch it.' So we stayed and we watched it, and it was the full three hour forty two minute cut, which was shown at the Cannes Film Festival the night it first opened, where it got, I'm not kidding, a twenty minute standing ovation. It was stunning, *stunning*."

James then described his reaction at seeing the full cut again, all those years later. "It started deliberately... I won't say slowly, but deliberately, with the music. And I thought, 'Oh my God, when this movie is seen the way it was supposed to be seen...' It just lulled you into this other world, this opium dream really, that was so mesmerising. I mean, the musical score, for my money, is perhaps the best musical score ever written for any movie. I just think that music is beyond anything I have ever heard. Ennio was sitting behind us and I turned and said, 'Maestro', and he nodded and said 'Maestro' back to me, which I thought was really sweet."

During our talk, I mentioned to James that the collaboration between him and De Niro often feels like one performance, and it is these two men and how they are portrayed by the two iconic actors, that give the film its edge and its tension. "Yes I believe that," Woods said, "and I have to say that Bob is an incredibly generous actor. And so were the other actors too, they were just a great bunch of people. Everybody has their balance; Deborah does, being in love with one man; the other man is powerful, and she wants to get away from the stench of the place, which she feels Noodles will always have. She has her balance. Certainly, Tuesday Weld's character (Carol), she goes from being married to being my mistress. They each have their own dynamic pull, and that triangle of Noodles, Max and Deborah is a very strong ménage of moral quandary."

James then explained what it really meant to collaborate with Robert De Niro, already America's most respected film actor.

"You have to remember too, that when we were making Once Upon a Time in America, Bob had just come off Raging Bull, one of the greatest performances ever put to film. And I was a virtual unknown. But I was playing a character where I was actually the strong and more ruthless of the two of us. So I not only had to be equal to Bob, to go toe to toe with him, I had to have the courage and confidence as a character and frankly as an actor, to be able to stand up and throw my punches against the greatest. I have to say that Sergio gave me that confidence. He felt that I was on to something; he loved my character and was very encouraging of my performance. And Bob was wonderful about letting me go headstrong into it. And I actually went against some of Bob's ideas. I remember we were doing the hospital scene, and I just kept staring at Bob all the time. And Bob said 'You know, maybe you shouldn't look at me all the time.' I think he was afraid that one actor was too concerned with another. But I knew that Max was preparing this catastrophe that was coming, and that I was in a sense almost longing to connect with him, to tell him even though I couldn't; that the only way I could save him was by sacrificing any love or trust we had had all our lives. The greatest tragedy is that in the end that love is denied to Max by Noodles, by doing the strongest and strangest thing possible; literally, to ignore his existence. So it was like a contest between a mongoose and a cobra, constantly snapping and dodging each other. It felt that way in every scene. And Bob and I became very good friends. I love Bob. We

110

hung out a lot which was something I was very pleased about. We ended up spending time together. Yet when we worked, the dynamic went right back to that sparring dance that those two characters had. As we tried to explore our own characters, we found ourselves exploring each other's characters as well.

"Bob was great, because he was always open to other actor's ideas. And he could never do anything false; it's not in his nature as an actor. He has a very difficult time doing anything unless it feels authentic - as do I, and all those wonderful actors in that film. We all felt we knew we were stepping up to the plate with the big hitter of life. You gonna work with Bob De Niro, you gotta be on your A-plus game in every minute. 'I'm working with a legend here, I'm gonna try and do a legendary performance within my own realm of ability or aspiration.' Not in a competitive way, but in a co-operative way, meaning that he is inspiring all of us; he is our muse to be our very best, and you hope that when you walk away thirty years from now, you'll say to people, 'That was my greatest performance because I was inspired working with a giant.' And I dug as deep as I could to give him what he deserved."

One part of the film which fans discuss and dissect is the ending. Is it Max/Bailey who goes into the back of the garbage truck? Though James has been asked about this millions of times, I could not resist. "Sergio had a photo double of me on set," James said. "You can't tell if it's me or not when Noodles looks back. Sergio wanted it that way. We want Bob to not be certain. To my knowledge I'm the only person Sergio ever explained the ending to. When I asked him why he used the photo double purposely, he said he wanted the audience and Noodles to be somewhat confused. I said to him that it obviously worked because I indeed was also confused. When I asked him point-blank if it was my character, Max (now Secretary Bailey) who jumped or was pushed into the garbage truck to his certain death, Sergio's exact words were, 'It's like Jimmy Hoffa. You don't know, but you know!' The Hoffa reference is a very important part of American organized crime urban legend. For decades people have speculated about the truth of how he was kidnapped and murdered, right up to the making of The Irishman by Martin Scorsese, one of Sergio Leone's greatest admirers."

When we came to the film again, Woods expressed more of his views on this masterpiece. "Forget that it's me for a minute," he said, "that James Woods is not I. I just think the casting of the two characters is great because they are so fundamentally different. Yet each yearns to be the other in so many ways. It's important that those characters be so different, yet have the same yearnings in so many ways. Yet with Max, he just wants more, more, more. While Noodles is just like, We've got enough, we've got enough... But just imagine I'm not in the movie. Imagine I am a film critic who happens to look like James Woods (laughs), I think this film is a masterpiece. It was the pinnacle of my career and it will eventually be seen as one of the greatest movies ever made."

The Godfather and Goodfellas may top more lists of the best crime movies, and both films might be more quoted, but for me the surreal, wistful poeticism of Once Upon a Time in America, coupled with its harsh ugliness, makes it one of the finest films of the 20th century and beyond.

OUT OF THE WOODS: 1984 - 1985

After Once Upon a Time in America, Woods was on quite a roll, and he found himself embarking on a very varied set of movies. In the two year period of 84 and 85, he popped up in some curious, interesting, occasionally brilliant films, and each role seemed to be totally different from the one before it.

Though some people may not automatically link Woods with 1984's highly successful Against All Odds, he does have a key role as Jake Wise, a seedy gambler who owns a nightclub and has quite a grand vision. The film, directed by Taylor Hackford, begins when Jake "helps" out his old chum Terry (Jeff Bridges) after he is let go by his football team, but ends up pulling him into the kind of situation he never wanted any part of. He actually hires him to pursue his girlfriend, Jessie (Rachel Ward), the rich daughter of the owner of Terry's football team, but does not suspect that Terry will fall in love with her and start an affair. This leads to all kinds of trouble.

Against All Odds is remembered for a number of reasons these days. Firstly, and most superficially, it's Phil Collins' eponymous, mega hit single, which comes at the very end of the film. People also recall the section of the movie in Jake's popular club, which includes performances from King Creole and the Coconuts. But perhaps most of all, the thing that most people remember about Against All Odds is the car chase scene between Bridges and Woods that comes early on in the picture. For me however, it has always been a picture to enjoy for its performances and its intriguing development. Bridges and Rachel Ward put in solid efforts, but for me Woods steals the show. It's not that he is competitive or purposely attempting to upstage his co-stars, but he gives Jake a curious mystery which makes him interesting. It's the classic Woods intensity at work, though his

Jake Wise is not quite what he seems. At first we deem him a master manipulator, a man who can own anyone with the right amount of money. But it's clear by the end that he is little more than a pawn himself, at least when we see his real status when it comes to the underworld's hierarchal structure.

"First of all, I loved working with Taylor," Woods recalled to me. "And of course I loved working with Jeff Bridges, who was just great. And it was a big production. People don't realise that. We were in that club doing those scenes for weeks. Taylor does a ton of coverage to get things right. It was at a time when Jeff and Rachel were huge stars; and I was too actually, we all were. We were at the top of our game. It's got one of the great race scenes of all time. I have to say, Jeff and I drove a lot of that. It was really fun but a little scary. But Jeff - you take for granted when you work with someone like Jeff, and Rachel too. Jeff and I had a natural rhythm together. He was very all-American and I kind of wanted to be him - I mean the characters, of course. I liked controlling him and in many ways lamented that my path had gone a certain way. One of the things that made that movie work - and it was a choice I made and a personal contribution to the movie - was making me really love Rachel's character. Jake was really in love with her. Yes he wanted to be powerful and in control of his woman and didn't want someone to take her away, but I think that he was genuinely heartbroken that she was stolen. Jake really loved her and she broke his heart. And an irony of the movie is the fact that Rachel's character kills more people than mine does. If you add it up (laughs), she kills more people than I do!"

One thing I like about the Jake character is the fact he isn't really as powerful as he hopes he is and we believe he might be at the start of the movie. "Yes," Woods agreed. "And he is outfoxed by them both. He's a bit of a pawn, and again, I think he would have realised he was a pawn had he not been so twisted by the triangle with her and Jeff Bridges' character, Terry."

After Against All Odds' success, Woods then lent his subtle comic skills to Cat's Eye (1985). Written by the masterful Stephen King, this darkly comic anthology film is one of the finest horror flicks of the 80s, even though it's not all out scary and has its tongue firmly in its cheek. With a screenplay by King himself, and two of the tales adapted from his own short stories in the Night Shift collection, it's consistently engaging from start to finish. Each story is linked by a cat which roams the streets, stopping in the city during the first instalment, entitled Quitters Inc. It stars Woods as a family man named Dick Morrison (Drew Barrymore plays his daughter, who also links the three tales in a more ambiguous manner), who goes to a mysterious company run by the shady Dr Donatti (played by Alan King) to help him quit smoking, and finds himself becoming increasingly paranoid and tortured by his addiction and the company whose service he has paid for.

The tale has some genuinely hilarious scenes (the party sequence alone makes the film worth watching, with the giant walking cigarette packs tempting Woods back to the demon nicotine) and for me (and some critics too) it is by far the finest of the three. It does differ from the original story quite a bit, and Woods is given the chance to stretch the part a little, but I have to say it might have made an interesting full length feature in its own right.

That said, the film is a showcase for Woods' comic talent. He gives Dick a certain nervy edginess, a jumpy laugh at key moments of embarrassment or disbelief. Also notice, in one particular scene, his cartoonish walk, that sneak he does when he's in his pyjamas and is convinced there's a man in the closet. But he also plays the creepier moments brilliantly too, like when he realises he is being watched from the next car as he lights up another smoke. But above all this is a comedic performance which he pulls off magnificently. After playing Max in Once Upon a Time in America, the sleazy cable station owner of Videodrome, and the mastermind criminal in Against All Odds, this light comic offering proved Woods had range.

"Ah, Cat's Eye!" James said with a hint of surprised enthusiasm when I raised the subject of the movie. "Yes, that was an offer that came through my agent. Drew had just done E.T. obviously, and everyone was in love with her. She was genuinely adorable. I played her dad in Cat's Eye when she was like, 9 or something, and then again when she was in her twenties in Riding in Cars with Boys. I have to say she was invariably just one of the sweetest people. She has a very kind and gentle nature, Drew. She is very sensitive. I loved working with her both times. As a kid she was so hilarious and cute. But in Cat's Eye I had very little to do with her, because as you remember, it was mostly me and Alan King. I love Stephen King, wanted to work with Drew and it was just a nice offer. I mean, everything about it was like, hey, this should be fun! It was at that period when I was getting a lot of stuff offered and I had some time open. I mean, you always wanna do Stephen King, because he is a wonderful writer and he's so prolific. But the irony is that when I did the movie I had quit smoking, and I do a movie about quitting smoking, end up smoking in the movie and it got me smoking again. It happened to me twice, this; on Cat's Eye and Another Day in Paradise (released in 1998, covered later in the book). So every time they suggested after, 'Do you mind smoking for the character? We'll use fake cigarettes.' It's like, 'No, I'm not smoking for the character ever again. No (laughs), just not doing it!'

Woods then told me some tales about working with the great Alan King, the legendary comedian who was here on more sinister form. "But I had a fabulous time with Alan King. He was a classic, good old

Vegas comedian. He was delightful to work with. I mean, he was an unabashed drinker. He said to the prop person, 'Could you bring me a glass?' and he would fill it with vodka to the brim. He would drink all day. He never missed a line. He never slurred his words. It was uncanny. It was like a guy taking his medicine. Honestly, he was as sharp as a tack. Just delightful. I loved working with him. Usually people who drink A LOT are not as fun as they think they are, but Alan was amazing. You'd never have known he'd taken a sip of alcohol."

On the subject of doing a comedy, James said, "It was fun doing a comedy. It's especially fun if you're the guy who's usually doing the serious parts. Dino De Laurentiis, who produced Cat's Eye, did quite a few low budget horror films. This one was actually released in cinemas and did pretty well, I think. But, you know, you're not doing it expecting to win an Oscar. But on the other hand, you're doing a comedy, you're having a blast, you're working with wonderful people. I was working with one of the top young stars of the day. We all went through the separate bits in read-throughs together, so I saw Drew's natural talent. I thought she was a delightful child, and so sweet to everybody."

Ted Kotcheff's Joshua Then and Now (also released in 1985) is one of Woods' most obscure films from the mid 80's. A low budget Canadian feature, it was based on the book by Mordecai Richler. Woods plays the adult Joshua, while Alan Arkin is his father. A semi-autobiographical slice of life, it begins with Joshua, tired and weary, looking back over his life and where he perhaps went wrong. Back in time, we experience Joshua's early years in a Montreal neighbourhood. His father's an ex-boxer turned shady type and his mother's a stripper and loose woman. He becomes a writer after an eventful Spanish trip (he's been obsessed with the Spanish Civil War since his childhood, and has even kept a scrap book of the conflict), and gets married to the daughter of a man of influence. Things then get more complicated, and Joshua judges his life against his school friends who are now more conventionally fulfilled. Can he come to terms with what his life has become?

This faintly melancholic but often darkly funny film is a quiet joy from start to finish. Woods is fabulous throughout, first as the tired, gaunt looking, fatigued Joshua, then in flashback through his twists and turns. "I don't understand how I got from there to here," he says. "I don't understand anything." He sums up the lost weariness of many men in their forties. What happened? How did it come to this?

Joshua Then and Now is beautifully directed by Kotcheff, and the screenplay, by Richler himself, is consistently engaging. Woods' voice over helps keep the whole thing together, acting as a kind of guide through the strange life we witness. He makes the part his own. Contradictorily, the New York Times said that Woods did a good job despite the material being totally unsuited to him. What this means is anyone's guess. If the material is unsuited to him, then why is he so effective in the part? It also makes you wonder just what he is deemed suitable for. Woods once recalled that he had asked the producers who their first choice for the part was. "They said it was Dustin Hoffman," he recalled. "But Dustin Hoffman now costs $6 million or something like that, and so the film would have ended up costing $15 million or $20 million. A small film like that can never earn back that much money." Now knowing the film as a Woods vehicle, it's impossible to imagine anyone, even Dustin Hoffman, doing it as well as James Woods.

Speaking to me about the film and Kotcheff in particular, Woods said: "Ted was one of my personal directors. I did Split Image with him and Joshua Then and Now. We had a great working relationship

118

and loved working together. And Mordecai was sort of the novelist laureate of Canada. If there was any one fiction writer who was pre-eminent in Canada it would be Mordecai. This was his personal story. And I got to spend time with Mordecai. It was based on his story actually, a nice narrative novel inspired by his background. He wrote the screenplay too. It was a bit heavy the way novel adaptations are. I expected that it was not probably going to be a big commercial movie. But we were gonna give it everything we had. Ted said he'd love me to do this character. And I said, 'Of course. But I think I'll have to do a bit of work to get it right.' It was a film about social strata and the impact of it on his life. And of course, I got to work with Alan Arkin, who was one of my heroes. So it was great. Alan Arkin, so great! I mean (laughs), I'm just thinking of the people I worked with!"

Woods then took me through a technical issue he felt robbed the film of a certain power: "The problem with the movie came with Gabrielle Lazure, who played Pauline. She was a big model in Paris and she learned to speak French. She spoke French a lot and preferred to speak it on set. All the make up girls were French-Canadian, so she would talk for an hour during make up, and then come to the set playing this English princess type, and her intonations would have a French override. We'd say, 'Sweetie, you got to stop speaking French before coming to set, it's affecting the accent.' So they made a big decision (the producers) after seeing the film that her accent was a big problem. So they got another actress to re-voice her entire part. The entire performance! Which meant that I had to re-voice a lot of my dialogue in all my scenes with her. I spent 8 days looping the dialogue. I had never done more than a day before that. It was very frustrating I have to say. I felt we lost a little bit, a lot of the spontaneity between these two characters. But the stuff we shot

119

in England was great. And me and Gabrielle were playing these young characters falling in love, and as actors we were really enjoying each other's company. It was nice. The feeling was genuine when we shot those love scenes. They were very sweet. The typical movie love scenes are of people humping, but this was sweeter, in front of their little gas fire in their flat in England. The romantic part was done very nicely by Ted. "

He also added a rather interesting detail about a project Ted approached Woods with before Joshua Then and Now. "And you might not believe this, but it is true, he offered me the part of Rambo in First Blood. I said, 'Ted, he's naked in the mountains for the first half of the movie.' And I said, 'Ted, I'm not a soldier, I'm a skinny guy.' And he said, 'Yeah, that's the thing. He's wiry but he knows how to survive and so on.' I was actually offered Rambo, and that's a true story, and it was a real offer. He was conceived as a guy you would never expect to be this clever, highly trained killer."

Woods has always dedicated himself to the highest quality television, from 1986's Promise through to 2000's Dirty Pictures and beyond. A stand out of his television work was Badge of the Assassin (1985). Based on a true story, this gritty and enthralling tale stars Woods as Assistant District Attorney Robert Tanenbaum, working alongside Yaphet Kotto and Alex Rocco on the case of a double cop murder in the early 1970's, acted out by members of the Black Panther party. One word which comes to mind when watching Badge of the Assassin is authenticity. This makes sense, for Woods' real life character not only wrote the book the screenplay was based on, but also executive-produced the film itself. It's another solid offering from the Golden Age of TV. Kotto is watchable as ever and Woods, always one to be loyal to his integrity, gives the part his all.

My partner Linzi had an interesting question for me to ask James, and that was if there were any characters from his career that he identified with. It brought us back to Badge of the Assassin. "Wow," James said, pausing to take the question in. After admitting that it was a great question, he finally came up with one man he could identity with, and that was Tanenbaum, his real life character from this very movie. "It was a true story and the fact he used his skills as a lawyer, his ruthlessness in seeking justice. I am obsessed with doing the right thing, and I think the fact he did the right thing and fought so hard to do it was important to me. And the fact he was victorious was very powerful to me. But I'm not a lawyer, so I can't really say I identified with him, but I did like his plight."

Though he was highly effective in all the films covered in this section, around the corner was a double whammy that completely changed his life and catapulted him into a whole new realm of acclaim.

James Woods in Salvador. Artwork by Linzi Napier.

SALVADOR (1986)

First off, I believe that Oliver Stone's Salvador is one of the greatest films of the 1980's. Acclaimed at the time, it is a film which has built up a reputation of its own within Stone's formidable filmography as the years have gone by. A bold and admirable feat of film-making, Stone was at the start of a fearless career as a director and a seeker of truth, a man who exposed the dark underbelly of what we have seen and think we know. His right hand man in this exciting era was none other than James Woods.

Salvador stars Woods as photojournalist Richard Boyle (the real life man who covered the troubles in El Salvador), a man down on his luck when he heads out to cover the Salvadoran Civil War. Accompanied by his friend Doctor Rock (Jim Belushi), the pair arrive in the chaotic land of El Salvador where Boyle hopes to scrape a living covering the conflict and meeting up with some former associates who may or may not be able to help him get some work. While there he reconnects with an old girlfriend, gets some genuinely exciting photos and ultimately winds up in a whole lot more trouble than he had hoped, stuck between the US-backed military and the revolutionaries. He exposes a truth that is way uglier than presumed, and becomes so connected to the land of El Salvador that he feels like a piece of him is torn away when he has to leave it - and some of the people there - behind.

Oliver Stone had first met Richard Boyle in the 1970's and became intrigued by the man. Years later, when looking in the chaotic back seat of the journalist's car, he spotted a stack of papers. Stone asked if he could read them, did so, and came across Boyle's account of his exploits in El Salvador. Stone, then known primarily as a screenwriter (he had won an Oscar for Midnight Express and caused quite a stir with his script for Brian De Palma's Scarface), told Boyle he wanted to make a film of his experiences during the Civil War. Boyle was adamant that no one would fund such a movie, so Stone promised him he would raise the money himself. A fire had been ignited within. This was the beginning of Stone's run as America's bravest political filmmaker, a dramatist both fearless and controversial.

When early plans for the movie involving Boyle playing himself went nowhere (Boyle was incapable of staying sober long enough to do a film), and John Daly came on board to produce, Martin Sheen had been cast as Boyle. James Woods was under consideration to play Doctor Rock, but Stone later wrote in his book, Chasing the Light, that his A type personality was too strong for a sidekick role. And the ambitious Woods, playing off the idea that Sheen was religious and might object to the graphic language and content (to be fair, Sheen had already expressed his discomfort), put himself forward for the part of Boyle. Woods convinced Stone he was the perfect actor to portray the chancing Boyle. He got the role, and the rising star Jim Belushi was cast as Doctor Rock.

Salvador was shot guerrilla style in Mexico on a low budget, meaning there was no room for spoilt movie star egos and extravagances. Thankfully, everyone involved believed in the picture and they gave it their all. Now firm friends, it's been well reported that Stone and Woods drove each other mad during the shoot, though it seems a lot of their anger was for the good of the picture, and their tension (and even insults) spilled over into improvisational segments of the film. And Stone knew the tension would do the picture good. Stone later recalled telling Belushi that Woods was the more experienced screen actor, and knew about being in front of the camera. "Watch out for Woods," Oliver warned him. Stone said Jimmy was the only one who was already a bona-fide star and he was out to hog the glory. With Belushi riled up and on his toes, Stone then went and told Woods to look out for Belushi, who might upstage him. "People say he's even better than his brother!" Stone exclaimed. Now Woods was coiled up and ready to go. Pitting them against one another, Stone brewed up the perfect mix of chemistry and competitiveness that ignited Doc and Richard's strange friendship. Even before filming, the two actors were wary of each other.

In the documentary on the making of the film, Woods speaks of a playful competition between him and Belushi. There was a sort of dance between the two, an upstaging, but as all three parties have noted since, this tension worked and made the relationship between Doc and Richard all the more believable. Let us not forget, he drags Doc to El Salvador against his wishes, bringing him round only by the promise of sex at a very affordable price. As soon as he realises how dangerous the place is, Doc freaks out, though he does eventually ease himself into the wild environment, and even settles down to stay there after Boyle's chaotic exit.

For me, Boyle and Rock are like a drugged up Don Quixote and Sancho Panza, two anti heroes, misguided souls perhaps, who head out on the road together against all odds. They may not be fighting with windmills and imaginary giants, and are in fact way above their heads, but there is the feeling that the world is their oyster, and there is a strange romanticism in the initial stage of the film when they drive out to El Salvador to the tune of Jackson Browne's Running on Empty. They are, however, ill-equipped for the events they become entangled in. In this case, especially with their hedonistic drug consumption, you might also compare them to the two main characters in Hunter S. Thompson's Fear and Loathing in Las Vegas. Indeed, the film has that Gonzo spirit running through it.

Years later, Stone spoke of his time with James on the shoot. "We joke about it now, we're friends, but I wanted to kill him a few times." In another Q and A, he said: "In the old days, I used to want to strangle Jimmy with my bare hands. But since that time Jimmy has mellowed out. And perhaps I have, too. And now I love him deeply. He has grown, actually, into a human being. And a fine one, too."

I asked Woods all about the legendary shoot. "There really wasn't trouble," he said. "Look, there was trouble making it in the sense that we engineered a kind of outrageous turbulence in the creation of the film. We all did. Jim did too, but I love Jim. And John Savage too, who I was responsible for getting that part (of the ambitious, daring, ultimately doomed photographer). And Valerie Wildman too, who was just wonderful. I think that the chaos of that movie reflected the chaos of the environment."

I had a long conversation with Woods about Boyle as a man who wants to expose the truth and will do anything to make sure the message about what is going on in El Salvador reaches America. Though only certain things were exaggerated for the film, one must remember that the heart of Salvador is based on the truth. "The murder of the nuns," James said, "they were essentially nuns but not nuns per se. Catholic Church workers. But that was an incredibly powerful true event that I remember moved me greatly when it happened. It was horrible. And the murder of the Archbishop and all of the disappearances. You know, to this day I still speak to people from El Salvador and they say, 'You made that movie and it's so powerful.' I ask them if they lost family and they say, 'Oh, I lost so many people.' So as I was making it, I was like, 'Shit man, this is an amazing true story.' Well, a 'true-ish' story, a dramatisation of this horrible time and place, and I just loved the idea that the hero was this kind of third-rate character who still had some heart. I never felt the real Boyle was like the Boyle I created. And me and Oliver argued about this. I said, 'Oliver, the real Boyle just isn't that interesting to me. And I don't think he's that heroic. But I think this character is heroic, a real journalist wanting to tell real stories.' And again, it's a prescient movie, because he is trying to tell a true story, and now, my contempt for the mass media in America is so profound. I mean, they have become these magpies, propagandists for one political party."

Expanding more on Boyle, Woods spoke about Richard in relation to the concept of the protagonist's journey and the protagonist's quest. "The quest always must be very important to the protagonist. It doesn't have to be so to the audience. They can still enjoy the story. Usually the protagonist is also embarking on a journey of which they may not be aware. When the quest and the journey either come together or the journey supersedes the quest, much to the hero's surprise, it becomes very fulfilling to the audience. What was interesting about the character in Salvador, his quest was to go down and make a few bucks, telling the story of what's really going on in El Salvador. But really, he's just trying to make a few bucks, have some fun, screw some whores and get drunk, smoke pot, hang out. And then the story becomes so compelling to him that he realises that he has a mission to share this story, because it is a horror story, a political one as well as a human horror story. And it must be told! So he goes from being a sort of opportunist bum, to becoming a very heroic man."

When it came to the startling finale, when Boyle cleverly smuggles the vital roll of film out of El Salvador, Woods explained it was not a conclusion which came about without a fight. "And Oliver and I ended up having a huge argument," Woods told me, "because at the border, all the film gets exposed that shows they are executing people. Oliver said to me, 'We got one more take, we are losing light, so don't fuck around in the scene or anything.' And I had my costumer build my boots so that I had a roll of film in the heel of my boot. And now we're buddies with the guards, drinking, and in the take, I get out the film and show it to them and go, 'Look fuckers, look what I got.' And Oliver was like, 'That's a fucking Hollywood ending.' And I was like, 'Oliver, she (Boyle's girlfriend) is going to be murdered. Boyle is going to have the shit kicked out of him and his life ruined. This movie is such a downer, it's OK that a little bit of good get through. And it is definitely not a Hollywood ending.' I think it's a good ending and Oliver eventually agreed."

Though Salvador is Stone's film and vision through and through, Woods is in some ways the beating heart of the picture, a vital, electric presence, jittery and sparking with nervous energy. He is a live wire, as if hooked up to electrodes, a blagger and a chancer who elbows his way to the centre of the conflict and comes out the other end somehow alive and in one piece, disillusioned with the media, with politics, with the establishment itself, and so called humanity. More specifically though, given it touches him directly at the film's end, Boyle is more ripped up about the treatment of ordinary people in the centre of this conflict. But when it came to portraying the real Boyle, Woods was not overly impressed by him, especially his lack of focus and vision (Stone said that as men the pair could not have been less alike), yet to add poignancy he chose to portray him as a man who desperately wanted to be someone extraordinary, the only man brave enough to capture the truth. The fact he is not the great man he wishes to be makes Boyle a strangely likeable character, at least as a creation in Woods' hands. Woods put to one side his personal feelings for the man himself (as he did with others, especially Roy

Cohn and the more monstrous men he's played) in order to give him depth.

When we spoke of the movie, I brought up one of my favourite scenes, when Boyle is drunk in the centre of five or six gun men, and he blags his way out of being killed. "I was supposed to be blind drunk but there was not a drop of alcohol," he recalled. "I didn't have nothing. I just played that scene - I mean, I would never play a scene drunk - but I was completely straight and sober. He's fighting for his life in that scene. And how did that guy survive? I think it's because I played it so crazily. I said to Oliver, 'I think if I play it crazy enough, I have to do it in a way so that they find it amusing, like, 'This gringo, we'll deal with him later.' I put a lot of work into the scene. And also the scene earlier when I scare Jim, and go 'Rargh!' and he laughs. Jim and I were a great couple in that I think. We quibbled on the set in a fun kind of way, but we liked the Hunter S. Thompson kind of journey into darkness, that then turns and gets really dark."

Though Woods and Stone had a certain friction, it needs to be said that their disagreements were to do with what was best for the picture. But Stone was also very open to Woods' ideas. One famous and very moving scene involves Boyle going to the scene of the crime where the Church workers were brutally raped and murdered. James had an idea, and he put it forward to Stone. "I had this Claddagh ring," he told me. "I wore it all the time. And the tradition with the Claddagh ring is that you can only give it to one person in your whole life. I said to Oliver, 'Wouldn't it be cool if I slipped the ring on to Cynthia Gibb's (who plays one of the murdered women, a character based on Jean Donovan) finger, when we find her body?' So Oliver said, 'Grab a camera and shoot it, I gotta go to lunch and stage another shot.' So on my lunch I went to Cynthia - and she was made up with all the murder make up - and I said to her, 'Cynthia, I know it's your lunch break and I hate to disturb you, but would you just shoot this scene where you lie down and I'm bent over you crying, and I'll put the Claddagh ring on you? It will be a great end to that scene.' We were in the parking lot where all the crew trucks were parked, and we said, 'Let's just shoot it here!' But the dirt was a different colour to the dirt in the actual scene, so I said, 'Get some darker dirt and put it down.' And she was like, 'Oh so I gotta get down on this dirt?' And I said, 'Please Cynthia, please do it for me.' And she did, to her credit, with all that horrible make up glued to her face. We got the dark dirt, we put it down, we shot the scene and, man, Oliver put it in the movie. It was one of my favourite, proudest little editorial things that I got to do. Oliver was very good about letting us create."

And of course, one cannot overlook the confession scene. Encouraging him to follow his gut, Stone famously rolled the cameras and told Woods that his character needed a confession. Woods' classic scene, made up on the spot to the priest, is a master class in film acting. He cannot promise to be a totally pure man, but will do his best, as long as he can still get drunk and smoke a spliff or two every now and then. He's doing this in a bid to marry his girlfriend (played brilliantly by Elpidia Carrillo) to get her out of El Salvador, so his intentions are good. But the scene illustrates Woods' acting genius and alone is enough to give him cinematic immortality. It's a magic moment and a flawless performance.

James had more kind words about Oliver, specifically about his influence on popular culture as a whole: "With Oliver, people talk about his political films, his conspiracy theories and his writing, but they are forgetting that Oliver actually created a lot of modern film grammar. He really was responsible for a lot of that kind of MTV craziness, you know? It was all Oliver. And in his book he teases me a lot, but actually, fundamentally we got along great about making a great movie. I broke his balls a lot on the movie and visa versa, but we became great friends and are to this day. We both got nominated for Academy Awards for Salvador, so we did something right, I guess."

In another chat, James went into detail about an on-set incident that could have turned seriously ugly. "Look, we were making a great movie. I think he's a brilliant filmmaker, a dear friend, and a pain the ass - and I love him. I defend him all the time, even when he is beating the shit out of me. But at the end of the movie, the scene at the Guatemalan border, the Guatemalan guards are basically thugs who are in collusion with the death squads. And after they torture me for information, trying to get the film which I hid in the boot... That was my idea by the way. Oliver didn't want any of that in. But I just did it in the middle of a take. Anyway, so they grab me into that old abandoned bus, put a gun to my head, I say a prayer, and they pull the trigger. But this is very important, the gun 'misfired', and here is what the word misfire actually means. A gun that is supposed to fire the bullet, the cartridge, does not fire. It misfires. It does not fire. So they put the gun to my head, and this was after Jon Hexum had accidentally killed himself playing Russian Roulette with a 'prop' gun (while filming Cover Up in 1984). He put the gun to his head, pulled the trigger and the blank in the gun fired. A blank has no slug in the cartridge, the bullet has no slug, just wadding and gunpowder. But the sheer force of the explosion of the gunpowder held against the head can actually cause brain damage - and in this case, death. So there is a difference between a live real bullet with gunpowder and a slug; a dummy bullet which looks the same with the gun powder removed so there is no way it can explode and force the projectile down the barre; and a blank which has gunpowder but no slug. In the story in Salvador, when the big thug guy pulls the trigger against my

131

head and it does not fire, that is to say it misfires, it gives me enough time for the ambassador to call and save my life. So while they were setting up the shot, meaning the filming of that scene, just before they are ready to go, I hear the guy - thank God I heard it - I heard him say to the prop guy, a word that sounded like 'blank'. I said to Oliver, 'Wait! Hold on!' And Oliver said, 'Jimmy, we're losing light for the shot, shut the fuck up!' So I said, 'Just wait! He just said the gun had a blank in here. You want me to put it to your head and pull the trigger?' He said, 'Ah you're whining.' We took the gun outside, pulled the trigger and it went off! It was a real blank, and it would have killed me. Believe me, that is what really happened on the set of Salvador. I stopped the shot because I knew something was wrong. I just heard whatever the word is that sounds like blank, and I was like, 'Wait a minute, it's meant to be a dummy, not a blank.' The fucking thing fired outside! It would have killed me!"

Woods' startling, edgy, highly intelligent performance in Salvador earned him his first Oscar nomination, though why he did not win is a mystery to me. Never has an actor appeared to be so on the edge while also being in control. Highly improvisational, Stone gave Woods room to breathe and bring Boyle forth in the way he chose.

Salvador took some time before it began to garner praise and was a slow burner with critics and audiences. After the smash success of Platoon later that same year, Salvador began to gain momentum. Many reviews were strong, but even those who were not fans of the film still had strong reactions to it. Roger Ebert, always a fan of Woods' work, wrote: "This is the sort of role Woods was born to play, with his glibness, his wary eyes and the endless cigarettes. There is an utter cynicism just beneath the surface of his character, the cynicism of a journalist who has travelled so far, seen so much and used so many chemicals that every story is just a new version of how everybody gets screwed. The heart of the movie is fascinating. And the heart consists of Woods and Belushi, two losers set adrift in a world they never made, trying to play games by everybody else's rules."

Salvador is harrowing, raw, unflinching, fearless, terrifying, darkly funny, exhilarating, exciting, tragic, ugly, and everything in between. Documentary-like in its realism, it still packs a punch to this day and is one of the most unforgettable film experiences of the past fifty years. We can look at it retrospectively as a vital start-off piece for Stone's career to follow, going right into Platoon, Wall Street and beyond. Stone went on to become a master filmmaker, a genius perhaps, but the rawness in Salvador is strangely compulsive, despite the horrendous acts and events that take place.

One can also look at the picture within the body of work that James Woods has given us. Undoubtedly, it's up there with his finest performances, a motor-like whirlwind of activity, movement, emotion and action. As great as Salvador is, it's impossible to imagine anyone else playing Richard Boyle. As Woods told me: "I embraced the spirit of Oliver's vision and brought it to life in a way that wasn't really on the page." It is the ultimate example of actor as co-filmmaker; or more specifically, as a true collaborator.

Speaking to Los Angeles Times in 1987, Woods said: "Salvador was made for pennies. You'd do something really big in one take because the light was going and you couldn't do it again another day. Oliver said after one take, 'Jeez, man, you know you did a tracheotomy in that scene!?' Well, yeah. It's like the Beatles, playing eight to 10 hours every night in a Hamburg basement. You get to know how to do it. You get to know everybody else's instrument. And when you've been in that basement, nothing later on throws you too much." To me, James said; "Salvador was the moment I became the James Woods I am proud to be, associated with relevant, political, cultural filmmaking."

It was nearly ten years until Woods and Stone worked as actor and director again, when he cast James as Haldeman in Nixon. "He offered me a couple of movies," Woods told me, "Wall Street and Platoon. With Platoon, my words to him were, 'Oliver, I just got out of one jungle with you, I don't think I can go into another right away.' I just had this image of being in a helicopter in the fucking jungle in the Philippines. Oliver's a genius and he's also a crazy man. Simple..."

OLIVER STONE ON SALVADOR
AND JAMES WOODS

Oliver Stone, one of the most influential and controversial filmmakers of all time, talked to me about working with James Woods on Salvador, the film's turbulent making, its rocky release, and its legacy within the Stone filmography.

When you came to making Salvador, it's well known that you had Martin Sheen ready to play Richard Boyle. What was it about James Woods that made you sure he was actually the right man for the part?

Jimmy basically torpedoed Marty for the role, when he started making fun of Marty's stiffness as a Christian. He was right in the end. Martin was not the right guy to play Richard Boyle, who was the Antichrist of the whole thing. It would have been a mistake. But

135

beggars can't be choosers and I was very happy to have an actor of Martin's calibre. But I'm very happy that it happened. And he did avert him in the way I described. You never know how it would have gone down with Martin Sheen, it might have had a different charm. But I don't think about that as much as I think that Jimmy just ended up being the right person.

Was there a tension between the real Richard Boyle and James Woods? You've said that as people they were the complete opposites.

Yes there was tension, certainly in every way (laughs). I think one of the philosophical issues was that Richard, who never really knew how movies were made, was so spontaneous and irreverent, and out there. He was not disciplined in the way that movies are made. So we always wanted Jimmy to be grungier, looser, crazier, and Jimmy had to deal with the problems of discipline. And Jimmy would often talk about empathy for the character, and of course it also concerned me at some point whether Jimmy was the one sanitising the thing too much, selling it out (laughs). We ended up with a film that worked at the end of the day. It was a difficult film to edit as you know, with all the interference. In the end, Jimmy gave a performance that got an Academy Award nomination. So it worked! It worked, that is the key. You never know what else could have worked. At one point Richard Boyle was going to play the role, after that disastrous screen test we did. I don't think Boyle would have worked and John Daly (producer at Hemdale) pointed that out. We needed an actor. I was desperate to make that movie in any way I could. There were tensions on every fucking level. And Jimmy would get annoyed if Boyle was around, and he'd think that Boyle would be critical of him. And Richard resented him because he was a movie star and getting paid more than he was. 'Who the fuck is he to do this?' All kinds of shit was going on the whole time. I had other problems too beside those two. But I think the film benefited from the chaos.

Salvador is such an exciting film to watch and I know the making of it was so turbulent. But was there a point, maybe once it was finished and released and people were reacting to it, that you started to think it was all worth it?

Oh yeah it was worth it. I knew what I wanted to do. But other people had doubts.

How was it working with Jimmy, with the ad libs and all the ideas he brought to the film?

As an improviser he is brilliant. Brilliant. I would always encourage him, within our time limits. And if he came up with something I would be the first to go with it. But he never gave me a problem on the content. It all worked itself out. We never really clashed fundamentally, except in the way which was, how grungy should we make the character? I was always trying to make him more sleazy, while Jimmy was always on the side of caution. Boyle's face would be a different colour everyday, so you have to understand we were dealing with a madman. I loved Boyle, but he was difficult. He'd be up and down, lecherous, greedy (laughs), wanting money all the time, scheming all the time, always complaining about something. Richard was a character, and he was the soul of the film in a sense. I wouldn't have been able to do it without him. It was his madness that drove it forward. Of course the critics got that confused with me, as they always do, saying that I was Richard Boyle. That's such bullshit. As I said, Jimmy was disgusted by him but I saw his strengths. And I think in the end Jimmy did too, although he has never expressed remorse about his death or anything like that. Jimmy is an actor, and he's great at it, and this is one of his best performances. In a sense he was free to do what he wanted, and he was exciting to have on the set. But he was difficult at the time. He always thought he knew best, and he often did (laughs), but it can be hard to work with a know-it-all. And his fear of getting hurt, I understand that. You know, an explosion next to your face, I do understand. I'm more sensitive to that now actually, but I needed an actor who was willing to take risks, and that was a movie full of risks. The film was constantly testing him. I wanted him to go to El Salvador before filming and I was pushing him, but he didn't want to go (laughs), because he was a germophobe and all that. He doesn't want to be in shit hole countries (laughs). He did almost quit, and then I'd have been up shit creek, because it was so difficult at that point with the money and all that. The only other solution would have been to get Gary Busey, and he was even crazier (laughs).

In your memoir, it's very exciting when you write of that period when the film starts to get a proper reception, it grows, and people start to laugh and respond to the Boyle character...

That didn't really happen at the start, no. I was pretty down after that when I left the country to go to the Philippines to shoot Platoon. I

138

thought it was over. It was flat, New York critics were snotty. It hadn't opened in LA yet. We were dead in the water in a sense. I mean, it was an art film. But as we were shooting Platoon, that's when I started getting news from the West Coast. That boosted my morale, because the West Coast were interested in the Salvador issue, and people were into it and laughing at the film. It was a big deal for me, after all the shit I had gone through with these studio types who'd seen the movie and expressed their disgust. They didn't see the humour in it. And then that witch, the critic (Pauline Kael), she didn't even bother to review it until months later and she was saying it was a scumbag film, but it was of interest, and that caught the interest of her crowd and brought it back to New York. It started making money on the West Coast, got good engagements in its second run, then her review led to it getting picked up again in New York.

But Platoon was the big thing that made people pay more attention to it. They knew Platoon was coming, then all of a sudden it was heating up, this invisible heat, that this was a hot film about Vietnam. My regret is that Platoon should never have been competitive with Salvador. The film crowd, the critics, were saying, 'Oh yes I think Salvador is a better movie.' It's like, God Almighty. Both were different films, both made under impossible conditions, and actually succeeded in spite of this. So you don't compare them, you just say thank you. It was all I could do. But it was quite annoying. And then in later years people would say, 'I think Salvador is the better film, because Platoon got all the awards, but it's not as good.' That's one thing I hate about the film business, its snobbism. I am not a snob director, I am a man of the people director. But Salvador was too disgusting a film for people, for middle America I guess. Even to this day people haven't bothered to see it. It doesn't have great distribution either. Hemdale went out of business and was sold off to MGM. Salvador was seen as a throw away after Platoon. So it never really had the shelf life of other films.

But with Jimmy, we ended up as friends. That took some time, it was a tough shoot and I did want to strangle him. But he did say those lines to me, as I noted at the time in my diary. He came up to me after the shoot and he seemed very happy with it and satisfied. Which was pretty good for Jimmy because he had been critical all along of the film ever getting out there. When I got Jimmy, you must understand that only The Onion Field had gotten notice. Once Upon a Time in America hadn't done business in the States. So no one was waiting on Salvador because of him. It didn't change the financing or anything like that. When it came out and he got the Academy Award nomination, we were all surprised, but we felt it was genuine on the part of the community. They were surprised by his performance. But unfortunately it was the seventh time Paul Newman had been nominated, this time for one of his lesser films, and he won. But I do think Jimmy was robbed. It does happen.

JIM BELUSHI ON SALVADOR
AND JAMES WOODS

Jim Belushi, comedy legend and cannabis farmer, spoke to me about his memories of Salvador with Oliver Stone and James Woods.

Do you remember how you felt when you got the part of Doctor Rock?

I was shocked. Oliver said he saw me do the White Guy Rap on Saturday Night Live. I had no idea how he bridged that character with the Doctor Rock character, but I was thrilled to be part of this important movie.

What did you think of the real Boyle and Doc when you met them?

The real Richard Boyle is one of the most fascinating people I've ever met. Fucking crazy and brilliant in the same moment. Big eyes, big smile, filled with information for a character actor to build on. He was a history lesson. Although he did repeat over and over, "I was the last one out of Cambodia! Not (whatever that guy's name was)." Richard was a war junkie and he loved the chaos and he was so clever on how to work through that chaos. Jimmy captured him perfectly because Jimmy is chaotic. The real Doc drove me crazy. I remember leaving dinner in Mexico, speaking to Oliver. I said, "If you want me to play him, he's going to be the most un-likeable character in film history." How I played the role was not how Doctor Rock was in real life. How Jimmy attacked the role was very similar to Boyle.

It's well known that Oliver riled you and Jimmy up, going to one and saying to "watch out" for the other. Do you think that tension between the two characters would have been as intense without all that beforehand?

Oliver was terrible! He whispered in my ear, "Jimmy has been playing supporting roles for a long time. He knows the camera like a hawk. Watch him." Later I found out Oliver went to Jimmy and said, "This Belushi guy is better than his brother. Watch him." So yes, he set us up right off the top. Jimmy and I fought for the first couple of weeks until we figured it out. Then we turned it around on Oliver. While Oliver was speaking to us and giving us direction, one time I said, "You know Oliver, I think what this scene really needs is a HAND." And I would run my hand up from my belly to my face. Oliver had directed his first movie with Michael Caine called The Hand, which didn't do very well. Oliver would get very defensive. "That was my first movie! I can't direct people older than me! I don't know what happened!" Let's just say we had a good time busting each other's balls. Oliver hadn't done Platoon yet. But the truth was, Jimmy did know that camera like a hawk. I had to watch him. And we had quite a few fights where he would pull out a switch blade in the middle of a cross two, forcing the cut to his close-up while I was talking. After that take, I turned to Jimmy and said, "You do that again, the next time you talk in the scene, you see all these watches in the glove compartment? I'm going to count them during your cross two." We had some really good fights. But the lie was that I'm certainly not better than my brother John.

What are some of your favourite memories of filming? And also some of the scariest?

My favourite scenes were me, Jimmy, and the car. We improvised a lot. I was a trained improviser and of course Jimmy's good at everything. "I'm really good at comedy! I'm really good at comedy!" At dinner and at conversation, Jimmy is one of the funniest people I know. Delivering a joke, well... he could have used a couple of classes. When we improvised he always over talked. That's a classic beginner's mistake in improvisation. But come on, we all know Jimmy. He always over talks! But he's funny and wicked smart. By the way, he'll let you know how wicked smart he is — MIT, bullshit bullshit bullshit, my IQ, bullshit, Mensa, bullshit. I love this fuckin' guy. The scariest memory was not the actual filming of the scenes, but the emotional toll of standing at the grave site of four nuns who were raped and murdered, being in the church when the archbishop was assassinated. And the hardest scene was walking through El Plato, a real location where the death squads dumped their victims off the side of a cliff. Jimmy and the John Savage character went there to photograph it, and I stood there with a crow who was trying to take my food away from me. Oliver had landscaped that cliff side with extras, bodies. And they laid on that hill all afternoon in the heat. Many of the extras were the real victims of the mutilation that happened in Salvador. There were people with arms, legs missing. It was a horrific sight and the images live with me still today. And the depth of sorrow and sadness and anger over the sheer brutality of civil war. It may have been staged for camera, but it transposed me emotionally as if it were happening right then. I'll never forget it.

Jimmy told me about some of the ad libs. What were some of your favourite spontaneous moments from filming?

Jimmy won't shut up. Fucking guy doesn't know when the scene ends because he's always gotta have the last word. I think we were in the back of a Jeep, having been arrested, and the Boyle character was 'skimming and scamming' to get us out. And I had some lines in that scene, apparently Jimmy forgot. So I'm trying to get my god damn lines in, Jimmy won't leave me a breath, so I just started yelling at him and telling him to shut up, telling him he's dramatic, telling him, "You've always got to have the last word, don't you!" And he would sure enough say, "Yes, I always have to have the last word." I just had to play it real. I wanted Jimmy to shut up, I wanted him to stop overacting, and I wanted him to let me play in the scene once in a while. I don't want you to think by the way I'm writing... There was nothing hostile between us. I admire and love Jimmy Woods deeply and our on screen conflicts were so real, so fun, it was such a pleasure to act with somebody as powerful as Jimmy. Because he gave me such an inspiration to bounce back and go toe to toe with him. I adored my time with Jimmy. Although he never fuckin' shuts up.

He's just Jimmy. Quick witted, fast talking, agenda-driven, powerful on the set. And if you don't stand up to him, he'll run over you like a thresher at harvest time. He's a powerhouse. And I loved being in that bubble with him.

144

PROMISE (1986)

The same year he was seen stomping through El Salvador with Oliver Stone (actually Mexico), James Woods also starred in Promise, one of the finest (and most awarded) TV films in history. What is most remarkable about Woods' work in Promise is how different it was to his role as Richard Boyle. Granted, he is a very good actor, and any actor who respects their craft will pride themselves on their adaptability. But if there are any two films which highlight the versatility of a single actor as Promise and Salvador do (bearing in mind the two pictures were released in the same year) then I would like to see them.

The story concerns James Garner as Bob, a man who upon his mother's death inherits both her home and custody of his younger brother, D.J., played by Woods, who suffers from schizophrenia. Bob was not so close to his mum and had been enjoying the life of a care free womanizer, living day to day without responsibilities. Suddenly, he finds himself carrying a bigger burden than he ever thought he would. At first, the relationship is strained. Bob, a straight forward, fun loving guy, can't understand his brother's complexities, his mood changes, and what to him is pure frustrating irrationality. D.J. can go for days sitting in an arm chair, cigarettes burning to the ground between his fingers. Disturbed by D.J.'s behaviour, Bob doesn't know what to do with him. He is like an alien, a total mystery to him. After a while though, they begin to bond. One day they decide to go stay in the country by a lake they frequented in their younger years. D.J. comes to life while there, and dreams of living a pure life by the water. He'll start his own business, pull himself round. His positivity is moving, but also unrealistic. After dark, he heads out to the rubble remains of an old building and re-enacts childhood memories, nearly falling from a great height as he does so. Bob grabs a hold of D.J. and takes him back to their lodgings, but D.J.'s rowdiness alerts the attention of the local law enforcement. This incident leads Bob to some serious questions. Is D.J. capable of an ordinary life out in the real world, or would it be more responsible to send him off to a secure home where he can be monitored, properly cared for and encouraged to engage in positive activities?

Promise was directed by Glenn Jordan, written by Richard Friedenberg, and was shot in two months in September and October of 86. Garner himself co-produced the picture. He wrote in his memoir: "It was an easy decision for me and my producing partner, Peter Duchow, to join forces with Hallmark." Garner knew that he was at the right age to play Bob, a man who "never grew up" in his eyes. He had a hand in casting Woods, having fondly recalled their work together on The Rockford Files. They would team up again on 1989's My Name is Bill W., and became firm friends for the rest of Garner's life.

As had been the case with Holocaust and The Onion Field, playing D.J. must have been a somewhat intimidating task for Woods, but again he had a responsibility to the subject at hand. "I had all the misconceptions," Woods said at the time. "I thought all schizophrenics believed they were Napoleon or Beethoven. One of the patients I met said to me, 'You can't imagine what it's like to hear a voice or to see a person and you know they're not there, but they are as tangible and as real as the person next to you.' That's what schizophrenia is. You not only have the day-to-day reality of the disease. You also have the dread burden of knowing even when you're well that you can lose control at any time. It's like being an emotional epileptic, like having a seizure of your soul or your mind."

146

Woods himself, rightly so, won both a Golden Globe and an Emmy for his performance, which is absolutely brilliant from start to finish. But it was a performance that nearly didn't happen. His agent had come to him with the project. "We have this offer for a TV movie, where they want you to play a retarded kid. Can I pass?" James was immediately intrigued. "What do you mean, 'to play a retarded kid?' What does that mean?" James told me that it was the best script he had ever read. Yet his agent insisted: "You are not doing a TV movie!" James' reply was equally straight forward: "Yes I am. I am doing this."

It is a tirelessly committed piece of work, multi faceted and well observed to the point that at times we forget we are watching Woods at all. He gives D.J. dignity, but does not shy away from both the ups and downs of his manic personality. When weighed down by his troubles, Woods is almost frightening in his intensity, his silences, and his stares. When overjoyed by the idea of living a normal life, his energy and sense of hope are extremely moving. He lifts you up, makes your heart genuinely ache, and then breaks it when it becomes clear that, despite all his best efforts, he cannot function like an everyday person.

Woods once said that Promise was perhaps his personal favourite out of all the roles he had played, stating, "It was a perfect part for me." Speaking to Charlie Rose in 1992, he explained: "I think my best performance actually was in Promise... When people ask me, I say, the one that I nailed for a perfect 10 as far as what I wanted to achieve and what I achieved. The one where I would not change a frame was Promise. The script was miraculously, beautifully written. The writing was to die for."

Speaking to me in 2021 about the role, James went into detail about his approach, specifically the scene where the brothers return to the lake they frequented as children, and Woods climbs up the rubble of the castle ruins, excited by his prospective future. "Oh God," Woods recalled, "that to me was an amazing scene. Yeah, you know, that was really interesting, because in that scene Jim Garner's character is afraid of heights. And I am on top of this stone castle, singing and acting crazy, while in fact I have horrible fear of heights in real life, not Jim. And it was way up on this thing, and if you fall, you die. And it was rainy and it was slippery and wet. But I was up there and I was in the moment. So it was a perfect example of him losing his mind a little bit."

James also looked back on the scene where his character gives his brother some insight into what it's like to be schizophrenic. "I had spent a couple of months with three guys who were actually really schizophrenic, and they really helped me a lot. They were at this halfway house. But this scene was sort of the championship speech that my character had. And my line to him was, 'Bobby, do you want to know what it's like to be like me?' And he said, 'Yeah', so I then explain what it's like to be a schizophrenic. One of the lines along the way is, 'I've never had a job and I never will; I never kissed a girl and I never will; I never had any friends and I never will.' And it was a very tragic and sad speech and any actor would do it and start to cry. Any male actor in Hollywood cries whenever they get the chance to, it's just astonishing to me. You know... Glenn Jordan, who was a great director and friend to me, I said to him, 'Glenn, this is such a big speech, and I have a weird idea. I am gonna give this speech as if I'm the older brother explaining something to the younger brother, like his first real lesson about why his dog has to be put to sleep, or why his Grandma died. In other words, I am gonna explain it in a kind and paternal, almost peaceful - and I won't say happy, but a caring way.' So what I did was I shared horrible explanations of the reality of schizophrenia to the one person who promised he would care for me.

It gave him the courage to do it through knowledge. And I did it almost with a warm smile on my face, and honestly it was probably the best two minutes I had in my life, on film.

"And what's interesting is that everyone was silent, and the crew were so quiet and respectful to the actors, but some member of the crew outside started to play basketball during the speech. Every now and then you can hear it in the speech. Now ordinarily - and we've heard actors, famously, on You Tube screaming at the crew... I said to myself, 'He is being so benevolent here to his brother, that there is nothing that can stop him in this moment of kindness.' So even as an actor, what would ordinarily have been very upsetting and kind of painful - you know, to have a beautiful take ruined - I just talked my way through it. And I think Glenn said, 'I loved that take so much that I am not gonna do it any other way. Of course, someone outside just didn't realise we were rolling, so we're gonna go out and shoot a picture of a couple of guys playing basketball outside. We may not need it, we may be able to wipe it in the editing.' But the thing is, I would have been thrown off by it. But my objective and goal in the scene was to be a person of such kindness and consideration, that though I have a devastating mental illness, which can never be cured and at best maintained, I did find within myself a spiritual strength that really defined the heart and soul of the character. And it brought us together as brothers. I mean, Jim and I LOVED doing that movie. To this day it is still the most honoured TV movie. It was amazing, just amazing."

While other actors might have looked down on TV in this period, Woods saw it as an opportunity to tackle issues dead on, to not have to think about promotion, box office takings and whether people were going to see it or not. After all, the airing of a TV movie goes out to millions, and there is an urgency about that. Woods said he and the station did have disagreements, but it was all down to his insistence on detail. He urged them to dye his shirts greyer, to highlight the dullness of D.J.s' life. "In the end," Woods said, "they indulged me."

Woods saw Promise as both an important story that needed telling, and a way to stretch himself and his public image in the process. "I'm proud that people can come up to me and say, 'I think of you as so scary.' That shows I have some technical virtuosity. But a film like Promise is more than technical virtuosity. It's a glimpse into my heart and soul."

Promise aired in December of 1986 to great acclaim. It won various awards, including the prestigious Peabody Prize, and an Emmy for Outstanding Drama. After its airing, the New York Times raved: "The story - and the film - belongs to Bob and D. J. as they circle each other warily and painfully. Mr. Garner does come through powerfully as he delves into a character very different from those in his familiar repertory. He is equally matched, however, by James Woods as D. J. Hailed for his work in such films as The Onion Field and Salvador, Mr. Woods is thoroughly riveting as he flits through a staggering range of emotions, sometimes in a single scene."

Promise is an engaging and very beautiful story, and the acting is often breathtaking. But most of all one comes away with the strong feeling that it does wonders for our collective understanding of mental health. Though we are initially disturbed by Woods' struggles, we learn to understand them and look beyond his psychological problems to the man who is at the core of this husk, who is buried inside the shell. It becomes a film about understanding, about being caring and open, and most of all, stepping up to your responsibilities as a decent human being. When you make a promise, as Bob does, you have to keep it.

BEST SELLER (1987)

One of the least talked of, yet most impressive 80's films to feature James Woods, is Best Seller (1987), where he found himself once again alongside the late and great Brian Dennehy. Another independent Hemdale production with John Daly (he had also produced Salvador), this sharp thriller has Woods as a hit-man named Cleve who wants the help of seasoned cop Dennis Meechum (Dennehy), who also happens to be a best selling writer, to adapt his admittedly fascinating story into book form. Things aren't straight forward though. Years earlier, as part of a masked gang, Cleve had killed two of Meechum's colleagues, and once this fact is revealed he is adamant on busting him. At the start of the film though, Woods appears out of nowhere during Dennehy's pursuit of a criminal and saves his life. Meechum is therefore torn and also genuinely intrigued by the tale Cleve has to tell him, that he was a paid assassin for Kappa International, a huge empire run by David Madlock (Paul Schena). What follows is a strange game between Woods and Dennehy, a kind of dance of psych outs and double bluffs. Is this relationship, this weird friendship that has developed between the officer and the criminal, at all healthy? Will he turn the hit man in as soon as the book is finished?

Larry Cohen's original script for the picture went about the place for years, and was originally intended for Burt Lancaster and Kirk Douglas. John Flynn then re-worked it for the 1980's and cast two of the most dynamic actors of the era. Cohen was pleased with the casting and the choice of director.

Woods himself was always intrigued by the script and saw much more in it than a thriller, but a film full of shady morals and tricky choices. "I thought, this guy can really write," Woods said to me of the screenplay. "I thought, What a great script. What a unique idea. Because of course I had known Joe Wambaugh, and thought, Shit, what if a killer came to Joe with a story? It's like the same problem I had with The Onion Field; do I talk to Greg Powell to create this character? So it was part of his moral dilemma. Brian Dennehy's dilemma is a very complex choice, a series of moral choices actually. Like, is it possible that you could become friends with a hired killer? Is it possible that the killer can finally make important choices of his own? I mean there is no redemption for him, but he does seem to be reaching for a reconstruction of the moral universe that at least gives him a personal redemption, even if he understands he will never have a global redemption from others, or society or even from Dennehy's character. But Dennehy's character is torn. There are a lot grey areas in that movie; the end justifying the means, all that type of stuff. The moral universe in which these two characters were operating was very disturbing for one of them, and an outlet of redemption to the other."

As anyone who's seen it will know, there is much more to the film than a straight forward thriller. One can look into hidden subtext a little too intensely, yet I feel there is something being said about 80's America here, the era of aspiration, of success being all, of suited yuppies making everything a commodity. Woods, speaking about this period in his career (and his independent films specifically) told Den of Geek that he liked the murkiness of the films, Best Seller in particular, because they presented something that was happening but was never pulled out into the open. "I liked doing them because they had a genre overlay for me," he said. "In other words, you really had an updated film noir feel, and at the same time the film noir underbelly of the yuppie decade. So while people were out there thinking life was good, because they could drive around in fast cars and have second vacation homes, there were still criminals out there doing their job, in updated, clever ways."

The idea of Woods' character being a personification of certain criticisms of that era is clear in one particular scene, when Cleve breaks into the house of Dennehy's female publishing agent. Clearly a wealthy woman, Woods holds her at knife point and in her bedroom, as she's cowering on the bed in her underwear, he talks about hard working families who will never have the money to buy the kind of expensive items and clothing that she takes for granted. "What makes you better than them?" he asks. "Nothing," she replies. Cleve agrees and then takes a knife through one of her pricey dresses. In this moment, he is almost the one man army against the Capitalist engine of the 1980's, the concept of greed being good, more being more and less being less. In his mind, though a killer himself, he's become a moral crusader, the only one brave enough to reverse the injustices of a corrupt Capitalist America while also reaching out for a personal redemptive pay off of his own. Of course, Cleve is no communist, he's just as driven as the next guy, but he is at least attempting to rebalance the scales.

I asked Woods if he thought I was looking too much into Cleve by seeing him as a man reeking vengeance on yuppie America. "I think his point was that everything is commerce," he replied. "I remember seeing a play that Al Pacino did when we were both young actors. And I will never forget this character saying, 'Well I'm a junkie and a whore and everyone thinks I'm a terrible human being, but how different am I from these trophy wives with their jewels and their fancy cars, and all their gifts? They're basically negotiating a better deal.' So it's that concept. I think he hated the hypocrisy of people who thought they were morally superior but didn't mind profiting from a killer, winning some awards and climbing the social ladder.

Rather than thinking, Is this the right thing to do? To mix with a killer?' It's the same as, was I tempted to meet Byron De La Beckwith (Woods' character in Ghosts of Mississippi, the vile white supremacist who killed Medgar Evers in the 1960's) or Gregory Powell? Yeah I was! But if I do that they now have a bargaining chip which in their small world makes them a little closer to royalty in their environment. You know, 'A movie actor came to me, I'm really special.' In the prison world that makes them a big shot."

But even as we learn a little more about him, Cleve is still a man of mystery. He appears out of nowhere in the building site early in the film (saving the cop's life), in his dark sunglasses and his sharp suit, just as a real life hit-man might. He looks like your regular businessman of the era, a city high roller perhaps, and it is this fact which makes him so interesting, not to mention the scary things he is capable of. (It also makes you ask what the difference is between a ruthless businessman and a killer.) The problem with many 80's movies was that such characters were so often a larger than life, muscle bound colossus who, yes, may have been able to punch someone over a table, but might have been a little too inconspicuous to make a decent assassin with genuine enigma and stealth. Woods' wiry Cleve is closer to the truth, and this was a fact not lost on James himself when he took the part. He liked the fact he was a "believable Superman" and was a professional in every sense, with a set of skills that were all his own. The fact he clings on to Dennehy's character, a man he can use in some ways to right various wrongs, adds another dimension to his character. Woods saw him as a sociopath yes, but perhaps one who had reached a point in his life where he wanted to do the right thing, expose some corruption for the moral good of his country. Woods gives Cleve a believability, and not once do we roll our eyes when he takes a man down with his gun with ease, or breaks another's neck because he is in the way. We buy it, and also swallow the fact he could quietly leave the room without you even knowing he'd been there. It's a subtle performance.

It helps of course that he was cast opposite an actor as good as Dennehy, who also settles into his role with apparent ease. Cleve sees them as soul brothers, is adamant they have a bond. "Cop and killer," he says, adding "two sides to the same coin." As he did with De Niro in Once Upon a Time in America, Woods plays off Dennehy splendidly, and Dennehy works against Woods' snake-like deviousness with a stony determination.

"It was great working with Brian," James told me. "We would laugh all the time. He was one of those people that the more I teased him, the more he laughed. He loved that I teased him all the time. And of course I would go to town on him, but he had an ego-less appreciation of life. He had no sense of self reverence, which I loved about him. He was a wonderful man, I just loved Brian. And there was a scene at the end when I was dying in his arms. And they do my close up and I die. And then they're gonna do his close up and he makes the mistake of saying, 'Well I finally have a close up where Jimmy Woods won't be bumping into it and trying to steal it.' The crew laughed and we were shooting his crying scene. All of a sudden I reach out and tug at him, pat him on the face and go, 'Just one more time!' He loved that (laughs). I loved Brian."

On the Meechum character, Woods shared his thoughts with me: "You believed he was the cop who had an end game in mind. So no matter what I did, his character never betrayed his sanctity. He was a cop and he was never gonna let this bad guy get away with this. But also, he was sure he was gonna step ladder Cleve to get to another man who was even more dangerous, someone who was delicious prey if you will. He was the guy who was worth making some wobbly moral choices for to get to and bring to justice."

Best Seller had originally been written as Hard Cover, and after the picture was released someone came forward saying the story had been plagiarised. Flynn recalled: "Then a woman sued us all - me, Larry Cohen, James Woods and producer Carter DeHaven. This woman claimed we had stolen the plot of a book she wrote called Best Seller. We went on to prove that this could not be the case, because Larry Cohen had submitted a treatment to Columbia prior to the copyright of this book. It's amazing, though, because there were plot similarities. Her book was about a killer who writes a best seller incriminating the people who hired him. Turns out this lady didn't want money. She asked for a three-picture deal with Hemdale Films."

Best Seller is not the standard 80's thriller it looks to be on its DVD cover. An intelligently written and constructed cat and mouse game, as Woods noted, it's a film about morals, about motives and personal redemption. At its centre are two wonderful performances by a pair of actors who work so well together that you wish they had teamed up more often. For me, Cleve remains one of James Woods' most fascinating figures.

COP (1988)

Then there was the seminal Cop (1988), written and directed by James B. Harris, who had worked with Woods earlier in the decade on the buried gem, Fast-Walking. Cop, based on James Ellroy's Blood on the Moon, has Woods in the role of hard-assed Police Detective Sergeant Lloyd Hopkins, who is trying to get to the bottom of a brutal murder in LA. The mystery leads him to the world of feminist literature, when he meets the owner of a poetry store and finds possible clues to the identity of the real killer, who in the mean time strikes again, and in an even more brutal fashion.

Cop is not your regular action thriller of the era, and Woods' character is unlike any lead cop you've ever seen; he gets VERY personal with people involved with a case; he goes home and tells his 8 year old daughter vivid details about the crimes he is investigating (though he has a valid reason for this, at least in his mind); he goes against orders everyday, but only in order to get justice. Lloyd is another multi dimensional man in the Woods gallery of unconventional faces, someone who is good in the sense that he wants to lock the bad guys away, but doesn't always go by the conventional book when doing so. In the hands of another actor, he would have been the typical 80's cop, the renegade with a mullet, the gun happy maverick repeatedly given stacks of paperwork to fill in after whacking some scumbag. But Woods makes the cop an individual; a maverick yes, but one who doesn't really care about the personal consequences his actions will have. For him, work is life and life is work. Unable to separate the two, he loses his family, but keeps his focus on busting the killer. He is not a wise-cracking hero, and this is no buddy cop movie of the breed that were all the rage at the time (even though there are some lovely interactions with Charles

Durning, who plays his partner). No, this man is something of a lone wolf, totally single minded and intent on catching the bad guy. Again, like Best Seller's Cleve, Woods' cop is a believable character, not a phony, phoned-in Hollywood creation born out of various clichés rolled into one. He ensures the film itself transcends the genre and becomes more of a character study than a police thriller. Woods turned down the lead in Oliver Stone's Wall Street for this, so it was clear he was committed to the script and the part he was to make his own.

When we came to Cop in one of our interviews, James seemed especially fond of it. "I mean, James Ellroy is a wonderful writer. And Jimmy Harris and I were friends. I mean, I was offered Wall Street and we certainly discussed it. Jimmy said, 'You got to take that part,' but I said, 'I promised you I was gonna do Cop, so I'm doing Cop.'"

When I raised the point of it not being a daft, quotable romp, Woods agreed. "I particularly like it because it's not clever, fun, high octane studio jokes and high-jinks. This is really very procedurally how it is. You got a cop who is of the same ilk; ruthless, misunderstood, passionate about justice and who has a certain code of ethics. He's not gonna let go. He has his opinions, like about the feminist library and all that, but basically he has one mission. And you know, some of it is deliberately slow, other bits are fast and high paced. I think it's a kind of a hidden gem that movie. A lot of people come to me and say, 'God I love that movie, it's so weird and dark.' But it's like that, especially when you watch the documentaries on those serial killers. When you get beyond the sensationalism of serial murder and you start to examine the psychology of the killer, the forensics of the crime scene, the judicial aspects including the difficulties of prosecution, the police investigation techniques and the restraints which make solving crimes that have a ticking clock more

158

difficult... When you have to solve a single act murder, you know, the pressures and those various issues are much more suppressed. But when you have a guy who's killed six women, and he's about to kill more, you have a ticking clock. And you are being restrained by the judicial elements of our legal system that will later come to haunt you if you don't honour them, and they can also cost people their lives. Police are aware of that and they are in a terrible dilemma, when they can surely be tempted to break the rules to get evidence they need, but if they do the guy may get off and it makes it more complex and therefore interesting as a film-making subject."

Cop has one of the coolest endings of any thriller I can think of. After the shoot out with the killer in the old school gymnasium, Lloyd, who's had his badge taken from him, manages to get the murderer with his hands up. Expecting a quick arrest, the killer is smug. But Lloyd is in no mood to piss around. He gives him the good news and the bad news. The good news is that he is indeed a cop and he has to take him in; the bad news is he's been suspended and he doesn't give a fuck. The killer's smug smile is wiped off instantly. Woods pulls the trigger, the gun fires, he aggressively reloads and the film goes to black.

"I improvised that whole ending," James told me. "That is not the original ending of Blood on the Moon. And James Ellroy was on the set a lot. He was there everyday. But the ending was my idea. We were supposed to have a big fight and all this stuff and I was supposed to arrest him. But I said, 'I know it sounds corny, but what if we just do a good news/bad news joke?' You know, the bad news is I don't give a fuck! I can't tell you the amount of people, especially cops, who say, 'You know, we would never do it,' but man, every cop secretly cheers when they watch that.' There are certain killers who

Cop (1988).

get away with it, and you know they're gonna get away with it, they literally get away with murder."

Critics greeted Cop enthusiastically. Roger Ebert, always a Woods admirer, wrote a rave review of his performance: "Anyone without a history of watching James Woods in the movies might easily misread Cop. They might think this is simply a violent, sick, contrived exploitation picture, and that would certainly be an accurate description of its surfaces. But Woods operates in this movie almost as if he were writing his own footnotes. He uses his personality, his voice and his quirky sense of humour to undermine the material and comment on it, until Cop becomes an essay on this whole genre of movie. And then, with the movie's startling last shot, Woods slams shut the book."

Ebert, who in the same piece called Woods "the most engaging and unconventional of leading men", also added: "Woods was born to play this role. He uses a curious and effective technique to get laughs, of which the movie has plenty. Instead of saying funny things, he knows how to throw in a pause, just long enough for the audience to figure out what he's really thinking, so that when he says a straight line, it's funny. The result is creepy; he invites us into his mind and makes us share his obsession. Cop is a violent movie, all the more so because it is so casual about the violence. It sees its events through the mind of a man who should never have been a cop and who has been a cop much too long. Yet the Woods character is not stupid and not brutal, just several degrees off from normal. It's as if Woods and Harris watched a Dirty Harry movie one night and decided to see what would happen if Harry were really dirty."

New York Times nailed Woods' persona at that time, and also the dedication and commitment he gave to each role. Writing of his work in Cop, Janet Maslin mused: "James Woods is more frequently seen

161

eating on-camera than just about any other actor, but he's so edgy and thin that there's nothing voluptuous about this behaviour. If anything, it's borderline rude. So is Mr. Woods' smoking and his wisecracking; so is virtually everything else he does. Combine this taunting manner with the fierce, obsessive dedication Mr. Woods brings to almost any role and you have the makings of a perfect Elmore Leonard character, which Mr. Woods is bound to play some day. In the meantime, he has arrived as the detective hero of Cop... Far and away the best thing about it (Cop) is Mr. Woods, who served as co-producer and demonstrates a clear understanding of what makes great movie detectives great."

Cop is one of the great police thrillers of the 1980's, but it is also a prime example of how Woods is able to take a part, make it his own, and redefine everything you previously thought was set in stone about film performance.

THE BOOST (1988)

In 1988, he was back with The Onion Field director Harold Becker for The Boost, a very fine drama which acts as the best anti-drugs statement you've ever seen. Here he plays Lenny Brown, a man working a low key job while living a modest, quietly happy life with Linda (Sean Young) in New York. Full of ambition, Lenny takes the plunge and gets work in California with Max Sherman (Steven Hill), a lofty businessman who runs a scheme working with shady tax shelters. Lenny and Linda are suddenly on the up, earning lots of cash, living in a swish pad and dining with prosperous yuppies. Just as quickly though, their luck turns around and they are in debt. Receiving a "boost" from a friend, the pair become addicted to cocaine. Though they try to shake off the drug and the lure of the big city, Lenny's aspirations take over and it becomes clear that in his misguided ambitions, he might just lose the thing that is most dear to him - Linda.

The Boost moves at a healthy pace and takes us through the dangers of wild ambition in a series of effective twists and turns. Young and Woods' chemistry shines off the screen, and their performances are rich and highly convincing. We genuinely like and care for them too, which makes the most harrowing moments all the more distressing. Woods is all vital electricity throughout, a man with ambition bursting out of him, who wants more and more, bigger and better, despite the fact he knows this drive is dangerous and may just kill him. It's a statement on greed, on insecurity, on materialistic hunger, but it does not hammer home a message in any overt way, nor does it drown us with slogans or ask us to condemn the main characters. Young and Woods, but Woods in particular, give their parts multi-dimensions, so that we both sympathise and become frustrated with their actions.

Woods has some terrific scenes in The Boost, in particular the first heavy OD scene which sees him land in hospital. The "wrong table" sequence, which comes near the closing chapter, is also classic Woods. The best sequence of all though comes at the very end, when he knows he's blown it. He has hurt the one he loves, ruined his life and his talent, become so hooked on the hard stuff that he can't see a way out. He's living in a dump, on his way down with no chance of a comeback. He looks exhausted, he's unshaven, he's a wreck. Woods plays it as if his real life depends on it.

When we came to talking about The Boost, I told James that Lenny was one of my personal favourites of all his characters, and that the performance was among his finest. "That is absolutely one of my favourites," James said. "I thought Sean was great too. She was fantastic in the movie. I loved working with her. I think she's a mercurial artist. And you talk about working with people; Amanda Blake, playing the old drug dealer, this is Kitty from Gunsmoke! When people ask me what it's like to work with icons, to me, working with these characters who I grew up with is... unbelievable in so many ways. I mean, I always remember working with Amanda Blake and she was wonderful to work with. I thought, Isn't this wonderful? She was this iconic character on this iconic TV show and now she is willing to do this movie where she's playing a chick who is freebasing two characters because, as an artist, she thought it was a cool character and a really cool movie. "

Woods then enthused about the film, and ultimately highlighted its message about addiction and how insecurity can drive someone over the edge: "It was based on a true story, but it came from Ben Stein's great book called Ludes. It was about quaaludes, but we turned it into being about cocaine which also had its own horrible epidemic and still does obviously. It destroyed America in many ways. I understood that years later Lenny (Woods' character) was still alive and was a drugs councillor, but that she got killed during a drug deal. But I thought the screenplay by Darryl Poniscan was terrific, and I thought Harold's direction was great. I thought Steven Hill was magnificent. But the relationship between Sean and me in that movie, I thought it was great. And I loved the character because he was such a classic Shakespearean character. He could not help but be hoist by his own petard. And his petard was never feeling he was worthy of this woman who he loved so much. And when you feel you're not worthy of love, it's that you don't understand love. He needed her to validate him so much. And if he had realised how much he loved her... It's like the metaphor for the wrong table at the end, those guys who wanna make the deal with Lenny, they're like, 'Look, the table's fine, we don't give a shit about the table.' And she was saying basically the same thing to him. It was like, 'Lenny, we have everything we want. We don't need a private plane. We don't need all this crap. We love each other, let's just love each other!' The scenes in the little house, they were so happy there. They never had to leave that beautiful little love nest because he had his nice job and she could have done whatever she did, and life would be good.

"And later when he's recovered and he's surfing and selling surf boards - it was so charming all that part, I loved how it was shot - and she comes and the two of them turn up (their friends from LA who get them into coke in the first place) and you just think, Oh fuck, don't do it! And of course now having a taste of it, she missed that wild life, and that's the nature of addiction.

"But the film didn't get released properly, unfortunately. I loved Hemdale, they were great. They did a lot of movies with me - they did Salvador, they did Best Seller. I loved John Daly, he was a character, and he was a rascal, but he was certainly good to me. But Harold was very upset that John cut four scenes out of the movie to shorten it, and he just could not forgive him. And I think it was too bad the movie didn't get more of an opportunity. But to this day I've had an unimaginable number of people say to me that it helped them quit an addiction. You know, like, the first thing is you're at a party doing some coke and the next thing you know you're in a crack house sitting with a gun on the table, snorting coke and talking about your life, where did it go... I always say Lenny had died of starvation because he couldn't see the feast that life had put in front of him. Linda for him was a feast. His ability to sell and charm was a nice ability, he could have done well. But it's like the drug, the way it is never enough for an addict, is also the way Lenny's appreciation of his gifts and his love for Linda, it was never enough. He loved her and she loved him back and it's like, Dude, take yes for an answer. How can you not be happy with what you've got? And this is a sickness in Hollywood too, everybody always needs more."

James then spoke about a certain technique used in a film that heightens the tension but also builds the story in an organic manner. "It's all about the slippery slope. The slippery slope is a great technique in movies. In Videodrome you had a slippery slope. You know, let's turn people on to a channel where things come alive. It's like, did you not think that maybe this isn't something you wanna fuck around with? When you start pulling flesh guns out of your stomach, you might be in the wrong place. You might wanna think this over. Even in Cat's Eye, that little comedy, it's like you have one puff of the cigarette and suddenly you're on a pack a day. So in The Boost you had a slippery slope. There was always a consequence, and that is very Shakespearean."

IMMEDIATE FAMILY (1989)

Woods was totally against type - at least as the public largely saw him - in Jonathan Kaplan's subtle and understated drama, Immediate Family (1989). In this warm, appealing and moving picture, he plays Michael Spector, a veterinarian married to Linda, played by Glenn Close. They have a pleasant life in the suburbs and are both successful people in their careers. The only thing they are missing, though, is a child. Linda is desperate to be a mother and is tormented by the mothers around her, her friends who are vocally proud of their children and don't mind saying so. Feeling left out, Linda becomes depressed. She and Michael then make the decision to adopt a child. When they go to the adoption agency, they meet Lucy (Mary Stuart Masterson), a pregnant teenager who will gladly give them the baby as soon as it's born. The Spectors take Lucy under their wings, and a strong bond develops. Kevin Dillon plays Sam, the father of the unborn child, and the four of them become very familiar, perhaps too much so. Inevitably, Lucy begins to doubt whether she wants to really let go of her baby. She changes her mind, taking her child away from Michael and Linda. But will she have yet another change of heart and realise that she and Sam aren't ready to be parents?

What I really like about Immediate Family is the fact it doesn't resort to clichés or over-schmaltziness. Yes the situations are familiar and had been seen in TV movies and features numerous times up to that point (and of course later), but the tone is different, more matter of fact, less sensationalised. The script by Barbara Benedek steers clear of sentimentality, even if the film is touching in a more organic and authentic manner. The acting, too, is splendid, and each performance elevates proceedings. Masterson is excellent as the torn young teen, while Close eases herself naturally into the part of the woman with a giant hole in her life. Woods is understated to the point that we don't even see the performance. One of Woods' gifts is always to make the technique look invisible, and here he becomes the character from his first frame onwards, perfectly believable as the everyday working guy, who comes back from his city job to relax in his unshowy but pleasant suburban home. He too is looking forward to being a parent.

"A lot of people were surprised to see me do Immediate Family," James told me. "That was a leading man image of me that people didn't expect me to have. Some people loved that movie. I mean, Immediate Family had Glenn Close, who is phenomenal. I got to work with my old friend Jonathan Kaplan. I love Jonathan."

Sadly, Immediate Family didn't cause much of a stir, but then it wasn't the kind of film of the era that did attract a lot of attention. Fans of hyper-Woods may be puzzled at first, but within minutes they will grasp that, as ever, he gives Michael a realness other actors might not have been able to achieve. He has some brilliant moments in it too, some of which are so un-sensationalised they may at first seem inconsequential. As ever though, these little touches make the performance. There is one particular scene when Close and Woods' characters are getting to know Masterson. They have dinner together and discuss the famous people they've seen in the streets. Close recalls her sighting of Fred Astaire. At first Woods doesn't take part, but Close presses him. "What about when you saw O.J. Simpson?" "Oh, the Juice!" he says. Close then reveals that after spotting Kareem Abdul-Jabbar, he followed him around town for an hour. Woods' embarrassment and meekness in this scene really defines his character. He's an everyday guy, pure and simple, even the kind that might get a thrill out of spotting a celebrity.

168

There is another great scene later on, when they meet Dillon and Masterson in a cafe, and Dillon's character reveals his career ambitions - to be a roadie. Woods' silence and patient listening is genuinely played to perfection, especially as we can imagine what kind of thoughts are racing through his mind at that moment. Yet he absorbs the naive young man's plans with quiet respect. But what makes this scene so cleverly played is the fact that Woods doesn't even need to say a word. It's all in the eyes and controlled body language. That said, his Michael is no snob. He's a straight forward middle class guy (middle class in the English sense), and his keenness to become a father (or more correctly his excitement) is extremely moving.

The scenes with Woods at his most tender are perhaps the best. When Masterson comes to see the baby in the newborn ward she is almost turned away by the nurse; until Woods, fussing over the baby, insists she can stay because, as he firmly announces, "She's family!" There is a hint of anger in his voice, adamant that this girl, who has chosen to give up her kin, be accepted and welcomed into their unit. Perhaps the most touching scene however is at the very end, when Woods and Close, with their shaggy pet dog, pose for a picture with their son for his first birthday. Inevitably, the perfect snapshot doesn't come to fruition. The dog runs away, the boy follows it out of the room and the proud parents scramble after their son. The dog returns just in time for the flash bulb to capture the golden moment - of the dog eating the birthday cake. It sounds schmaltzy but in the way it's played it's anything but that. In fact it's very real and heart-warming.

When I brought up the fact that Immediate Family feels genuine, Woods offered me valuable insights: "I appreciate that you saw that. We went out of our way to be unsentimental in the telling of that story. And I think one of the reasons it wasn't more successful is because it avoided sentimentality. If it had trod that sentimental line it would have been more successful, but it wouldn't have been as a good a movie. But I'll tell you why it felt that way. Barbara Benedek, who wrote that screenplay - though it wasn't a true story, it was based on her personal experience of trying to get pregnant and adopting. So it was a very personal story for her. Glenn Close loved having her on set as an adviser. And the producers were women too and they really were a wonderful bunch of people. I think Barbara's passion about what she experienced helped - even though she wouldn't talk literally of the facts of her own situation. But I remember it very fondly, because my friend was directing. He'd always wanted to have me in a big movie, and he liked the fact that I had a sense of gravitas in the way I worked. He didn't wanna do a sentimental greeting card version of the story. He wanted to say it was a big issue for women. You know, it is a tough situation for women. This was kind of a generation who had embraced feminism, they had entered middle age and they were like, 'Whoops, we forgot to have children!' And it's about the harsh cold reality about it being easier to have children at 20 than it is at 40 for example. Biology is a cruel taskmaster. I think all that made this story much more intriguing and interesting. As a man working on it, listening to the women around me talking about it, it was really quite enlightening, quite frankly. It was something I really enjoyed. And Kevin and Mary brought a childishness to their characters, they were just children having a child. And here is an adult woman not able to have a child. So I thought it was a really brilliant screenplay. And Jonathan Kaplan, I just love him as a friend and he's brilliant."

OTHER SCREEN HIGHLIGHTS:
1987 - 1990

By the mid 1980's James Woods was already a famous, acclaimed actor, one recognised for his very own type of intensity. After a string of acclaimed, enthralling performances, he was emerging as one of the world's most reliable and exciting actors. It should be noted though, that no one part was the same, and every man he played had something distinctive to separate him from the next one. Indeed, Woods even seemed to adopt a unique physicality to suit the character in question, perhaps in a bid to get to grips with their psychology. There are no fall backs with Woods, no predictabilities, even if there are comforting traits that come and go.

For instance, you might notice that trademark eye roll that Woods often does; in Casino, when he is pretending to be taking down De Niro's phone number; also in The Boost, when being wheeled out of the hospital after an OD, and is impatient with the orderly pushing him out. Then there are the expressive hand movements he uses for either intense or up-close interactions, but these are perfectly natural. And do not forget the familiar Woods crossed arms, which present a man in control, as in Contact (1997) and the Shark series (2006-2008). Yet if you study closer you will see such subtle changes that it's as if Woods has created a new interior thought process for each man. This may seem like over-analysis (after all, Woods is an intuitive actor and not a method man at all), but it is in fact these subtle little touches that give the roles their individuality.

One cannot help but draw attention to these little flourishes. For instance, there is one particular scene in Salvador where he is surrounded by armed men. He pulls out a knife and, as he is clearly intoxicated, he begins to flash the blade around. He knows he's in trouble, but he's blagging his way through the scenario. But look at his feet; he almost dances, as Oliver Stone later noted, and there is even something of Chaplin about that moment. I also think of the sadness behind his eyes in Once Upon a Time in America. There is a key scene when he smiles at Noodles and puts his hand on his shoulder, but the smile fades and a strange longing comes across his face. It's a tiny detail, but it tells so much about his love, competitiveness and secret wish to connect with someone, Noodles in particular. And I think of the early parts of The Onion Field too, when his Greg Powell looks at Jimmy Smith in an animalistic, almost vaguely sexual way, but more as sexual power than attraction. These little things do add up when considering his performances and what makes them so rich.

Though he had proven himself time and time again before this period, from 87 to 90 he expanded his range even further. To begin the credits covered in this section is the startling TV film, In Love and War (1987). Woods plays real life Navy Commander James Stockdale, who was held prisoner by the North Vietnamese for 8 years. Jane Alexander wonderfully fills the part of Sybil, James' wife, who became the head of the National League of Families, an organisation that dealt with the families of Vietnam veterans who were prisoners or missing in action. The film charts her struggles on the outside trying to get justice for her husband, contrasting with his tormented life as a prisoner thousands of miles away.

Directed by Paul Aoron, and adapted from the Stockdales' book by screenwriter Carol Shreder, In Love and War features a harrowing, authentic and ultimately powerful feat from James Woods. Had this been a theatrical release, he would no doubt have been given an Oscar nomination. He did earn a Golden Globe nomination however

172

and critics were enthusiastic about his work. Led by his efforts, the film is an engaging drama which, according to reports, attracted 45 million viewers when it first aired on TV. It is also a hugely important story that needed to be told.

James himself found the shoot a genuine challenge. Seeing as he is locked up for most of the picture, and subjected to torture and beatings, it was far from a pleasant experience, proving extremely uncomfortable and tiring for Woods. "We filmed in South Carolina on an aircraft hanger that is now a museum," he told me. "We only could film there at certain times, we had no other time and we had to be there. We had worked brutal weeks, 18 hour days, 20 hour days, me being tortured, and it was horrible. I rarely complain as an actor, but doing torture scenes is miserable, just getting the shit beaten out of you all day. Even if it's being done with you and stunt doubles, it's still all day long! And of course, you always end up getting hurt somehow. We'd been working until 4 in the morning. We were leaving Sunday to shoot on a Monday, and Saturday we had to come back and finish work. But my turn around was 12 hours. I couldn't come in until 4 in the afternoon. I was exhausted, and they were gonna come in at noon and shoot pick up shots. They just didn't have the time to do it. So I came in at 11 after, like, getting home at about 5 or 6 in the morning. I was back in at 11. I remember Jon Avnet (the producer) getting on his knees and saying, 'Thank you, thank you, thank you!'"

Director Joseph Ruben's True Believer (1989) is another solid movie featuring yet another committed Woods performance. Here he excels as maverick defence attorney Eddie Dodd, a man who, slightly disenfranchised with the legal system, finds himself stirred once again by a prison murder which takes him back to a Chinatown killing from a decade earlier. Way back when, Dodd was a man excited and enthralled by the very idea of seeking justice. In the late sixties and early seventies he was a famous civil rights lawyer, but twenty years on, at the end of the yuppie era, he's slightly burnt out. He still has the long hair, but it's tied back in a weird mullet. (In a later interview, Woods joked that he had kept the wig as a pet.) He is still on the edge, but he doesn't have the faith and passion he once had. This case however, immediately landing him in hot water, gets his blood flowing again, and he is in his element once more, as if the 1980s never happened.

Robert Downey Jr. is effective as the rookie straight out of law school sent over to work with Dodd, but this is Woods at centre stage. Of course this does not mean he chews scenery and asserts himself over the rest of the cast, but Dodd is such a charismatic role that there was no way Woods wasn't going to make him the heart of the picture. Embodied in this one character is the hope of a whole generation, one that believed that justice would win in the end, that truth and integrity were absolute. The fact he's frazzled, let down by the system, only makes his resurgence all the more exciting. Woods plays it with perfection.

"What you've got to understand about True Believer," Woods told me, "is that it was actually a movie that got kind of screwed. It was based on a guy called Tony Serra, who was this hippy lawyer whose kids were named, like, Crystal or Chime or Summer or Winter or whatever the fuck their names were (laughs). I'm joking of course. And he was this ultimate San Francisco hippy who happened to be this great lawyer. And they created this story based on a real case but they decided to make the story with the revelation that the crime had been committed by a District Attorney. Well we got word that the District Attorney was like, 'We weren't crooked. Are you crazy? You can't say this in a movie! We're gonna sue.' So we had to stop filming, change the name of the characters, set it in New York and base it on a random case. Which was fine, because it was still a great story. But it would have been wonderful if it could have been the real Tony Serra. But I did get to spend a lot of time with Tony. I even got to go into a big murder case, to spend time in the court with him."

Again, the reviews were glowing for Woods. Roger Ebert, a man I believe truly appreciated Woods' intelligent way of approaching a role, wrote in his review of True Believer: "Let us now consider the case of James Woods, a name on that brief list of actors whose presence more or less guarantees that a film will be interesting. Woods works a lot. In the last year he has made Cop, about a dangerously out-of-control homicide detective; The Boost, about a salesman who gets swept away in the Los Angeles fast lane, and now True Believer, about a radical lawyer from the 1960's who has recently specialized in defending drug dealers. The characters in these movies are not all the same man, although they all share some of Woods' high-energy restlessness. The high-flier in The Boost, for example, is not nearly as intelligent as Eddie Dodd, the fast-talking lawyer in True Believer. And yet all three characters are hypnotically watchable, because Woods talks fast and is always thinking, and his performances assume that the audience can listen and think as quickly as he can. In the season of the Idiot Plot (the plot that doesn't work unless everyone in it is an idiot), Woods makes movies in which the audience has to be on its toes to keep up with him. It's quite an act, and when I see Woods on the screen in the first shot of a movie I sort of smile to myself because I know that something strange and offbeat and maybe even inspired is about to happen."

At the very end of the 1980's, Woods took on a part that was to become one of the defining performances of his career. He deservedly won his second Emmy (and another Golden Globe nomination) for his part in My Name is Bill W., a gripping Hallmark drama based on the true life story of William Wilson and Robert Holbrook Smith, the founders of Alcoholics Anonymous. Alongside - once again - the great James Garner, this is another example of the fact that American TV has always had the ability to deliver product as good as - if not better - than that of the big screen, while putting across important messages and sociological themes in the process.

Woods delivers a terrific performance and in his bold fearlessness he takes us and himself on a complete journey. At the picture's start William is a stockbroker living a successful life, happily married to Lois (JoBeth Williams). A World War 1 veteran, he has however developed a drinking habit that slowly spirals out of control once the Wall Street Crash takes the country by storm. Once his fortune is gone, his drinking takes over his life and even threatens his marriage. When playing the drunk, Woods is one of the most authentic I have seen on the screen. Nowhere in sight are the corny slurs and the cartoon burps, but a man shackled to the bottle, who will do anything to get a drink and then do anything, no matter how degrading, once inebriated. He loses his self respect, and then ultimately the respect of his wife. But there is hope on the horizon. Once he is committed to recovering, he sets in motion the formation of Alcoholics Anonymous, dedicating his life to helping others.

The centre piece of the film is the famous speech William delivers to his wife when trying to kick the bottle, which culminates in the sad conclusion: "What I want more than anything is another drink". Remarkably, Woods had to fight to keep this long but vital monologue in the film. He felt, rightly so, that without it the film would have lost much of its power and the message would be diluted. He even called up the head of the network to highlight its importance and fought for its inclusion. Thankfully, his integrity won out and the speech remains in the film for eternity.

Though Woods gave a stellar effort, many thought that the Best Actor Emmy would go to Robert Duvall that year for his work in Lonesome Dove. "It was understood," James told me, "that the unbelievably remarkable actor and man Robert Duvall was going to win the Emmy that year. It was sort of a given. My mom had come out from Rhode Island with my stepfather, and of course the nominees sit down in the orchestra but unfortunately my mom and stepfather were up in the mezzanine where your guests go. I said, 'Mom, we're not gonna win anything, but it'll be fun and everything, going to the Emmys, but we're not gonna win.' And Jim (Garner) said to me that he wasn't feeling well and he said, 'I'm gonna sit this one out, but what I am gonna do is give your mom my tickets.' I said to Jim, 'That's fantastic.' And my mom said, 'You're gonna win!' 'Mom, I promise you, I am not going to win. Bob Duvall is a great actor. It's had twenty nominations this show, trust me he is gonna win.' And in fact he was in the front row (laughs)! 'It's a big clue mom, he is sitting in the front row!' So they had a big movie screen that year and they put the camera on whoever won and they froze their reaction. So when you went up to get your award there was a HUGE image of you hearing the news. So of course, I won, and I was so surprised that I leant back and slapped the front of my head. Like, 'How did this happen?' And at that point I was Mr Hollywood Tough Guy, but I look up and there's my mom running down the aisle. It still brings a sweet tear to me eye, thinking of her running down the aisle. I gave her a big hug! Of course, it was all on camera. So, you know, it was a great moment. So lovely. So I go off and Bob Duvall is there, and I salute him and he graciously smiles and nods, giving me his salute back. Such a great guy. But I was just totally surprised. I really did feel that way, just in shock. It was a great moment in my life."

Though over thirty years old, many people still recall the film with fondness and are aware of its reputation as a highly important piece of work. Still shown to recovering alcoholics to this day, it has contributed to help improve the lives of thousands of people. James told me he regularly has people approach him to say the film helped them beat their habit. Once, a gentleman even told him he had a gun on the table and planned to kill himself while watching the film in a darkly ironic final act. Seeing the picture to the end however, he immediately contacted AA and began to get help. Now that, I feel, is quite a legacy for a movie.

While there are many films Woods made which get singled out in retrospective articles on his career, one that is completely ignored is Women and Men: Stories of Seduction (1990). A three part anthology made for TV and adapted from short stories from great writers, Woods' segment is based on Ernest Hemingway's Hills Like White Elephants. Directed by British great Tony Richardson, this perfect little short (the final one of the film) stars Woods and Melanie Griffith as Robert and Hadley; he's a writer, she is his partner along for the ride as their relationship comes to an end. They are in blisteringly hot Spain and the tension between them - while she is toying with a great choice ahead of her - makes for compelling viewing. The brief story as originally published may have been expanded with additional dialogue here, but Woods and Griffith have such chemistry and are so genuinely enjoyable to watch together that even a full length feature wouldn't have dragged in the slightest.

The other segments are directed by Ken Russell and Frederic Raphael, but though enjoyable these two parts pale in comparison to the finale. And reviewers felt this way too. Entertainment Weekly wrote in their piece on the movie: "These are the classiest TV credits of the summer: Short stories by Ernest Hemingway, Mary McCarthy, and Dorothy Parker have been adapted by directors Tony Richardson, Frederic Raphael, and Ken Russell, respectively. The stars include James Woods, Melanie Griffith, Elizabeth McGovern, Beau Bridges, Molly Ringwald, and Peter Weller. The results in Women & Men, however, are mediocre. The best is last: In Hemingway's Hills Like White Elephants, Woods and Griffith portray a couple waiting for a train in Spain, debating whether the woman, who has recently discovered she's pregnant, should get an abortion. The adaptation, by Joan Didion and John Gregory Dunne, takes many liberties with Hemingway's dialogue, all of them sensible ones that capture Hemingway's spare prose style without falling into parody, no mean feat. Director Tony Richardson has shot this half-hour movie in a crisp, straightforward way that complements the dialogue. Given the talent involved in Women & Men, one good film out of three is disappointing."

"Yeah, we shot that in Spain," Woods recalled to me. "We were hours from the nearest airport. We shot it in Caen, the middle of nowhere. Nothing but olive trees, and this old rail-road and this little station. We went all the way over there to film this scene and Tony was looking round and he said, 'You know, I love this wall.' So he put us against this wall. Now the producers were sitting at a little table out on the edge, and they said, 'Tony, we've brought an entire cast and crew out 5000 miles, the middle of nowhere, to shoot against a wall?! We could have done this on a sound stage in Hollywood! Are you crazy?' But he said, 'This is where I want to shoot it.' But they talked him into doing the scene where we're walking through the olive trees. And then we see the train coming, and it's like, in one 15 minute lay over, we see the end of a relationship. Brilliantly written and brilliantly performed by Melanie. I thought she was great. And we were living in this hotel. And there was a church there, and she decided she wanted to take the new baby - and this is when she was with Don Johnson and it was a big deal, with all the paparazzi. There was a bounty for, like, $250,000 for anyone who could get a picture of the baby. But Melanie decides, 'Let's go to church on Sunday.' And I said, 'You know the paparazzi are everywhere right?' And of course she wanted to taunt them. And they'd be there, jumping over the chairs. It was so crazy. And there we were, out in Spain in the middle of nowhere. But honestly I thought that was a wonderful piece of film. One of my favourite things I've done."

And there was something rather poignant about the making of this film. James and I had a big discussion about British films of the late 50's and early 60's, the era of the kitchen sink drama, and he expressed his fondness for the rawness of vintage UK cinema. One of his favourite filmmakers from that period, who inspired him early on in his acting career, was none other than Tony Richardson, who had made such seminal works as Look Back in Anger (1959), A Taste of Honey (1961) and The Loneliness of the Long Distance Runner (1962). So here was Woods, all these years on, in Spain of all places, being directed by one of Britain's true greats. "I had always wanted to work with Tony Richardson," he said. "I remember being there and thinking, 'Jesus! I'm working with Tony Richardson!' And it was actually one of the last things he did before he died. I was very glad I got to work with him."

"ESCAPIST ENTERTAINMENT"
WOODS ON SCREEN, 1990 - 1991

In the early 1990's, Woods went through a phase of choosing all-out, good old fashioned entertainment. The films in this era, from 1991 to 1992, may be light, free of controversy and feel-good to varying degrees, but they are rich, hugely enjoyable pictures, excellently put together and performed by the respective casts. What is interesting though, is that Woods chose to abruptly follow these breezy but enjoyable films with one of his heaviest, Citizen Cohn, which happened to contain one of the bravest and most compelling performances of his screen career.

Before that though, Woods was in the midst of a rush of good natured entertainment, at least for a while. Speaking to Charlie Rose in 1992 as Diggstown hit theatres, he explained: "I think when times are really bad, people want to have fun. I think we're in a really slow, sludgy depression, incipient depression. I think when people want to go and just let out that steam, which everybody has to let out, they kind of want to go and have a good time. I, of all people, have always been on, I think, the cutting edge of doing more politically or sociologically or philosophically or psychologically interesting films and right now, one of the reasons in the past year or two, I've really been interested in doing more escapist entertainment, because I think people just really need it..."

When I asked James about this, he said: "Honestly, I think that was my agent at the time. He said, 'Look, you're doing all these independent movies but you're never gonna get to do the bigger movies until you have a box office hit, a BIG box office hit, so you know, try doing something a little more commercial.' So I said, 'OK, fair enough.' I didn't wanna become one of those guys who will only do the little movies. And the independent movement was getting suppressed at that point. It was getting harder to get financing and stuff. So it was a bit of a conscious decision, but also I'm not gonna go turn down working with Michael J. Fox. Who doesn't wanna make a movie with Michael J. Fox and be directed by John Badham? So yeah!"

The first in Woods' escapist trilogy (my term, I might add) was 1991's The Hard Way. In the John Badham-directed hit, Woods plays John Moss, a NYPD cop having to deal with both a sick killer who calls himself The Party Crasher, and spoilt movie star Nick Lang (Fox), who is hanging round close to Moss in preparation for a Hollywood film role.

What I love about The Hard Way (or one of the things at least) is that the city feels truly alive. It's a place with many shades, of gritty streets, awe inspiring sights, dangerous neighbourhoods and lots of atmosphere; and the characters, even the extras and minor parts, are all so full of colour and appeal. This nostalgic, ludicrously entertaining film is worth seeing mostly for the charisma and chemistry of the two leads. Michael J. Fox was just leaving behind the iconic Back to the Future series at this stage, and was at the height of his fame. Putting him against Woods, the edgiest actor of mainstream American cinema, was a very inspired choice. They play off each other beautifully, the tension and humour bursting off the screen.

Fox and Woods enjoy many memorable moments together, and at least two of the scenes are classics. One is the hot dog scene, with Woods lapping up the unhealthy snack from the car park vendor, Fox the Hollywood health freak reluctant to even take a bite. Then there is the hilarious "seduction" scene, when Fox acts as the girl and Woods the man trying to hit on her. Even though the sequence seems so natural, it turns out that Woods and Fox worked hard to get it to work. Woods told Den of Geek: "We were doing the scene, and you would think it was hilarious, but we couldn't get it right. We just didn't feel it was funny. And I was embarrassed, he's playing the woman... and John sort of was focused on Michael imitating Annabella Sciorra. And Michael came up with the idea. He said, 'You know the problem here? I'm just trying to be a girl'. And he was right; you're not specific to what her problem would be, which is that she was really, really pissed. It's not that she's a girl, it's that she's really pissed. So Michael came up with this ad-lib where he said, 'Don't you take that tone with me', and that's when it opened up. It's like sometimes it just takes a fucking moment where a great actor like Michael, who has comedy timing like I can't believe, and he just came up with that 'Don't you take that tone with me'. Then it becomes funny, but we struggled to get that scene."

What people may forget about this much loved buddy picture (released during what you might call the golden era of the buddy picture) is that it's a "big" film in the truest sense. There are crazy stunts, shoot outs, dangerous car chases, explosions, all against the turbulent comedy bouncing back and forth between Woods and Fox. Woods actually performed one of the most dangerous stunts himself, when he's hanging out of the truck chasing the killer. And there he is, James Woods, utterly convincing as the mainstream cop, pursuing the bad guys through the hustle and bustle of the busy streets.

"That was me the entire time!" he said. "And I had broken my finger in a stunt earlier and it was taped. I was holding on with four fingers! And they said, 'If you fall off the truck - they'd never allow us to do this now - don't go sideways 'cos you'll hit the car behind. Try and aim for the wind-shield and you'll go through the wind-shield and you'll survive.' I was like, 'Okay...' And in fact, I fell off the truck once going about 40 miles an hour, and dislocated my shoulder. So that was the end of that! I mean, people get injured doing movies. I've been injured a lot on movies."

I brought up the fact that The Hard Way was one of the biggest, most outrageous movies of the time. "Are you fucking kidding? There was more dangerous stunt work on The Hard Way than any movie I have ever done times ten," he added. "We were on that fucking hat (during the climatic scene at the top of the building). They said, 'You guys will do all this stuff below". My stunt double however was on that hat ten stories above Times Square. For, like, seven or eight of the shots he wasn't even tied down. He was literally walking up there with no rope. No harness. Nothing. I said, 'Steve (Lambert, Woods' stunt double), you cannot do this!' He said, 'Nah, it'll be a great shot.' So he did it. I mean it was insane. I am gonna give him credit. I've seen him do things I never thought I'd see in my life. I used to get sick to my stomach watching him. But we'd (Woods and Fox) still be three stories up doing it. I mean, three stories is sixty feet above the floor. No harnesses, up there fucking running around. I hated it, because I hate heights. I. Hate. Heights. That is my one thing I hate. I hate it. But I've done it a million times in movies!"

The Hard Way is, at the end of the day, a perfect star vehicle, highlighting the skills of the two leads. Woods is terrific as the tough cop who finds it hard to express himself unless it's through anger. Here he is as intense as can be, but this time he channels that intensity for the good. Upon the film's release, Roger Ebert nailed it when he observed in his review: "Woods plays the kind of role where, if they hadn't been able to hire him, they would have had to shut down the movie. Who else could play this rapid-fire, angry, violent, foul-mouthed, insecure, sneaky and lying but lovable rascal? He's the toughest cop in New York, the kind who rams his police car into the back of a truck because he's late for a date. I have seen some James Woods movies I didn't enjoy, but it's hard to remember them - the names of few other actors give you more of a guarantee that you will not be bored and will possibly be electrified."

Though another one of his live wires, this time Woods is on the right side of the law. Contrasting against his jagged edges, Fox is hilarious as the pampered celebrity roaming the mean streets, ultimately seeing the drastic differences between gritty real life and the sheen of the movies. The Hard Way was a massive hit upon release, making back 66 million at the box office. Today, it hasn't aged at all, and is one of the finest of the late 80s/early 90s buddy movies.

When I asked James about working with Fox, his voice was suddenly filled with genuine warmth and affection. "Ah, Michael... I mean, I have worked with so many people, and the first thing I am able to say about them is everything you love about them on camera, they are that times ten in real life. Michael is just the nicest guy, the sweetest; funny, cute, adorable, really cool. My late brother Mike was on set with us a lot, he had a little part in the film. We would just hang around a lot. Michael would be in our trailer all the time. We just had fun every day! Annabella Sciorria too, she was great. LL Cool J was so cool, so great. Delroy Lindo, fantastic. The villain, Stephen (Lang), I'd worked with him before, and he's a great guy. He's always the bad guy, but he's like the nicest guy (laughs), and so fun. And John Badham, the director. John was wonderful to me. I loved him. He was a really good friend of mine after that. A wonderful director to work with. I'd always wanted to work with him. That was so much fun doing The Hard Way. I loved doing that movie, loved it!"

And on working with Woods, director John Badham had this to say in 1991 not long after the film's release: "Jimmy's terrific because he has such tremendous energy. Now, as he himself will readily admit, he knows more about everybody's job than an actor really ought to, and he spends more time *doing* other people's jobs. At some point you want to say to him, *Jimmy*, you know, don't worry about what lens we have on or where the focus is or where the light is on your face.' But he just can't help it. The thing is, he's right there with you. He's not some guy who's just showing up to do the scenes and collect his check."

Woods then took on the breezy Straight Talk (1992), starring alongside, unexpectedly as it may have been to some people, Dolly Parton. Though it seems a rather unlikely pairing from a distance, the duo work brilliantly together and actually have a chemistry that borders on electric.

Straight Talk is another one of those films which, given my age, has that sweet nostalgic feel to it. It was in some ways a freer, even simpler time for movies, when boxes didn't necessarily have to be ticked, when the filmmakers didn't have to over-think things. In short, they could deliver good old fashioned entertainment, with no message and no ulterior motives. Straight Talk is such a film. In this light, instantly likeable comedy, Dolly Parton is Shirlee, a Southern gal who leaves her boyfriend Steve (Michael Madsen) and heads for the bright lights of Chicago. At first over awed by the streets and the activity around her, reality soon sets in when she runs out of money and is about to be without a place to stay. One day, during a mix up when applying for a receptionist job, she is mistaken for a new radio therapist at the city's biggest talk station. Though she is sketchy about her past, Shirlee is taken under the wing of Alan (Griffin Dunne), who helps carve a neat PR package out of her down to earth personality. Woods is Jack Russell, a wily reporter who meets Shirlee early on, "saving" her from apparent suicide on a bridge, where she is actually reaching out for a twenty dollar bill that's blown away. He comes across Shirlee again once she's a radio star and begins to get close to her, firstly as a means to use her for a good story at the newspaper, before genuinely falling for her.

Straight Talk did well at the box office, being a hit in both America and a Number 1 success in the UK. Reviews were mixed, but even those who weren't won over by the story itself could not fault Woods and Parton, who are, it has to be said, fantastic together. It was actually Dolly herself who wanted Woods for the part of Jack. She had always found him "magnetic and sexy", as she told Bobby Wygant, and it was her and director Barnet Kelman who pushed for his casting, despite Hollywood Pictures not thinking him an ideal choice.

Speaking on Larry King Live, she explained: "James Woods is my leading man. It's an unusual role for him to play but I think he did it real well." When King said it didn't sound like a James Woods movie, Dolly replied: "But I think he wanted to do a more light hearted script than some of the more intense roles that he's known to play. And he's a very fine actor as you know, and a very intense person, but he was very gentle, very sweet and he was quite romantic, and a wonderful kisser. It's true!"

"That made me feel great," Woods said when I brought up the fact that Dolly pushed for his casting. "She was the star of the movie, and I was her co-star. But it was her movie. And for years after that she would go on talk shows and say, 'James Woods is the best kisser.' And respect to her, she never wavered (laughs)! If you ever wanna feel good about ever having been a leading man, and they ask you what's the best thing someone could say... I'd think, Hmmm, if Martin Scorsese or Oliver Stone said I was the greatest actor that ever lived that would be pretty good. But when Dolly Parton says you're the greatest kisser? That's it! That's the one! Put that one on my plaque."

187

"Dolly Parton," Woods told me, "is just literally the nicest person I have ever met in the business. She's just this angel. She is so wonderful that you wanna be around her every minute. And she's the same to every single person she meets bar none. Funny as hell too. I mean, she'll tell dirty jokes and everyone will go, 'What?' But she does it with such a smile."

Woods recalled his memories of Dolly with a lot of warmth and much laughter, and you could hear in his tone that he was smiling with fondness as he spoke. Between shots Dolly would take James to the trailer and preview him her latest song. Not having a guitar, she would scratch her nails together to make percussion and then take him through a rendition of a future hit. Definitely a perk of the job, if you ask me!

"The crew loved her and she loved the crew. I loved her too. We had a fantastic time making that movie. Everybody was just so great to work with. Dolly was gracious and wonderful to everybody. All the people in Chicago treated us great, and we'd go to these little restaurants with the Teamsters. I don't mean the chic area, I mean like some little neighbourhood place where the mom would be in the kitchen cooking and it had been there for a hundred years. It was just great. I got along with all the Teamsters, they were wonderful to us. They've always been wonderful to me and I've always had a great time with them. They work so hard; they get there at 3 o' clock in the morning, they don't leave until 11 at night. People say, 'Oh the Teamsters are asleep.' And you'd be like, 'Well yeah! They've been working a twenty hour day! Let them take a nap!' So anyway, I just had a great time. I know it sounds like I had a great time on everything, but I really did."

He also fondly recalled the joke Dolly told him on set: "How do you circumcise a hillbilly? By kicking his sister in the chin!" (Movie geek

188

note: Woods must have loved this gag, because he tells it later in 1998's Another Day in Paradise.)

When you line up the sociopaths and psychos Woods has played against the more everyday, normal, decent men, I think you will find that it's much more of an even match than people might think. Straight Talk in particular proves that he is just as capable of convincing and entertaining as a regular guy than as a creep or odd ball. Straight Talk is joyous fun, a real pleasure from start to finish, and among the most openly enjoyable films of Woods' career.

Something of a favourite among hardcore Woods fans is Diggstown (1992). Directed by Michael Ritchie and written by Steven McKay, the film stars Woods as Gabriel Caine, a con man who's just got out of prison and has a fresh scam on his mind. Fitz (Oliver Platt) is his partner in crime, and together they travel to Diggstown, a town that puts boxing on a pedestal. Bruce Dern is John Gillon, a high roller who owns most of the town and once managed their most famous export, boxer Charles Diggs. Fitz challenges the city's claim that Diggs once KO'd five boxers in one day and insists that Gillon will pay him $100,000 if he can bring to town a boxer who can floor all ten of Diggstown's best fighters. Gabriel chooses Palmer (Louis Gossett Jr.) for the job, an ex-boxer nearing fifty whose glory years are behind him. Can Palmer rise to the challenge, or have Fitz and Caine pushed it too far this time?

Diggstown works on many levels. Firstly, it's the classic underdog story, where the man least likely to succeed does so in the end. Dern is the establishment, smug and complacent, and Woods and Gossett Jr. are the little men, the rebels standing up to his cruel greed. Though the feat seems impossible, we genuinely root for them and want them to come out on top. The script is fine of course, but the acting is what makes the picture a winner. Woods is at his motormouth best, a man who could talk his way into and out of anything. This is the kind of role no one else could have played. Woods is the star here, the central figure, and it's a thrill to see him as the leading man in a major piece of mainstream entertainment. The fact he carries it (aided of course by the brilliant Louis Gossett Jr.) is a credit to him.

Woods promoted the film extensively, appearing everywhere to encourage people to go see it. Speaking to Charlie Rose, Woods explained he had seen the movie with an audience, and had enjoyed their enthusiastic reactions: "I saw the movie in a small screening room. We saw the movie and said, God, this is really a fun movie. A couple of weeks later the producer called me and said, You've got to see it with a real audience. I said, Why? He said, Just trust me on this. They sneak me in because they don't want the audience to see that I'm there and the audience literally does stand up and cheer 3 times in the movie."

Woods also said that, though he liked the script, he felt that some additional, unneeded dialogue and subtext should be cut, for he saw it as pure escapist fun, a case of the simpler the better. The audience didn't need any extra baggage. What they did get in Diggstown, though, as well as in The Hard Way and Straight Talk, was an actor giving it his all. It wasn't the genre he is most associated with of course, but he proved he was genuinely funny. As Michael J. Fox noted, "What people don't realise about Jimmy is that he's funny. Sick, but funny!"

CITIZEN COHN (1992)

And then, as if to break off the run of feel good cinema, James Woods starred as Roy Cohn, Joseph McCarthy's Chief Counsel during the Communist witch hunts in the 1950's. A controversial figure if there ever was one, Woods brought him to life (and then some) in the remarkable TV film, Citizen Cohn (1992). Putting in another tour de force, this is one of Woods' strongest efforts in all, a spot-on portrayal of a man who doesn't always deserve our warmest wishes (massive understatement), but does keep us hooked and alert from the beginning to the very end.

Based on Nicholas von Hoffman's book of the same name, and directed by Frank Pierson, it begins with the aged Cohn dying of AIDS in a hospital, haunted by memories and ghosts from the past. And with the word "ghosts" this is implied literally when it comes to the Rosenbergs, the couple who Cohn delighted in seeing hung after they were caught spying on the USA for the Soviet Union and giving them vital secrets. They are at his bedside, physical manifestations of a deeply buried guilt that may or may not have been there beneath the harsh, spiky exterior. The film then goes back in time through his ambitious career on the world stage, not shying away from his most cold hearted and merciless behaviour during the McCarthy hearings in 1954.

Woods' effort is often overpoweringly good, and stands for me as one of the finest portrayals of a real life figure in the history of film and TV. From his pure, undiluted and frankly quite terrifying rage in the opening sequence, this is a staggering piece of work. Woods does not do an imitation of Cohn, but transcends impressionism, bringing Cohn into his own realm, his own stratosphere. A rigid copy would have been missing the point. In Woods' hands, Cohn becomes a firework of anger and resentment, a closeted homosexual taking out his insecurities on the world around him. He's a Jew who persecutes Jews, a gay man who condemns gay men. Self hatred drives his bigotry. This was not lost on Woods himself, who told the New York Times: "He is so complex and contradictory. He once addressed a fund-raiser and delivered a diatribe about gays, and then promptly jumped into a limousine for Studio 54 and was flamboyant on the dance floor with his gay friends. This guy was so self-loathing."

But there is a pathetic side to his Cohn. In the hospital for instance, when he tries to escape and nearly collapses, he is lifted up like a frail little boy, an injured bird, and carried back to his bed. For this moment, he is vulnerable, pitiful even. As the film progresses though, and we are reminded of the man's dark past, our pity goes out of the window.

Woods earned himself Emmy and Golden Globe nominations for his dedicated portrayal of Cohn. Why he didn't win both is a mystery to me. I must add too, that had this been released on the big screen, he would have also been up for the Oscar. It's a formidable piece of work and there are few characterisations of the period (or any period for that matter) to rival it in terms of affecting the viewer and giving us so many emotions and feelings.

In one interview, Woods spoke about being offered the part. "I read the thing on Cohn and said, 'You know, just playing another really evil man is something I really just want to shy away from,' but then I did Straight Talk and I did Diggstown and I thought, Well, I can't pass it up."

On his portrayal of Cohn, he explained: "I faced this kind of strange dilemma. If you're going to be playing somebody who's a real person, and I've done this before when I played Gregory Powell in The Onion Field... There's an old rule in acting, which is you don't play the part, you let the part play you. I think when you mimic the persona of someone, you tend to lose the heart and soul of what the character really is... I said, I'm not going to do any research on how Roy moved. I mean, I've seen him before and I want to try to forget it. I'm just going to play the material, and me and the material, because the material is so rich..."

Oddly, when Woods stumbled upon a TV interview with Cohn, he was thrown back at how much the real Cohn matched his own interpretation. Everyone assumed Woods had watched the clip in preparation, but this was not the case. Following his gut and intuition proved to be the key to capturing Cohn. Had he studied more archive footage, tried to replicate his movements, his voice, his manner, then something more important at the core of Cohn would have been lost. What Woods does is capture the charm of the sociopath, making us ponder on why we are taken in by the psychos and narcissists of the world. The fact they know how to charm us though, that they know what to say and which buttons to press, is their secret. Woods' Cohn is your trademark sociopath, a man with a singular vision; that his view is right and everyone else is wrong. He wants to change America to suit his ego, not change America for the better. And without Cohn, it is important to note, McCarthy himself (played excellently here by Joe Don Baker) might not have gone half as far as he did during the witch hunts and hearings.

The performance has gone down as both one of the boldest in Woods' oeuvre and in TV history. The work has lasted because, as with other monsters, James did not choose to approach him as one. "Roy Cohn is finally an enigmatic figure," Woods told the New York Times at the time. "I didn't necessarily want to portray him as an evil character, although the rational part of my mind knows that he probably was."

If you are ever wondering what it might be like for a director to direct James Woods, Frank Pierson, speaking after the release of Citizen Cohn, once defined the task thus: "What is it like to direct Jimmy Woods? I wouldn't know. You don't direct him. You surf him. It's like surf-riding the biggest wave you ever saw. A moving mountain of energy and inventiveness and intelligence. And if you stay standing up, it's the biggest damn thrill of any director's lifetime."

"In Citizen Cohn," James told me when we came to discussing this wonderful film, "I was working with Frank, who I loved. And HBO wanted to work with us as a team. We did Citizen Cohn, then we did Dirty Pictures. But he was getting old. It was like, Why didn't I find this guy earlier in my life? I would have done films with Frank my whole life. He was a fantastic director and we got on great. The direction was so great. Frank did an amazing job. I wish Frank had gone from being the great writer he was and had been able to direct sooner. If I could have picked that one director, who I could have been 'his guy', it would have been Frank. We just got along so well. I loved him, and visa versa. We got along so well. I so admired him and he admired me as an actor. We did important work together. I believe that if Citizen Cohn had been a feature film - I mean, HBO was doing top quality work and the world agrees with me. And I was sort of the HBO darling for a while. I loved them and they were always great to me. I was happy to help them and I was a part of the first movement where they were doing cutting edge movies. But anyway, I think had it been a feature film Frank would have been nominated as a director, and David Franzoni for the screenplay. It would have ranked up there with any great political film ever made. I think it was as good as that. Not because I was in it of course, but the movie itself, the direction and the production values. It was up there with the great political biographies."

Woods also pointed out his favourite scenes from the film, ones he felt highlighted Cohn's weird, often monstrous character: "But there were two moments I loved in Citizen Cohn. There was the scene where Cohn is testifying and he's had the surgery and he's still got the sacks dangling from his ears. Fucking brilliant, and actually based on truth by the way. But the other scene I loved is when he walks out when they've failed, because Joe McCarthy went too far. And he says, 'Loyalty Joe, a thing called loyalty.' And he was passionate. So here's Roy Cohn, this weasel, but he was passionate. Frank didn't want to make him a caricature, even though Frank was a liberal guy. I said to Frank, 'I think I got to do this bit like Cohn means it. It can't be another one of his scams. Let's do it so he means it. It'll be a much more interesting character that way.' But Cohn's twisted relationships too - he's spreading his mother's ashes and he's got all these boys on the yacht. I mean, the screenplay was just fucking great. That was film-making at its peak. But everybody hated Roy Cohn. And he even hated himself. He was a self loathing bigot. He was a hypocrite. But to himself he was also a patriot. A vile human being and a mockery of what I believe is patriotism, which is believing in the law but not manipulating it for political gain. But I thought, I'm playing this universally reviled character. How can we portray him if he sees himself as the villain? He has to find something about himself. So when he says it's about loyalty, it was a case of, if we could magically have a scene where an angel comes to him and says, 'Roy, how do you see yourself?' He'd say, 'Well, I'm a patriot, and I believe in this country.' He would believe he was not only a patriot, but on the barricades of the revolution of patriotism.

He saw himself as a revolutionary hero at a time when communism was taking over the country."

"And high intensity acting is exhausting," he continued when speaking of his performance. "Citizen Cohn was a lot of work. I was always wearing make up, people don't realise that. When I was young I had my hair dyed. And then when I was older, they put a bald cap over my hair, did the make up so my skin matched the cap. I was wearing prosthetic make up all the time. But you get used to it. And I know it sounds crazy to be complaining about make up, because honestly, I am not complaining. And the make up artists are superb artists. And the final word on that is, yes it's uncomfortable, but it gets you into the character."

Woods then expressed his admiration for the cast. "This cast was unbelievable. I mean, every single one of these actors was just brilliant. Like Jeffrey Nordling, who was playing this sweet dumb guy, it was a great performance. But then, they all were great. Karen Ludwig playing Ethel Rosenberg. Allen Garfield playing the guy at the beginning, he was always good. I mean, Pat Hingle, Lee Grant. And that scene I did with Daniel Benzali and Joe Bologana, where we're at dinner and I'm eating from their plates (laughs). That was one of my favourite scenes I have ever done. He's totally oblivious to the fact that people are just like, 'You're eating all our food!' But Cohn really did that. I found all this out in my research. I mean, it was a very accurate portrait of him and what he did."

And the key to Woods making Cohn multi-dimensional perhaps comes in that one key word - loyalty. It's mentioned there in the opening scene with his parents, his mother pressing its importance in the restaurant, while his father is a little more passive. And Cohn himself comes back to it, that word, and it shows that he truly believes in what he is doing. This belief, the loyalty he has to his head strong conviction, gives Cohn a drive so determined that we at least grasp his conquest. He is a man possessed by his own idea of justice, of what is right. Being loyal to that drives him forward. We don't agree with him, but we at least understand him. And as Woods stated to me about another character, when such men believe they are the hero in their own stories, it makes their journey all the more interesting - and chilling - to watch.

But despite his vision, we don't remotely like Cohn, the egotist that he is. He is a man who can't stand making mistakes. Notice his anger and the way Woods plays it when the House bring in a supposed communist by the name of Annie Lee Moss, who actually turns out to be the wrong Mrs. Moss. Though clearly an innocent woman, a Democrat who's been suspended from her job (she certainly hasn't been sending codes to the Russians as accused), Cohn will do anything to not look silly in front of his colleagues. Desperately rifling through papers, he insists she could still go to prison for perjury. The very idea of being wrong, and being seen slipping up, is not something Cohn can bare.

Another facet of Cohn's sketchy personality that Woods perfects is his closet homosexuality. When he first meets David Schine (played by Jeffrey Nording) at a party, a far from bright young man who he ends up pulling into his world, the attraction he has for him is so obvious that even McCarthy seems uncomfortable with the way Cohn stares at him. Worse still, Cohn has a female date with him, a woman clearly there to help keep up the façade that this "anti-homosexual" is straight as a dye. However, when his interest is piqued by Schine, and he is clearly developing a school boy crush on him, he asks the lady to be excused. "Go powder your nose or something," he adds. It's a brilliant moment, with Woods' Cohn defined ultimately as a man of denial, but one who genuinely doesn't care about how his arrogance affects others.

This remarkable film, led by Woods' powerhouse effort, won the prestigious Peabody Award. At the ceremony that year, producer Doro Bachrach said the film was made because "James Woods had the courage to embrace this infamous American villain." When Woods stepped towards the microphone he commented that Doro had missed out the most important person in her speech - herself. "I think people like Doro Bachrach and all the people in this room, not like many people in our industry... you are indeed all changing the world."

Citizen Cohn does sum up the power that American television once had, not just as entertainment, but as an enlightening, thought provoking and progressive art form. Citizen Cohn and films like it held up a mirror to society, forced people to look at themselves in terms of their history, in a bid to remind them how far they had come and how far there still was left to travel. This was, indeed, a golden age of TV. While a lot of television is entertaining, it seldom says much. The best of James Woods' work for the small screen is anything but small; it's big, makes statements and dives head-first towards the truth. Citizen Cohn may be an ugly reminder of what we were once happy to deem acceptable, what people were willing to turn their heads away from, but it's vital that the past is brought up in the context of our modern times - just as long as we don't try to re-write it.

TREASURES AND HIDDEN GEMS
1991 - 1994

James Woods committed himself to a lot of high quality TV and film in the 1990's. Some of these were lead roles, others odd ball cameos, and some showy supporting roles where he stole the show. This period of time seemed to enhance Woods' reputation as a go-to actor, someone who was reliable and always delivered the goods. To filmmakers he was a safe bet, a man who could be trusted, even if his methods and results were far from unflinching and complacent. His rich and varied experience on TV, film and stage meant he had turned acting around in a way, redefined and stretched it beyond the expressive or the merely competent. James Woods' style became an art form in its own; forceful without being over the top, strict without being stale, playful without appearing unruly. All this sounds contradictory, but it applies to Woods' way of working.

This said, the early nineties were also a changing time for Woods. Dissatisfied with the work his agents at CAA were getting him, and their insistence on the pay check being hefty enough for them to get their neat percentage, Woods shifted representation. The turning point for him was when Quentin Tarantino came up to him one day and asked him why he had turned down the Mr Pink role in Reservoir Dogs. Woods thought it was a joke, but Tarantino insisted it was true. Apparently, the CAA guys had said Woods would never do a film for $50,000. "Man," Woods said to Tarantino, "I would have made that movie for free."

With his new agents at ICM, Woods laid out some new ground rules. "I said to the new agents, I feel like I'm just out of the business at this point. People didn't really notice because Citizen Cohn had come out and had fourteen Emmy nominations and so on. And I said to them, probably in a more polite way, I want to read every script that's out there. I never want anyone making my decisions again but me. It was all part of a campaign that I launched to get back into the zone I wanted to be in, which was to work with the best directors in the world on good material with other good actors. I didn't give a shit about the size of the part, the salary or anything else. It was one of the best decisions I ever made. Because there's one absolute, unequivocal equation for success in this business so you can last: just do good work, every time you act. When they do my contracts, I don't even ask what my billing is. I say, 'Do the best you can but I want to do this picture.' I was in a big lull because I wasn't doing what was true to myself as a man and as an actor."

Woods has been known to provide a cameo here and there, and they are always highly effective. One of the best came in Richard Attenborough's rich re-telling of the life of Charlie Chaplin, titled, simply enough, Chaplin (1991). The picture earned mixed reviews in its time, mainly from those who found it overly dramatic when compared to the life which writer David Robinson wrote so eloquently of in his acclaimed biography, Chaplin: His Life and Art. However, most agreed that Robert Downey Jr. gave a good performance as the Little Tramp in his journey from silent film star to acclaimed director, from beloved icon to American outlaw forced out of the States for his so called communistic leanings.

In one effective scene, James Woods plays the attorney Joseph Scott, the man who openly insulted Chaplin during the infamous Joan Barry paternity case, a brief but memorable turn. I told James that I felt the film really came to life when he entered it. Though it's a strong biopic, there is a fire in the Woods scene which is absent from the rest of the picture. "I think Sir Richard - he said, 'Call me Dickie.' I am sure he liked to be called Dickie (laughs). So, Bob Downey Jr. and I had done True Believer together. We liked each other and were pretty good friends. He was brilliant as Chaplin. I remember meeting him in New York and he was standing there just playing with his hat like Chaplin. I thought, Wow that's great! I think he had said, 'Hey, why don't we see if Jimmy will do this?' And I think there was a request, like, 'We know it's one day's work, but Bob and Sir Richard would really love if you would do it.' So it was like, Hmmmm (Laughs), let me think it over! I'm joking of course. Richard Attenborough and Robert Downey Jr. would like you to be in a movie? Of course I'm doing it.

"I've done a few cameos that turned out to be pretty successful for me. Now this one was a pretty conventional part for me to play, the tough lawyer. But I think it was important for the audience to immediately have an impression of something. If you use an actor who is pretty well known or pretty well respected, also who is known to have a certain ability... Like a case of, 'You know, we'd love someone to play this tough lawyer. Ah, maybe James Woods could do that.' And then if you're there, and you're the opposing lawyer, the audience thinks, Oh Shit, we got a problem here. Mr Chaplin has a problem. And that was what I think they were after. The lawyer on the other side was pretty tough, but then I walk in and they think, Oh, now we have a problem. That was the general idea. I'm like a music cue, ominous music plays and enter the opposing lawyer. And I have to say that was one of the few roles where I didn't feel there was a lot I could do with it to put my own stamp on it. And remember that when you are playing period stuff you've got to be careful not to smell of contemporary morays or accents or styling. You want to make sure you behave in a way those characters would behave at that time and in that place. So it was one of those situations where it was like a case of, Don't drop the ball, put it in the hoop and call it a day. And that's what I did. You know, kick that fucker into the goal and go home."

James at the 1992 Emmy Awards.

Another overlooked gem is The Boys (1991), in which he co starred with John Lithgow and was directed, once again, by Glenn Jordan. Written by William Link, the script was based on his own writing partnership with Richard Levinson, who had recently passed away. In the film, Woods plays Walter and Lithgow plays Artie. They are, like Link and Levinson, a writing duo who've been together for two decades penning scripts for TV and film. Artie's a big smoker, but Walter isn't, and this fact has caused some tension. The dark irony comes in the fact that while Walter has lived a clean life, he has developed lung cancer from his friend's habit.

The Boys is not merely an anti-smoking campaign in the form of a two hour movie, as one reviewer glibly claimed it to be. In fact, it's a very engaging, at times blackly funny film led by two sharp performances. Yes, the message is clear - that our actions do not only affect us, but others too - but as entertainment the film is a joy, mostly for the two actors, who have a great rapport. They enjoyed working together so much that they immediately began looking for ideal vehicles as a duo. When Lithgow commented that they had told their agents to put their heads together, Woods replied, "And they'll probably come up with some fabulous script, and then give it to Redford and Newman." Sadly, the pair never worked together again. This is a shame, because the chemistry is alive throughout The Boys. Besides, I like the idea of that double act, Woods and Lithgow.

Woods grabbed our attentions in several high profile pictures in the 1990's, but there were weird oddities in there too that today take a little more digging around for. He appeared in the TV series Fallen Angels, in a brilliant episode called Since I Don't Have You (1993), adapted from a James Ellroy story. The 30 minute short stars Gary Busey as Buzz Meeks, a man who divides his time between two jobs; one for Howard Hughes, the other with mobster Mickey, played brilliantly by Woods in a performance which earned him a CableACE Award nomination. From his first appearance, standing before the mirror being fitted for a suit, he is every bit the 1930's power mad mobster. He sends Buzz out to look for a woman he's been searching for. When Buzz asks for more money for his assignment, Woods goes nuts and takes his rage out on his tailor. "Vents but no cuffs!" he yells, pulling out a gun and kicking his tailor out of the room. He has a swagger here that is like his Once Upon a Time in America's Max on cocaine, calling everyone in ear shot a putts or a piece of schmutz. It's yet another hidden gem of a performance.

He also popped up on TV in Dream On (1993), but another stand out which is easier to track down is 1994's Next Door. A darkly funny black comedy made for TV, it stars Woods and Randy Quaid as two neighbours who at first get on despite their huge differences, which are apparent from the get go; Woods, married to Kate Capshaw, is a college professor, Quaid a crude butcher who makes love with his wife (played by Lucinda Jenney), very loudly, in the garden. As the film progresses, the feud becomes more intense and in the end reaches a destructive level bordering on thriller territory.

A sort of class comedy of contrasts, it resists getting too broad and entertains uproariously. In the opening scenes it seems that Quaid is playing an extension of his role from the Vacation films, yet this man has a more scheming edge and a ferocious intelligence. He is absolutely hilarious and at times frightening as the boorish neighbour, while Woods is lower key, more of an ordinary middle class dad dealing with a nightmare over the picket fence. He excels as a normal guy once again, someone who refuses to raise his fists to this ape before him.

Variety liked the film and were most impressed by Woods' effort: "Woods' comically edgy performance holds things together. He and Quaid create a stark contrast... Woods and a sparkling Capshaw emphasize the humour."

Woods reflected on working on Next Door during one of our interviews: "It's a suburban spoof, but it's also a movie about escalation. It goes from, 'Hey could you not have your sprinklers ruin our flowers?" to (laughs) all out warfare. It was a case of appeasement, but the guy next door is a nut-case. And our guy goes from being a civilised guy seeing if he can soften the situation, and of course - as

Neville Chamberlain taught us, and more recently Joe Biden - sometimes appeasement is just not a good idea. So this was a suburban comedy of manners that also had reverberations for geopolitical truths about appeasement and aggression. It was a pretty cool story actually, and I just loved working with the three leads."

Woods has always been highly effective as the flash villain, but the same year he did Next Door he was also given the opportunity to show a softer side in more low key fare. In the TV movie Jane's House (1994), he played Paul Clark, a widowed sports shop owner who with his two children, a son and daughter, struggles with the loss of his late wife. One day he meets Mary Parker (Anne Archer), a former tennis star now working as a sporting agent. After she does a favour for Woods (getting a well known baseball star to appear at the store's grand opening), this career woman who's never had a relationship last longer than a year develops feelings for him. She enjoys being around him, finds his presence comforting and frankly thinks he's a breath of fresh air. They begin to fall for one another, but there are sensitive issues to confront; namely his children who, still heartbroken over their mother's death, perhaps aren't ready for a new woman coming into their lives. Mary too has a lot on her plate. When she moves in with the family, she feels like an outsider, as if she doesn't belong there. But will time and perseverance pay off?

Jane's House is a beautifully acted little drama, understated and light but also poignant and thought provoking. There are some important issues raised and questions asked. When is too early to move on after the death of a partner? Isn't it every widow's right, regardless of the children, to be happy? Does anyone think of the hardships for the partner coming into the one parent family? Jane's House doesn't enforce these thoughts on us of course, but they come up subtly as the drama unfolds. It helps that the screenwriter is Eric

Roth, and the script steers clear of predictable manipulation. Glenn Jordan (who worked magic with Woods on Promise and The Boys) directs with assured professionalism, letting the actors do their thing. And the performances are splendid; Archer is appealing and charming, while Woods slides neatly into the father role as if he was born to exclusively play such men. Only those who know Woods' psychos and sociopaths will be surprised that he could pull off the part of an ordinary father, but those in the know understand the wide variety of his abilities. He is warm, loving, and totally believable as an ordinary, low key, mild mannered father.

The film was greeted with warm notices and many critics were pleased with Woods' efforts. The Chicago Sun Times wrote that James had softened his image and taken a gentler approach to the role, while New York Magazine put much of the film's success down to Woods. "None of the story would be remarkable except for the quiet performance of James Woods," they wrote. "After so much raw meat, this is vegetarian James Woods: baffled, decent, tentative, nostalgic, romantic, domestic. As his suffering was sotto voce, almost parenthetical, so his brand-new love is a hum, not a crescendo. Instead of raging, he accommodates. In the hesitations of his portrayal, Woods leaves us room to imagine all kinds of things."

"Well I had personal experience in this area," Woods said to me when we came to Jane's House. "My mom was widowed at a young age. I came from a beautiful loving family where our parents really loved us and they loved each other. It was like Jane's House in a sense that they were decent people who had lost someone through death. And there is nothing crueller or more difficult for each person who has to make that journey. I always love the expression in Jane's House. I say something like, 'I think I'm progressing well here,' basically expressing to the daughter that he really believed he was growing in a direction where he was getting beyond the grief so he could live a productive life, to not be dragged down by his sorrow. And she says to him, 'Then why is mom's robe still on the back of the bathroom door a year later?' To me that was a great piece of writing. And Eric Roth wrote that screenplay, the man who wrote Forrest Gump! It's not like this is just some TV movie. There was a lot to this movie. I got to work with my great buddy, Graham Beckel, and Anne Archer was just lovely, she was just great. And she was great for that part too. It was a very universal American story. First of all, Glenn Jordan is a director I really love. Just a great director and a dear, dear friend. He asked me to do it. I mean, I might not have done it for another director, but I wanted to do it with him. And it was kind of a departure for me to be able to play a character like that. But it was a story I had a personal experience of. I saw what it is like for a person who has been widowed to try and climb back into life and embrace it after being destroyed by an unanticipated loss, a real stumble in life, to lose a mate. So it was an important story for me."

Jane's House has never been released in any commercial format, meaning that if you do want to watch it, the only way is to either track down an old VHS recording or an online upload. If you do put the effort in, Jane's House will prove a treat for anyone who likes lower key Woods.

Curse of the Starving Class (1994) is one of Woods' overlooked pictures from this period; which is indeed a shame, as it features a very powerful, assured performance that, though not receiving much credit at the time of release or since, is a contender for one of his finest. It's a multi layered, full-on effort, and it seems a crime it should be so neglected.

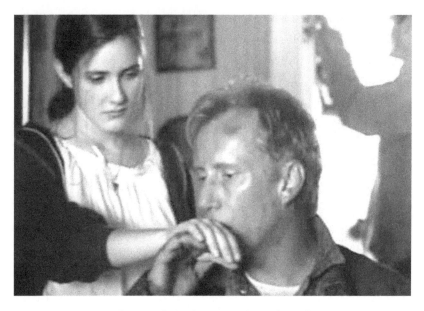

Curse of the Starving Class (1994).

Adapted from the acclaimed play by Sam Shepard, and scripted by Bruce Beresford (perhaps best known as a director of such films as Last Dance and Double Jeopardy), it focuses on the Tates, a desperately poor farming family who face the sort of rough challenges many clans do who try to live off the land in these changing times. Woods is Weston Tate, the hard drinking father who, at least in the first half of the story, is no good to anyone. Kathy Bates is Ella, the wife and mother, who on the surface makes out she is committed to the country life, but is secretly having a fling with rich businessman Taylor (Randy Quaid) in a bid to encourage him to buy the farm. Henry Thomas is the son, Wesley, who rejects the idea of giving up the farm despite not really wishing to contribute towards its up-keep, and Kristin Fiorella is the rebellious daughter, Emma.

With his careful script, Beresford made Shepard's play cinematic, and definitely opened up the original text, making it ideal for film. The direction by J. Michael McClary is free of fuss and does not get bogged down in fancy flourishes, therefore making room for the performances, which are, it must be said, extraordinary and the main reason to view this adaptation. Bates is perfect as the seemingly sturdy mother, who keeps ploughing on despite her secret longing for a glamorous life in Paris. Henry Thomas is very strong too, and Louis Gossett Jr. has a great part as Elliot the barman.

The strongest work here though is from Woods, who is staggeringly good. In the opening segment, he is near terrifying as the rowdy, foul mouthed father, drinking himself into a stupor at the local bar. What strikes me is the raucous laughter he adopts early on in the film, the red cap, the manic eyes, and the overcharged manner. The other drinkers seem to like him, at least on the surface, and they laugh at his jokes. They are unaware though of his true demons, his inner darkness, and his memories of combat in Vietnam. At home he is a tragic figure, and his rage at the world, his dissatisfaction, those plaguing demons, come to the forefront during the remarkable, overwhelmingly powerful scene where, naked, he takes to the field in tears, screaming in torment. It's one of the most moving and striking scenes of Woods' career, and regretfully it's hardly known at all.

What makes his performance even more impressive is how he turns himself around, totally believably, in the second half of the picture. Here, he looks the clean cut dad, as if he hasn't touched a drop of beer in his life. This transformation does not jar in the slightest, and Woods makes the transition completely natural.

Performances aside, there is a lot of meat here. Leaning towards Eugene O'Neill territory, it explores the weight of responsibility on those who live off the land (or hope to), the purity of a commitment to the soil, the frictions between father and son, the inevitable revolt of the teenager and the destruction of the nuclear family. Yes, we may have seen these themes on screen before, but here they are encompassed in a film that does not drown in its own lofty ambitions. Thanks to the performances, this overlooked gem soars. When I mentioned this film to Woods, and the fact it was so often overlooked, his words were: "I am perplexed about that. It's as if it had never been made. But the house was meant to burn down at the end. And the problem was, again, we didn't have the budget to do it properly. We had a great cast - Kathy Bates, Henry Thomas, Randy Quaid. It was sad because we couldn't finish it properly."

But then there was a bit of Woods gold that has gone down in legend and will forever be enjoyed across the world. Ever since it first aired in 1989, The Simpsons proved to be ideally suited to celebrity cameos. While in later seasons the famous voices began to dominate and sometimes overtake the show's plots, in the first ten seasons at least they were merely a witty addition to go alongside the equally witty scripts and larger than life main characters who, very quickly, became household names. In Season Six, James Woods put in a classic guest spot as himself in the episode Homer and Apu. When Homer inadvertently gets Apu sacked from the Kwik E Mart, the company begin to interview possible replacements. Enter James Woods. The interview scene is particularly good. When they ask him for his work experience, Woods reels off The Onion Field, Salvador, True Believer and The Hard Way as his CV. "This sounds like the resume of a Hollywood movie star," they say. Alas, he is hired.

There are some great scenes; in one, given he has taken the job as research for a part (itself a little nod towards The Hard Way), he quizzes a customer on whether he was convincing as a Kwik E Mart worker; later, he swears while on the phone to his agent trying to scrape cheese out of the oven; at the end, after Apu takes a bullet for him, Woods says he must leave to fight aliens in outer space. Homer says it sounds like a good movie. "Yes," Woods says, shifty eyed, "a movie..." But perhaps the funniest part is when Woods is excited to finally meet Apu. "You're a legend around here. Is it true you once worked 96 hours straight?" Apu says yes it's true, adding that he was so delirious by the end he thought he was a humming bird. "Yeah I know," Woods says, "I studied your tapes." Cue CCTV footage of Apu flapping his arms like a humming bird around the Kwik E Mart.

"Yeah, with The Simpsons," Woods told me, "they just asked me to do it, to play myself. It was a kind of caricature of a hot headed crazy actor. I'd played those kinds of parts at the time, so part of the spoof was that I had this uncontrollable temper. I played up to that in the press of course, around the time I was doing all those movies. I played the bad boy image a lot, which just couldn't be further from the truth. I'm a quiet law abiding citizen who just sits at home playing the guitar! So I helped with that image, not consciously, but just went along with it. You know, the press have to have a hook. But in The Simpsons that was the nature of that character. It was a lot of fun to do. I knew Harry Shearer already through Christopher Guest. And he was there. I got there and I hadn't even read the script. I just was going to read it cold. So everything you hear me do I was just reading cold actually. I like to do that, do it like a rehearsal. So I'd read it and say, 'Let me do it one more time', and then I'd do it better. But sometimes the first read-through was better than actually preparing for it."

I asked James if he had any opportunity to ad-lib during his Simpsons appearance. "It was so well written - not that when I've ad-libbed the script's been badly written. Sometimes the writing is so good it inspires you to ad-lib, and sometimes the writing can be excellent but so complete that you don't ad-lib. And of course The Simpsons has its own built in humour. It's very self-referential, so you don't wanna ad-lib too much because you'll take away from the cosmology of the series itself. It has its own flavour and its own tone, and to ad-lib would be stepping outside of that."

THE SPECIALIST AND THE GETAWAY

By 1994, Woods hadn't been the star of a major movie for a couple of years, and felt as if he had slipped out of serious contention ever so slightly. He told me that he had changed agents and was trying to get back on the right professional path, just as the offer came to play the bad guy in the new Stallone vehicle, The Specialist. "OK, it was a bit of a cornball movie," he laughed, "a bit of a B picture with a big budget, but it put me back out there. I mean, it wasn't exactly an existential exploration of the human condition (laughs), it was a genre movie. And I was playing THE bad guy. I really enjoyed it."

In the same year he put in a lower key but equally villainous turn in another mainstream action thriller, The Getaway, providing the dark charisma needed to contrast against the glowing rays from the glossy stars. In both pictures, he showed that even within the high budgeted constraints of major mainstream motion pictures, he could still be a dangerous, unpredictable and exciting live wire.

In The Specialist, he found himself alongside two mega stars, the great Sharon Stone and the iconic Sly Stallone, who plays an explosives expert hit man who falls in with a woman who wants him to help get revenge on the mob who killed her family when she was a girl. The Specialist is actually a very enjoyable, if a little daft, crime thriller. In some ways it's a showcase for the beauty and appeal of Stone, who only two years earlier had arrived on the world stage with her legendary turn in Basic Instinct. She excels in her more intense moments here and is the epitome of Hollywood glamour. But in other ways it's the supporting players who come away the best. Rod Steiger hams it up wonderfully as the crime boss, with his subtlety turned to zero, while Eric Roberts is brilliantly nasty as the object of Stone's hatred. But Woods, playing a former CIA colleague of

213

Stallone's now working with the mob (there are twists in the plot too which reveal he and Stone's character have other motives), walks away with the picture. He goes all out to make this guy a total nightmare, gets all the best lines, dominates the funniest scenes and turns it up to eleven without, somehow, being remotely hammy. (It was later reported that Woods came out so well in preview screenings and was so popular with audiences that extra Stallone footage was shot and inserted into the picture.)

Speaking to Total Film Magazine in 1995, he was asked if he had any qualms about playing a killer. "Well," Woods said, "in the first three pages of the movie I kill an eight years old girl, so I'm not looking for any redemption here. It's not even an issue. I'm just trying to make this guy as bad as possible, but he's so charming." Woods also said he saw the character as a typical bad guy of the era, a time when style reigned over content and it was difficult to tell who the bad guy was. "It's like in this day and age, as we know from the Menendez case, all you have to do is wear the right sweater and you can kill anybody... This character looks a very traditional guy from the 40s. A man for an America of the 90s - no morals, lots of public image. These days you don't know how to define the bad guy."

But define the bad guy Woods certainly did, especially in The Specialist. He is highly effective as the live wire and has some classic scenes; the opening sequence for instance, is perfect in establishing how evil he is, while also giving him the opportunity to have fisticuffs with Sly Stallone; the office scene when threatening to drop the explosive pen; his rough scene with Sharon Stone, slapping her as he does rather viciously. He is menace personified.

Woods proved that even in such tight boundaries, he was able to add personal touches and playful flourishes that not only showed what a great spontaneous actor he is, but also lifted the picture from

214

being too over familiar and cheesy. The moments that turned out to be Woods improvisations are stand outs. When he told me which ones he came up with on the spot, I realised that, funnily enough, these moments had always been my personal favourite highlights.

One of these wild ad libs James elaborated on comes near the end of the picture. When Woods and his men find out the floor Stallone is on in the plush hotel, they head for the elevator. Right then, an old couple come up to use the lift. Woods tells them to get lost and use another lift. He also abruptly orders the man (who is wearing what can only be described as an eye soar on his upper body) to "get a new shirt!" It's quick, so quick in fact that few people might notice it, especially in a film crammed with so many explosions, shots of Sharon Stone's physique and action packed set pieces. But this little bit of humour always stood out to me. Then Woods explained it had been an ad lib. The old couple had drifted into shot, seemingly unaware that a major motion picture was being shot. The cast and crew laughed, but director Luis Llosa was adamant that the scene would not make the final cut. Woods, however, knew that it would. "It won't," insisted Luis, "I am in charge and I say it won't be in the finished film." Woods bet him 100 dollars it would, and Luis agreed. As it turned out, Luis ended up paying James 100 dollars - the scene remains in the movie to this day. It's hard to imagine The Specialist without such moments which feel fresh and alive.

Another improvised scene is the one many people pick out as the highlight; when Woods illustrates what a nut job he is by making an explosive out of a pen and then says he will drop it and blow the whole floor to kingdom come. Woods told me they shot the whole thing on a whim one day, and when producer Jerry Weintraub ("An old fashioned producer," Woods dubbed him, "but a great guy.") found out, he went ballistic - until he watched the finished scenes that is. "That's great," he said, "but don't do it again!"

I asked Sharon Stone, who remains a friend of James', about working with him for the first time on The Specialist: "Every actor, every human is different. I have three kids, all super different; great family. It begins with acceptance and love. I believe when I come to work with you, I don't have to like you, understand you even, but I should love you if I've agreed to join your acting family and join in creating a common dream. Jimmy and I get each other on some deep level. He's so smart, and I love his weird humour, even my kids love his jokes. He is kind to my children. People might not expect how great he is with kids." The shoot only consolidated their bond.

Even though the film was a hit, it got terrible notices, unfairly I feel. The New York Times savaged the film, writing, "Though The Specialist is full of giant explosions, the biggest bomb is the movie itself. The Specialist is less than a movie than a celebrity photo session with special effects." Entertainment Weekly weren't fans either, but seemed to agree that Woods was great, writing in their review that he "steals this awful, awfully amusing production."

But how can you not love a film featuring James Woods, Sly Stallone and Sharon Stone? Besides, it's great fun, never claims to take itself seriously and remains a total treat from start to finish.

Woods was on similarly charismatic form in The Getaway (1994), this time playing support to another duo of Hollywood power players, Alec Baldwin and Kim Basinger. This blackly comic thriller, directed by Roger Donaldson, stars Alec Baldwin as hotshot criminal Doc McCoy, married to the beautiful and equally wily Carol (Kim Basinger). Michael Madsen plays Rudy, a shifty con who works with Doc from time to time. One day he comes forward and offers Doc 50/50 on a $300,000 payment for releasing a Mexican drug dealer's son from a prison van. The run is pulled off, but as the private plane waits on the runway, the police turn up. Rudy gets away, but Doc is left behind, and is promptly arrested. He is then locked up in a dingy Mexican prison, where he expects to spend the next twenty years of his life. When Carol visits him, he mentions a shady individual named Benyon. Doc says if she finds him, Benyon might be able to help release him from the jail. Carol goes over, and we get our first glimpse of Benyon, played by Woods. He is on the phone as Basinger/Carol walks in, takes one look at her and says to the person on the other end of the line: "I'll call you back." He agrees to help Carol and Doc, but for a "price", details of which we find out later. When Doc is released he is called over to see Benyon, who "asks" him to take part in a risky robbery at a dog track. Though Doc doesn't want to use the men Benyon has given him (none other than Rudy himself and another gentleman, played by Philip Seymour Hoffman), Benyon reminds him that, should Doc protest too much, he could easily end up back in the Mexican lock up. Though the heist is pulled off with relative ease, it's the getaway itself which proves tricky for Carol and Doc.

The Getaway, a stylish remake of the classic Steve McQueen movie (itself based on the book by Jim Thompson), is a typical action thriller of the 1990s. And as a guy who grew up in that decade, for me it's something of a nostalgic treat. It has some of the familiar hallmarks of such a film and the era; double crosses, frequent shoot outs, saxophone sound-tracked sex scenes, snappy dialogue, flashy performances. As a wild thriller, The Getaway is a pure joy.

The mood is frantic, the jokes are dark as can be and the cast are tremendous. Baldwin and Basinger are gold as a duo (they were still married at this stage and at the peak of their stardom), and it's hard to think of another Hollywood twosome from the time who could have pulled this off. Stallone and Stone did well in The Specialist, but the chemistry between Alec and Kim is electric. The rest of the cast are great too; Michael Madsen is pure bastardry personified as the vile Rudy, who meets along the way a veterinarian's wife (played by Jennifer Tilly) who soon becomes his accomplice and bedroom buddy. Richard Farnsworth has a nifty cameo at the film's end, providing his usual rustic charm, and though a smaller part, David Morse stands out as one of Benyon's henchmen.

Woods is fabulous as Benyon, but I feel, even though it was an unexpected twist (and it was a plot point in both the original film and the novel), that it was a genuine mistake to kill him off even before the first hour was up. He had a hold over Doc, beheld all the power in fact, and was ready and willing to use his dark secret with Carol against him. I feel that writing him out deprived the film of a certain edge, a dynamic it might have merited from in the second half. Freed from Benyon's claws, the film is what the title says it is, a getaway pure and simple. That said, in his few scenes Woods gives this mysterious puppet master a certain Max Bercovicz, a most shady individual appearing to the outside world as a straight business man. He has an empire of his own, his finger is in many pies and he employs a mini army of underlings. I feel that Benyon was such a strong character, and that Woods gave him such enigmatic qualities, that I would have loved to have learned more about his past.

In one of our talks, Woods actually spoke about the idea of his character having a back story of his own, and that being a key factor in fleshing out the role. "No matter how big my part, no matter how big or small, I always imagined, 'What if this movie was this character's story?' So I would build the entire story of this character's life in my mind." This method comes through in his portrayal of Benyon to the point that, yes, it becomes frustrating that this intriguing villain didn't get a movie all of his own. Once again Woods leaves us wanting more, not less.

"The Getaway was great," Woods said, his voice filling with excitement when he recalled his co-stars on the movie. "Just look at the actors I got to work with! Michael Madsen is another unique actor. And it's funny, when guys are really good at what they do, people just expect them to be a certain type of person. I of all people should know better! But I expected Michael to be kinda tough, like he is in the Tarantino movies. Then you meet him and he's this fabulous guy who's really fun and smart and clever. And Alec Baldwin is a wonderful actor. I love Alec. I loved working with him. And of course Jennifer Tilly. Madsen was just terrific. And David Morse. I mean, Philip Seymour Hoffman was in the movie! It's amazing."

He also looked back on his two scenes with Kim Basinger. "Those two scenes, the second when I get killed... She's just great to work with. She dialled in, 100 percent, and she was there! We didn't even need to rehearse, we just rehearsed the movements with the director, Roger Donaldson. I loved him, a great director. So she comes in, David Morse gives her that overly comfortable frisk in that skin tight dress. It's like, 'Dude, believe me, she is not wearing a gun under that dress that looks like it's been painted on!' But they played that bit great. So she comes in and we have our scene, and there is an undertone that we've been sexually involved. That was part of her deal. That was clearly there in the plot but also understated. My character being the ruthless crime boss that he is, he has this veneer of being a gentleman - and of course he isn't going to pass on the opportunity to compromise her character, because she's so gorgeous! It's Kim Basinger! Women like that in the world of crime, they're going to be between a rock and a hard place - if you pardon the pun - and that triangle was very important in the story. And you have to remember, Alec and Kim were in the middle of a big love affair themselves at the time, so there was a lot of drama going on there. A lot of drama! But (with that film) my attitude was, How am I going to turn down a Roger Donaldson movie, where I'm working with Alec Baldwin and Kim Basinger, both at the peak of their career, with Michael Madsen, Jenifer Tilly, David Morse and Philip Seymour Hoffman? Of course I'm doing the movie! I'm gonna be running over there with bells on!"

The Getaway was butchered by critics, for what reason I am unsure. Roger Ebert called it "nasty and mean spirited" - which, I am sure, it was intended to be, in order to show what the lives of these kinds of people are like. Yes it's unflinching, but it's hard to get too offended.

Though these two pictures were not Woods' very best work, they were great action movies, and they did get him back on the marquees and at the forefront of an industry that all too quickly seems to forget where the true talent is.

KILLER: A JOURNAL OF MURDER (1995)

Killer: A Journal of Murder is worthy of your viewing time for a number of reasons. Firstly, on a historical level alone. Adapted from the autobiography of Carl Panzram, the first serial killer in America, it offers a glimpse into the primitive roots of this most murky and disturbing of phenomena - the idea of killing for enjoyment, even fulfilment. Secondly, the film gives us an insight into the mind of a pure psychopath; not a sociopath or someone lacking empathy, but an out and out psychopath, which Panzram surely was. Thirdly, it is entertaining, genuinely intriguing and engaging as a stand alone film (even if it were fictitious it would be equally absorbing). And finally, it contains within it a breathtakingly authentic, at times extremely unsettling, performance from James Woods.

It has to be said that, as much as an actor can, he becomes Carl Panzram. We first see Carl when he is arrested for burglary and then imprisoned, though we know nothing else of his back story just yet. He then forms a strange bond with a new guard, Henry (Robert Sean Leonard), though the other guards despise him and give out regular beatings. One day Carl asks Henry for paper and a pencil so he can put down his "story"; he wants to confess on paper that he's a prolific serial killer. Henry provides the paper and begins to read Carl's graphic write ups of his exploits. But with the truth out, Carl must now face the consequences of his actions.

Tim Metcalfe (who found the killer's autobiography in a book shop and began writing the script) offers us a revealing look at the inner workings of a killer. His direction is unfussy, unshowy, but still up close and personal, and he imaginatively mixes real life photos and footage to enhance the authenticity of flashbacks. As this is all true, he relents from sensationalising events and presents them to us in a straight forward, almost documentary-like fashion.

As brilliantly put together as the film is, it's hard if not impossible to imagine anyone but Woods in the part of Panzram. He simply makes the role his own and is compulsively watchable from start to finish; equally terrifying and fascinating, as all such killers are. He gives him depth, though rightfully does not indulge the character's sins; nor does he invite us to like, understand or sympathise with him in any way. It's a warts and all portrait of an evil, sick man. But as the guard finds out, there is a root to this madness. Maybe he secretly does long for a connection, and realises near the end of the film, when on death row and ready to meet his maker, that no one has ever really been kind to him. He does recall a jailer from the past (Spud) who let him out on day release, but he let the man down and took advantage of his kindness by raping a librarian while out and about. He is sick, twisted, damaged beyond repair. Woods though, once again, somehow doesn't make him come across as a cartoon, even though he gives Carl no redeeming qualities whatsoever. A lesser actor may have turned him into a snarling demon, a devil on earth, but Woods keeps him human, though very much the embodiment of soulless evil at the same time. It's a fine line, sounding contradictory, but Woods never slips off.

The flashbacks are a wonderful addition to the film, narrated by Woods reading from the actual Panzram memoir. These parts are brutally frank, with Carl/James recalling his past adventures with a certain disconnected quality that makes them all the more disturbing. One image sticks in my mind; it is of Carl killing a man, in a black and white flashback. After the murder, Woods turns to the screen, snarling animal-like, blood all over him. For that moment, he embodies what a murderer really is, a man who takes life for gratification. He is more beast than man in those few seconds, and there is a feral quality about Woods, and a deep darkness in his gaze, which makes the scene one of the most disturbing I have ever seen.

Speaking to me about the film, Woods said: "Janet Yang really produced the film for Oliver (Stone). He was never on the set. But Janet's fantastic. I love Janet. And this was Tim Metcalfe's first film as director, and we are still friends to this day. He really needed my help on Killer, because he thought directing was just, like, 'Hey, action!' So he kind of got buried a bit and requested my help. We kind of worked together very closely directing the film. I'm not saying I directed the movie, but he asked my advice a lot and I'd say, 'Put the camera here, you can put the camera there,' because I had a lot of experience. Oliver supported it because he liked Tim's screenplay and he liked Tim as an auteur. He wanted Janet to have an opportunity to produce something, but our budget was too low. We couldn't make the film we wanted to properly. So it was a little skimpy. We were just under-budgeted."

But the film is effective and Woods himself is blisteringly good. In the scene near the end when the guard hugs him, Woods himself said that "though he was a complete monster, I don't think he ever had a moment of kindness in his life. And I think at the end with the guard when he gives him that moment of kindness, I think that it's not that he appreciates it as compassion, but he appreciates that someone opens the door and shows him what other lives must be like, that he will never understand."

Through talking about Killer, James also gave me an incredible insight into how he gets into a role. "I went straight from that into Indictment, which Oliver also produced, all about the McMartin trial (where Woods plays the lawyer Danny Davis). I literally left on a Friday on Killer in Connecticut, I went from there, flew to Los

223

Angeles, and on Monday we were on the set and I was doing costume fittings while we were doing filming. I gotta tell you, I don't do prep or anything like that. I get a feeling of the character that I can't explain. I just live the way the character lives. The scene is presented to me. If I read a script and I get a sense of who that character is - I don't know how he's gonna solve the dilemma he's in, but if I sense who he is, I just get out there and use Jimmy Cagney's dictum: Put your two feet on the ground, look the other guy in the eye and tell the truth. That's what I do."

Deservedly both the film and Woods were praised by the critics, with Roger Ebert calling it a "powerful, searing performance." Elsewhere, the Los Angeles Times could not have been more complimentary of his efforts. In their article, titled "A Triumph for James Woods", they wrote of his "galvanizing, Oscar-calibre portrayal. Carl Panzram is perfect for James Woods, who arguably has never had so rich an opportunity to express such bristling wit, passion, rage and irony, revealing the humanity--vulnerability, even in so dangerous, bestial a man. His Panzram is so full of energy and anarchic spirit he jazzes up the entire film. Ultimately, Woods is better than the picture, but he's so much the picture it scarcely matters." Upon release, the Metro said of Woods' performance: "Woods is the soul of Killer: A Journal of Murder. Woods communicates something that's important: how satisfying, how joyous, it must be to be a really first-rate actor."

In all fairness, it is a faultless piece of work and proof, if further proof were needed, that in my view Woods has given more committed, believable performances than any actor in modern times. Killer: A Journal of Murder is an essential stop on your journey through Woods' filmography.

TIM METCALFE ON
KILLER: A JOURNAL OF MURDER

I got the chance to speak to Tim Metcalfe, the writer and director of Killer: A Journal of Murder, all about the making of the movie and working with James Woods.

The film came about in a rather unusual way didn't it?

I was in a used book store, probably 1989, 88 maybe. I saw the book in the true crime section. Back then the true crime sections were maybe one or two shelves. So I saw it sticking out, staring at me. I picked it up and looked at it, and it had a terrifying picture of Panzram on it. I bought the book and just let it sit on my shelf for a year or two. Something scared me about it. There was something very creepy about it. I finally read it, and immediately knew I had to make a film of it. I contacted the publisher and got an option on the book pretty easily. But I wrote the script, got it to a producer named Melinda Jason, who was an agent back then who wanted to work with me. So I got it to her and she said it was wonderful. We tried it several places and finally got it to Janet Yang, who was running Oliver Stone's company. So Janet said she liked it, took it to Oliver. And the idea was that I would direct it. Oliver was backing a lot of first time directors, being very generous with his time. He had a suite of offices and got a lot of movies made with first time directors. With a star attached and his name we were able to get a 2 million dollar budget. No one told me the actual budget, it was always changing and I could never get an honest answer. But it was about 2 million dollars. It is not much now, and it wasn't much then! This was a film set in 1929, we needed period clothes, period cars, period sets. It was impossible, but we somewhat pulled it off. I think some of the scenes don't look as well as they could have, because we couldn't afford to shoot more than one or two takes of scenes. But I still think it came out as a worthy movie.

Was James Woods the first choice to play Panzram?

No, I wanted Ed Harris first, because physically he looks more like Panzram. They had a strong resemblance. I actually thought Ed would be good. I can't remember if he read it or we told him the idea and he said he didn't wanna play someone like that. He was squeamish about playing in violent films. We went through some other names and I met with a few actors who were interested in playing the part. One of them was Stephen Lang. I met with Joe Montagna who I think wanted to play the guard. I don't actually remember. I met with a lot of actors who wanted to play the guard, and a few who wanted to play the killer. Then Jimmy came up because of his relationship with Oliver. So Jimmy and I met for lunch, and he was very enthusiastic about wanting to do it.

James Woods is fearless as an actor I think. Panzram has no redeeming qualities, and Woods doesn't try to redeem him in any way.

I have to disagree with you in one sense. The character in real life, in the book, was far worse. The script, with some urging, made me soften him, if you can believe it. He was a monster, a real monster. Many of his victims were children who he strangled and raped. I mention that briefly, when the guard reads the diary and says,

"Children, how could you?" - but it was kind of obscure. He was horrible. His relationship with the guard was softened a bit, but it was true to the story. And I always think I shouldn't have done that. I should have kept him as hard as he was and as mean as he was, then it would have been more powerful.

I'm not sure what I'd have thought watching the film knowing all that stuff. The moment at the end when the guard hugs him might have jarred a little more.

Well that was not a real moment. The biggest fictionalising of the book that I did was consolidate two prisons Panzram was in into one. He was in Washington City Jail when he met Lesser the guard, he wrote the diary for him there, and then he was transferred to Leavenworth in Kansas, and they never saw each other again. He was hanged without Lesser being there. He did advocate for him to fight for his life and get a reprieve, but in letters, not in person. But that wouldn't have worked in the film. That was the biggest cheat I did. No one was actually there to say goodbye to him. So it was a bit of a cheat, but not one that I thought was wrong. But there was a time when after the film was done and out there - this is gonna sound nuts - but I felt like he was haunting me, and I had a string of bad luck and some things went wrong. I thought, It's Panzram, he's getting his own back on me for not telling his story right. Now, over the years I got over it. It was kind of superstitious, if not ridiculous, that this man was haunting me. But I did feel that way for a while. I had a framed picture of the book jacket sent to me by Henry Lesser's niece or nephew. I had it on the wall of my office. Everyday, Panzram was staring at me. So one day I called them back and said, 'I've had enough, I'm gonna give this back to you, I don't want this guy staring at me everyday.' So I gave it back.

Were you nervous about directing for the first time, given it was such a heavy story too?

No, but I should have been. I should have been more nervous and better prepared. We did wonderful story boards. They were put up in the art department, and my director of photography, Ken Kelsch, walked in and said they were beautiful but that we weren't gonna use them. He basically laughed at them. Because he knew that we didn't have the time to get all those angles. He'd made a lot of movies at that budget level.

How was it directing James Woods?

We didn't do much rehearsal if any. We didn't have the time for it. But he knew the script inside and out. He's a very good memorizer. He improvised but he knew all his lines. As you know, he has a frenetic, sarcastic way of speaking in his movies. There's often a bit of a trend, a theme that he might go to. So I said, 'I don't want you to do a lot of improvising, unless we discuss it. I don't want you to talk fast the way you do. I don't think this guy should talk fast. He's a slow, careful speaker. He says what he means. If he says he's gonna kill you, he means it. I don't want a lot of improvised remarks. I want you to understand this character as a toad, a snake or something, just sitting there, watching, and suddenly the tongue comes out and catches a fly. That's what I want.' And he followed that closely. There was one thing - I spoke to Jimmy about this recently - that if there is ever a time I need to laugh, I think about the scene when he is talking to the preacher at the end of the movie. He starts talking about Mabel's biscuits or whatever, and all of that stuff he said to him was improvised. It was in the script that he was supposed to outrage the guy by saying all these obscene things to him. But Jimmy said things that were not in the script that threw that actor off. We captured that on film (laughs), and you can see his face. He doesn't know how to respond to him, these obscenities he threw at him. That still makes me laugh twenty five years later. But when he is in the scenes with the Henry Lesser character, there was no improvising and no anal jokes or anything.

It is a very controlled performance. When he's narrating while writing the diaries, there is this detached air to his voice. It's so different to some of his other work that in some ways you don't even associate it with James Woods.

Yes, that's what I wanted. He has mannerisms that have worked well for him for fifty years. But I didn't want any of that. I remember Oliver Stone after the first screening, he said to Jimmy, "That's maybe one of your best two or three performances ever." He was very complimentary about it. People could see there was none of the usual shtick. He invented that style in Oliver's Salvador in many ways, that was often his thing. He did that style great in a couple of movies. But I didn't want that. But once Jimmy got the haircut and the costume he started to feel this character and really feel what I wanted. Slow down, don't talk fast, and be scary.

Jimmy was also somewhat of a co-director with me. There were times when the clock was ticking and I did not have the experience of how to get a series of shots in quick enough time. I was dithering and he was saying, 'Here's how we're gonna do it.' There's the scene where

229

Lesser comes into the cell holding a steel bar, this was in the book. Panzram thought he was gonna hit him with it, but he was just using it to tap the bars to see if they were loose. If you look at that scene there are a lot of complicated shots trying to get across the paranoia, and the simplicity of Lesser just coming in to tap the bars. That's his POV. From Panzram's view it's more like, this guard is coming in here to hit me with that. And Jimmy just came up with all the angles. It was like Artificial Intelligence. 'We're gonna do this, do this, and do this.' And we had the shots. I could have done it over a couple of hours maybe. He did it in ten seconds.

I love the paranoia in that shot from the back, just above the door, as Panzram reaches for the bar on the bed.

Yeah! And that was all him. A couple of other times that came about. There was another he really helped map out. It was the farewell scene in the yard, and he has his most emotional line when he says he wants out of his body. It was complicated for Ken to keep up with them, to stop when they stopped. Jimmy sort of worked that one out. We kind of worked it out together, and he was very helpful. And he was very helpful as a producer too. He had the power to say no to something. If a set wasn't good enough, or the bars looked like they were made out of cardboard. And he complained. I did learn that from him. If you are the director or the star, you have the power to say no. Generally you will win the day. It's a shame he never directed a film because he knows more about directing a film than most directors. I have no doubt he would have been as good as Robert Redford or other actors who became directors.

230

CASINO (1995)

Five years following their last gangster movie, Goodfellas, became a worldwide cultural phenomenon, and four years since their last actor-director collaboration all together with Cape Fear, Robert De Niro and Martin Scorsese teamed up again for a crime epic of a different sort, the wonderful and highly ambitious Casino. Based on the true story of a Jewish bookie appointed the role of casino-head for the mob, the film charts a decade at the top, taking in a mountain of excess from the years 1973 to 1983, that is destined to come crumbling down like a blood-drenched avalanche. It culminates in the downfall of the mob's hold over Las Vegas, the advent of Disney Land mentality, and the loss of a consequence-free playground. A violent gangster film it may be, but Casino really is so much more than that. It's a study of greed, lust and friendship, complexly explored in a devastatingly powerful three way drama between three very different people.

As Sam "Ace" Rothstein, De Niro brings a certain realism and, dare I say it, decency to the table. Here is a man who made his name making bets for the mob, but who was so serious about his job that "he never enjoyed himself". He's a strict professional suddenly thrust into the colourful, shady world of Vegas, seeing over the huge Tangiers hotel and casino. The mob send in Nicky Santoro (Joe Pesci), a short tempered enforcer, to watch Sam's back. But Nicky isn't happy just being the muscle for the casino; he assembles his own dodgy crew and starts robbing homes and businesses, turning the heat not only on himself, but on Sam and the whole mob. Then Sam meets and marries Ginger (Sharon Stone), a hustler who agrees to set up home with him once he promises her guaranteed wealth for the rest of her life. It's clear from the get go that she doesn't love Sam and this relationship soon starts to break down. On top of this, Nicky draws the FBI in with his increasingly reckless and violent escapades. As Sam yearns for a straight business role, shunning Nicky more and more throughout the film, it's clear that these three individuals all have separate goals which, when put together, can only tear the whole thing apart.

Nicholas Pileggi, the writer who penned Wiseguy, the book on which Goodfellas was based, worked alongside Scorsese for several months on the screenplay for Casino. Pileggi had read an article on the true story and thought it would translate well to film. The real "Ace", Lefty Rosenthal, wasn't going to cooperate on the film, until of course he learned that De Niro was going to be playing him. From then on, as Pileggi noted, he was all for the project.

The end result is a mammoth effort. Firstly, it looks amazing, and there is a wider scope to the story and narrative. Scorsese's directorial touches are even more imaginative and multi dimensional than ever before, bringing the story to life with never ending whirls of the camera and constant hypnotic movement. When conscious of it, you notice the camera barely stays still and there are clever edits by the brilliant Thelma Schoonmaker throughout. There are so many smart cuts, jumps and techniques that it is simply dazzling. The use of narration enhances further the feeling of being invited inside this murky world, this time by both De Niro and Pesci. The film is visually stunning, and the constant costume changes, bright lights and filming innovations make sure it never becomes slow. The acting is tremendous, with Stone undoubtedly giving the film's most intense and impressive performance, a tour de force which still stuns me to this day. Her character goes from care-free hustler, to dissatisfied mob wife, to disconnected drunk, and finally to all out crazy. It's one of the finest pieces of acting I have ever seen. At three hours long, the whole thing flies by and is constantly gripping. It goes through so many shifts, eras and dramatic set ups that one can only conclude that Scorsese achieved film-making perfection this time around. In time, perhaps Casino will be seen as one of his finest works.

And then we come to James Woods, who has a small but unforgettable part as Lester Diamond, a sleazy pimp who Ginger is still in love with from their early years together. The real life Lester was not actually a pimp, but Lenny Marmor, the real Ginger's LA-based con man boyfriend. A few alterations though (valid in my opinion) and the man is fleshed out into a real sleazoid. The fact that Woods only has a handful of scenes, and is only in the film for under ten minutes of screen time, is a testament to his acting. Many people recall Woods' performance in Casino as a highlight. Rather like Harvey Keitel as the pimp, Sport, in Scorsese's Taxi Driver, he fleshes out a barely written part and makes it his own. Lester comes in and out of the story, but his appearances are so memorable that people tend to look back on the film and swear he was in it more.

We first see Diamond when Ace is referring to him as Ginger's "old pimp boyfriend", and we are shown images of Ginger handing him wads of cash she's earned in her hustling. In the scene, she hands over the money. After pocketing it, he looks out of the window, shiftily, as if someone is following him. Then Lester gets in his car, disappearing out of Ginger's life for a while until he needs her money again. The way Ginger watches him leave in his sleazy auto, almost like a little girl observing her father leave the house for work, is strangely sad. It also illustrates the hold he has over this woman who seems so in control of her life.

The next time we see Lester is when he's speaking to Ginger on the phone during her wedding, feigning emotion while a hooker roams the room in underwear doing coke. (It's darkly funny, and certainly toned down from Woods' original suggestion that she should be blowing him.) Lester rears his head again, leeching cash from Ginger, but he gets beaten up by some of Ace's men. (Lester has the immortal line, "Why don't you do it yourself, you chicken shit cocksucker!"). Diamond then re-appears when he and Ginger kidnap Ace's daughter, but the plan doesn't work. Woods has some of the film's most memorable lines - all, I might add, improvised. Amidst this huge sweeping film, it's a credit to Woods that so many people recall Lester Diamond, despite his brief screen time. (In my view, there should have been a Lester Diamond spin off.)

Woods had been desperate to work with Scorsese for a while, and he put the word out to Marty: "Any part, any film, anywhere!" Scorsese called him one day and said there was a role in Casino, but it was only five lines. Woods didn't care, agreed to play Lester, and he was on board.

James later told me that he was once playing golf with Joe Pesci and Joe said to him, "I hear you're gonna do Casino. Hey, do you have a walk for him yet?" He suggested Woods do a pimp roll, and following his advice, James came up with a walk that defined the sleazy Lester. "I do it on the way out of the restaurant," James told me, "and it always gets a big laugh. He's trying to maintain his dignity. It's such a fun character."

Woods also told me the fun he had in improvising with Sharon Stone and the girl playing Ginger and Sam's daughter, Erika von Tagen. No holds barred, Scorsese, Woods and Stone encouraged her to tease Woods' character. She sticks her tongue out at him, tells him to shut up, and in response Max gets very wound up. "I'm gonna send her to Bolivia in a fucking box!" he screams.

"And I improvised all of it," James told me in 2020. "The voiceover to the wedding was another improvisation. We were just supposed to

234

cut to me at the end when he (De Niro) finds Ginger on the phone. So Scorsese put me in a robe with the Speedos, and there's the girl and she's topless and doing coke. We did this long improvisation."

Later, when Woods gave Thelma Schoonmaker her award at the Hollywood Film Festival, she said she was glad that he was the one to hand her the gong. In her speech, Schoonmaker recalled the fact that for the wedding scene they had no music set aside. Marty and Thelma came to the conclusion that a voice over of Woods and Stone on the phone might work better, his manipulative spiel contrasting with the visuals of the superficially blissful wedding.

"Nick Pileggi," Woods said, "told me that he was never happier to take credit for writing that wasn't his. And by the way he is such a great writer, the great writers like Nick are very open to improvisations that work. Sometimes an actor can own a part so well that they can create a response or even a whole scene that works."

One of my favourite scenes, not just within Casino, but of all time, is the one in the cafe when Ace walks in on Ginger and Lester as she's handing him a substantial amount of money. For me, a scene featuring Robert De Niro, Sharon Stone and James Woods at one table was always going to be a classic, but the dynamics between the three are so well-handled that the sequence is now a perfect example of how three powerhouses can make such a scene look simple and straight forward.

When I asked James about this moment, he shed some light on it for me: "Well that scene was really as written. There was a lot of information there, we didn't improvise and it really was as written. Remember, I had spent a year with Bob De Niro doing Once Upon a Time in America. And I had done The Specialist with Sharon, and I knew her from before when she auditioned for The Boost, and I thought she was a great actress. So now, here we are all together. It was really fun doing that scene, because we all knew each other so well. But we were there doing our thing together with Marty Scorsese. Marty did an interesting thing in that scene. When Bob comes in he sits down, and it's like, Shit, here he is. So I had my back to the door, and in the actual master, it was over Bob and Sharon's shoulders looking at me. This was sort of my introduction into the film. Bob comes in. And in one of the takes he stood standing, and I had to look up in a subservient position. And it was very funny actually. He's taking the money, this terrified weasel (laughs), this weasely guy. Marty said it was a great shot, of me looking up. So he said, 'I really wanna re-shoot the whole master to match that shot when Bob stays standing.' So we re-shot the master, and then of Bob sitting down in the seat afterwards. It was great. It was a case of, how can we make it better? Marty would always wanna do anything to make the scene better. And that was when we got to put that pimp roll in, which was great. When Marty saw me do that, he said, 'Right, we gotta get a shot of you doing that.' I remember in the movie theatre that walk got a really big laugh."

The poster of Casino famously shows Pesci, De Niro and Stone, but Woods' Lester is certainly the fourth most important character. This isn't down to screen time of course, but the impact he has on both the film and Ginger's situation. Had Ginger not been so tied and loyal to him, her relationship with Ace might have worked out better, and perhaps - a big perhaps - she might not have lost control and set the whole thing off the rails.

"I was never meant to be a major character," Woods said, "but I remember when Sharon won her Golden Globe for the film, in her speech she said, 'Such an honour to work with Robert De Niro, Joe Pesci and Jimmy Woods, all three of his personalities (laughs).' You know, as if I'm a multiple personality of something!"

236

After the film's release, and the Golden Globe win, Sharon Stone felt like she had finally proven herself. "It's deeply gratifying in two ways," she told the Guardian. "I see the film and I realise... I haven't been deluding myself all these years. I really can do it. And because I got up to bat with my dream people, that was the apex for me... and then Marty... And then to get the pat on your back from your peers is always pretty great. You know, you don't get a lot of that."

I asked Sharon Stone how she'd felt about going back to work with James Woods again after The Specialist, especially given the weird relationship between their characters in Casino, Ginger and Lester, was so different. "I knew it would be great because we got to go from me defying him, to me being obsessively in his control. Yet with the same strange compulsive obsessive base. There was a lot of deep psychological work layered in already. For me anyway."

On the dynamic between Ginger and Lester, she added, "He's the only family she's ever had, the only person who knows her from her childhood. And that beautiful kid and I had a ball teasing Jimmy. I think it added to the frenetic, cocaine driven mania of the scene. I have to admit to egging her on."

Sharon also shared with me her view on her and James' relationship as actors and friends. "Jimmy and I have wildly different ideas about masculinity and femininity and how they best manifest; that makes for fabulous screen chemistry: we duke it out on screen and I think it works because underneath it, we adore each other. He is a genuine genius, studied at MIT, and while he's a certified idiot about some things in my humble opinion, his genius has astounding range and it manifests itself in extraordinary ways in his acting craft."

Casino, like Once Upon a Time in America, is a gangster movie that transcends the genre, a film about people, about power, friendship, regret and betrayal. Another grand, awe-inspiring epic,

Casino is for me one of the best movies ever made. Woods' part in it may be smaller, but no one who's seen Casino will ever forget the name of Lester Diamond. And when I asked James if he'd have liked to have played any of his characters again, he did not hesitate for a second before saying Lester Diamond.

NIXON (1995)

Though many years in Woods' career highlight his knack of choosing a wide variety of types, 1995 proved to be one of the most varied of his career. The same year he played Lester Diamond in Casino, starred in Indictment, portrayed a killer in A Journal of Murder and a dodgy brother in James Alexander's For Better or Worse, he was back with Oliver Stone again in the towering, acclaimed biopic, Nixon.

Starring Anthony Hopkins as the dividing president, Stone takes us intimately inside the White House, starting affairs with Watergate and flitting back and forth (in a fragmented, tormented style, as if in Nixon's frazzled mind) to the past; his early glory years at college, his childhood, his initial political career, all before the rot set in.

Nixon really does transport the viewer into the president's orbit so well that, though not documentary-like (stylised as it is in the trademark multi-faceted, multi-layered Stone manner of his post-JFK work and beyond), we often forget we're in a movie. Hopkins may not do a spot-on impersonation, but that was never his intention. Hopkins tried the accent in a table reading (he later recalled Woods teasing him afterwards, complimenting his great German accent), but quickly dispensed doing a copy of Nixon's voice. He adopts a twang, yes, but he gives Nixon depth by putting his own intensity into the part. We totally believe Hopkins is Nixon, just his own version of Nixon. That said, we all have our own view of such giants, but Hopkins' portrayal is as true and real as the man we see on the old news reel footage. In many ways, he is Richard Nixon.

The film boasts a fine supporting cast, including Paul Sorvino, Ed Harris and David Hyde Pierce. Woods is on Oscar worthy form as Haldeman, Nixon's Chief of Staff, a role he seems to have dived right into and simply relished the chance to play. Here is a man of commitment, who was utterly devoted to the president no matter what he did or said. His loyalty is rather touching, but also tragic and perhaps misplaced, especially when you find out that Nixon never spoke to Haldeman again after everything went wrong.

For Woods, the initial idea of the film was an odd one. And he was not alone. Indeed, even when in conversation with Billy Wilder, the veteran director asked Stone, "Who wants to see a film about Richard Nixon?" But as filming commenced, and then even more so when the picture was edited, Woods saw what Stone was doing - adding humanity to the image of Nixon, the myth of Tricky Dicky. He was in a sense de-mystifying him.

Woods explained to Charlie Rose: "I, like everybody else about a year ago when Oliver Stone suggested he might be doing this film about Richard Nixon, thought, 'Why?' And as we were working on it, I started to get a sense of why we were doing it, and then when I finally saw it... It took my breath away, and I realized that what he did with Platoon, with regards to the Vietnam War, and the time to heal, the divisive spirit about that war, he somehow has closed a lot of the abscess about cynicism in government that came from Watergate and from the Nixon presidency. He's not saying that they were right or wrong, certainly. He's not even forgiving. He's just saying, You know, just walk for a while in their shoes."

Ultimately though, Stone does not make Nixon a man to admire, yet at times we pity him; pity his ineptness; pity him for what he went through in his younger years; pity his inability to connect with the youth of the day; pity his downfall; pity the collapse of his marriage; pity his inability full stop. We sympathise with the situation itself. But Nixon suffered mostly in the battle with his own ego, the fight for his own somewhat creaky reputation, and Stone makes this clear. Woods rightly dubbed him "a man who sat at a banquet of caviare and pheasant and complained about hunger." Though Stone himself, raised conservative by his father, did support Nixon upon his return from fighting in Vietnam in 1968, he had turned against him by 1972. Yet in this study he empathises with the man. And through Hopkins' performance, we are offered the kind of glimpse into Nixon's psyche we would otherwise never have had.

It is ironic that, for a film featuring such a strong Woods performance, Stone initially didn't think he was right for the part. Woods had been working on Killer: A Journal of Murder, which Stone produced, and looking in the mirror one day at the buzz cut he'd had in order to portray the convict on death row, Woods saw someone else... Haldeman. Cutting off a planned holiday, Woods went to see Stone and insisted he was right for the role. "No," Stone said, "Haldeman was straight, compressed, grey... You wear your heart on your sleeve, and you're emotional, you're like a roller coaster!" Woods kept on pressing and eventually Stone said he could audition. Other actors of Woods' calibre may see an audition as a comedown, but not him. He auditioned with pride, for he wanted to prove he was right for the part, that he could pull it off. Swallowing his pride, Woods tested for Haldeman and got the role.

"Yes he did lobby for it," Oliver Stone told me. "It was his idea. He wanted to be in the movie. His career had moved on and he was much more in demand than on Salvador. He was much more humble by then. He had done more films, was more settled into the Hollywood planetarium here. And he laughed a lot during the making of Nixon. He admired Anthony Hopkins greatly."

Woods' Haldeman is concrete, a firm fixture throughout the film. He is, as Woods said, tied to Nixon's hip at all times, his right hand man and organiser. He knows all the dirt as well as the shortcomings. He is almost robotic, a machine, an emotionless computer that serves

Nixon's every whim and does so efficiently. His dedication is tireless. Woods told me that he interpreted Haldeman as a kind of extension of Nixon and he used his own initiative to flesh out the character this way. "When Nixon reached for his coffee, I'd go for the cup first," is how Woods put it, and this comes across throughout the picture. He almost exists *for* Nixon.

For Woods himself though, given he was on set with Hopkins a lot, he had front row access to this extraordinary transformation. During one take, Woods was so mesmerised by what Hopkins was doing he almost missed his line. "I watched and I thought, 'I'm working with the greatest actor God ever created.' I mean, I had chills while he was doing the scene."

That didn't stop him playfully teasing Hopkins though, a man Woods told me really is the greatest living actor. After the said scene, when Woods watched his colleague in total awe, he publicly declared before the cast and crew that Hopkins was a master. But, he added, this was the last time he would compliment him in public. "We all know you can't act really," he laughed, "you fucking German ham." Hopkins loved Woods and his co-stars ribbing him, and Woods said they laughed until they ached on the making of the movie. One funny memory for Woods was when he asked Hopkins what he should call him. "I don't like all that Sir stuff," he said. "OK," Woods replied sharply. "How about I call you Lady Hopkins?"

Time has seen Nixon age much better than many so called hits of the same period. For me it's a solid classic in Stone's canon. Watching it now, and taking in all the time frames, all the sets, locations, characters faces, re-enactments, effects, heavy performances, fills me with awe that Stone could put such a masterpiece together. It also features an essential Woods performance, one of his best known roles which he pulls off to sheer perfection.

"THE HYPER WOODS TREATMENT"
1995 - 1996

The mid 1990's were a fruitful time for James Woods. Mixing his film appearances with TV, Woods continued to make the highest quality television. One of his finest was the Oliver Stone produced Indictment: The McMartin Trial (1995), which is also one of the strongest TV films of the 1990's - and beyond for that matter. A hugely gripping re-telling of the infamous McMartin trial, which centred around a family-run day care centre whose staff were accused of child abuse and satanic worship, it has a sharp script, a break neck pace and a cast of actors at their finest. Woods puts in a formidable effort as singled minded Attorney Danny Davis, who charges through the case with intensity and guts, a man who will do anything to clear his defendant's names. His lawyer has a real arc too, someone who begins the case with the typical kind of harsh coldness needed for law, and ends up as a genuine friend to the family.

Indictment received positive feedback and Woods in particular was praised for his work. Unfortunately though, some reviewers mistook his skill and hard work for coasting. Variety wrote: "By now, Woods could portray in his sleep the edgy, hack defence lawyer who finds purpose through the case, but no matter. He's well suited for the role and pulls it off without a hitch." Still, to make this kind of acting look easy takes a lot of work and focus.

The film is brilliantly acted by all the cast (Henry Thomas and Mercedes Ruehl are particularly strong) and excellently directed by Mick Jackson, who confronts in the courtroom and keeps activity fizzing, though not dizzying. Thankfully for the viewer, the tone is set early on, and we know whose side to be on; the rational, rather than

243

the sensationalist accusers. But a good point is made about how the word guilty attaches itself even to proven innocence. At the end, when Woods walks by the sea with the family, they are victims of verbal abuse, long after their trial is over. Mud sticks after all, and these people's lives will never be normal again.

"Indictment is very interesting," Woods told me, "because it was written by Abby Mann. When we were doing Indictment we were very fortunate to get Mercedes to play the prosecutor. She was fantastic in it, and she started to improvise and throw in facts. She had her opinions on the case. And I was one of the producers on the film. So we had to go and have a conversation with Mick Jackson, a great director, and we said, 'Look, there were 77 law suits associated with this case. The lawyers have vetted this script with a fine tooth comb. You know that I am a great champion of artists and artist's creativity, including actors improvising, but the problem we have here is we cannot change a single word of this script. And if we do, we would have to get the lawyers back in to go over it again. This thing is such a hot potato. So many people's lives were ruined and hurt by this, people are outraged on both sides of this experience. So you are gonna have to decide to agree, as you did contractually, to play the script as written, or if you feel you are being too bound. And I would understand each decision, and I wouldn't judge you for either decision.' She said, 'Yeah, let me think it over.' So she went away for half an hour, thought it over, came back and said, 'I thought about it and, you know, I understand your dilemma and I'm gonna stay with the show.' And I said, 'I understand it's a hard decision. I'm frustrated by it too, but we're in a position where we ordinarily would have some leeway and we just don't. We can't afford to keep vetting the script.' So that was that, and she gave a brilliant performance. She was great to work with."

To this day Woods sounds excited by working on the film and the whole McMartin case in general. "I tell you," he said, "people talk about the O.J. case. The McMartin case was even bigger. The passions involved in that case were astonishing." When I brought up Danny Davis' great journey in the film, Woods was passionate about the character. "Yeah, the great arc of that character is that his quest was - and this was the idea we tried to put across. It was an editorial choice, that he was a bit taken with himself. He was a successful, commercial lawyer interested in power, fame, glory and money. And after watching these people being tortured by the press - it was like a witch hunt! He actually was a part of understanding that these people were being tortured by the law, by the press, by every institution in this country that is a part of what makes it one of the greatest experiments in civilised political governmental behaviour. And yet it can be exploited and oft times perverted for the sake of profit by those very institutions. Especially the media. But yes, he went from having this quest - his quest is to make money, get rich and get famous in the process. His journey ends up with him growing into a more compassionate man and bonding with this family, and finding a greater humanity in himself and a greater calling. I mean, in real life, I am not sure whether that journey was there. But it was a good example of how you can tell a story with all the facts being correct and still choose to make it more dramatic by making one character's journey be richer and more emotional."

On the subject of getting it right, the idea that the McMartins were innocent, Woods told me that certain influential people later brought up the idea that the film may have taken the wrong angle. "But," James continued, "very qualified people throughout that trial, and afterwards too, were very adamant that they were to some degree right about their positions. It was a very passionate trial and I don't

245

think many people involved with it will ever change their minds of their opinions. It was a brutal, dehumanizing experience for them. If I had to guess, you know, it felt like there was something odd in that situation, but some of the claims of the children were so absurd and these so called psychiatrists - as portrayed in the film - were so suspect according to the experts... I just don't know, but I can tell you one thing, there was a lot of passion in that case. And there still is, to this day. "

The very same year, Woods had a lighter supporting role in Jason Alexander's totally overlooked directorial effort, For Better or Worse (1995). Alexander himself stars as Michael, a down on his luck guy who attends help courses, despite not suffering from any addictions, all in a bid to gain acceptance. Whether it be Alcoholics Anonymous or Kleptomania, he spends his spare time receiving rounds of applause to boost his ailing confidence. He also obsessively paints endless portraits of the woman who left him, owes months of rent to his landlord, and has to tolerate his harsh mother. Woods turns up ten minutes in as his charismatic though admittedly chaotic brother, Reggie. Fresh from his wedding, he's wearing a glittery blue suit, strutting into his brother's apartment and telling him, once again, he needs his help. Alexander is then dragged into a farce, proving once and for all that his eccentric sibling can never be trusted. Reggie leaves his drunken bride with Michael and is ready to plot the robbery of his mother's workplace, the credit union.

For Better or Worse is one of the most obscure films Woods was a part of in the 1990's, and it is totally forgotten today. That said, anyone who does manage to track it down might be pleasantly surprised. Granted it is no classic, but despite the horrid reviews it's received over the years, I think it's genuinely funny. Woods eases himself into the Reggie role brilliantly, and convinces as the wise talking brother able to charm the mother he could well be later holding up at gun point. He is lovably sleazy, the kind of character a lot of us know; the man who disappears for a while and comes back, unannounced, with a brand new scheme that he promises will change his and your life forever. Woods and Alexander are funny throughout

Larceny, lust and lunacy.
No ordinary trip down the aisle.

and I admit to even liking the weird musical score (those a-capela voices take a while to shake out of your head).

"I love Jason," James said to me. "He's so sweet and so great. He knew my sense of humour too, so I loved that he let me do it. But then he put that soundtrack on, the music, and every single person said to him, 'Jason, those guys - I guess - are great, whatever, but they are not right for this movie. They kill the movie. The soundtrack kills this movie' Everybody told him that. But he insisted on it, and said he was gonna sink or swim with it. And unfortunately he did. But I think that with a different soundtrack it would have been a completely different movie. It was really funny, a kind of Seinfield-esque story, but it just had the wrong music! That said, Jason is a comedy genius."

Reviews were not kind, and Variety harshly led the way with their blunt criticism, writing: "Virtually nothing goes right in For Better or Worse, beginning with the plot and extending to performances, direction and comic pacing. Alexander gets points for rounding up such scene-stealers as Woods, Rip Torn, Joe Mantegna and Rob Reiner, but he squanders their talents."

There is another overlooked gem in this era, the 1996 Hallmark TV film, The Summer of Ben Tyler. The same year he was the oppressive white supremacist in Ghosts of Mississippi, he was the polar opposite as Temple Rayburn, a 1940's lawyer in the Deep South, who hires a mentally disabled young black man, Ben Tyler (Charles Mattocks), to be his housekeeper. The film points out the blatant racism of the era, but doesn't do so patronisingly. Rather than making Tyler a victim through and through, he is presented as a decent, honourable young man, and is played with dignity by Mattocks. Woods, in a Golden Globe nominated turn, is sturdy as the lawyer who must choose between his own good faith and the corruptive nature of the complacent yet judgemental society around him. Made after he had filmed Ghosts of Mississippi, in one interview Woods said he took the film to cleanse himself of playing the evil Beckwith.

"I did some great films with Hallmark," Woods told me, "who kind of wanted to change their image a little bit. And one of these films was The Summer of Ben Tyler, which was based on a true story. Because I played so many quirky parts, villains that had less cliché and more depth and breadth to them, it wasn't really a massive step to play, quote, a good guy; and by the way, in neither case am I making that judgement. When I play a villain I'm not saying, 'Here's the bag guy!' And when I play a decent man I'm not saying, 'Here's the good guy!' It's like, Let's see what they do. So with Ben Tyler, it was literally like, this will be a nice change to say the least. I can't tell you how many great characters I turned down because, you know, I just didn't wanna play another villain. There were a lot of roles where it was, like, enough already, I've done this before. Enough. Fuck."

It is indeed refreshing to see Woods playing such a decent man, and critics at the time of release also appreciated his work. Variety wrote: "A sumptuously produced gem of a film with a refreshing message of moral heroism, The Summer of Ben Tyler is as poignant, heart-warming and superbly acted as any of the 189 previous Hallmark Hall of Fame productions. The absence of guile and purity of soul that define Ben Tyler's humanity serve as the metaphor driving the film, a radiant reminder that doing the decent thing is rarely easy but always necessary. Robert Inman's sharply focused script shines like a beacon. Jan Scott's evocative design work and the seamless photography of Neil Roach and his team, on location in North Carolina, make for a visually captivating work. Tech credits are all first-rate. But none of it would matter if not for the straw stirring this drink: Woods. He has the uncanny ability to lose himself in a role so completely that he has grown as convincing a saint as he is a villain. And his chemistry with the understated (Elizabeth) McGovern is surprisingly strong and real."

Brilliantly made and acted, The Summer of Ben Tyler is another shining example of how effective and thought provoking TV once was. And Woods was at the forefront of what I would call this movement. This was high production value TV with morals, not preaching as such, but making one aware of the bigger world out there. Of this era, and Woods' work on the small screen, TV pundit Howard Rosenberg rightly wrote: "James Woods is rapidly becoming television's contemporary version of Jimmy Stewart—always the perfect choice for a story about an ordinary man facing an extraordinary moral dilemma."

And the Stewart comparison is valid. He was a crusader of truth and justice in much of his TV work, and very much had that Jimmy Stewart every-man quality. In other ways, he is like a modern Cagney, carrying the idea of saying your lines like you mean them and standing where you ought to stand. But the great thing about James Woods is that this is only half of the picture. To contrast this sturdy reliability is the feeling the man you see before you is on the edge, dangerous, and taking risks at all times. The mid 1990's, and the mix of parts he took on in this period, define his paradoxical brilliance.

GHOSTS OF MISSISSIPPI (1996)

When film writer Gavin Smith interviewed James Woods for Film Comment in early 1997, following the release of Ghosts of Mississippi, he preceded the Q and A with the following statement:

"Has Woods reconciled himself to the fact that people don't respond when he plays sensible, decent citizens like the husband in Immediate Family, but can't get enough of his fast-talking live wires, sardonic creeps, and too-tightly-wrapped intensoids? These are seldom the province of stars (Jack Nicholson excepted), so does that make Woods, indisputably a leading man, a character actor, not a star? In the last few years, Woods has delivered a series of memorable, scene-stealing supporting roles - The Specialist, Casino, and Nixon, a vigorous creative renewal after a period of career drift. His extraordinary evocation of Byron De La Beckwith, Medgar Evers's assassin in Ghosts of Mississippi, caps these achievements."

The true ability and range Woods has as an actor is in complete contrast to Smith's over simplified idea of his public image, that of a man who specialises in psychos, sociopaths and monsters. Watching his lesser seen and appreciated work as more sensitive men (the afore-mentioned Immediate Family for instance, or Joshua Then and Now, Jane's House and the later This Girl's Life) shows us that he is just as comfortable when under the skin of everyday people. Yet it cannot be denied that the public laps up his intense side. Why is this? Is it a case of morbid fascination? The fact they want Woods as the sleaze, the narcissist, the merciless psycho, because he does the things they secretly want to but would never dare? Or is it just because he's so damned good at tapping into the darkness of the human soul? After all, he is a man who became an actor to explore the human condition.

Yet there is a difference between an intense rascal like Richard Boyle and, say, a despicable killer like Greg Powell. And when we are discussing characters with no redeeming qualities at all, his performance in Ghosts of Mississippi is on a whole other level. The fact he was so adamant on playing such a part in the first place is worthy of respect, but to go all in the way he did, with no holds barred, puts the portrayal in its own category, even when we are talking about the more deplorable characters he's played.

Ghosts of Mississippi, directed by Rob Reiner, tells the true life tale of the murder of Civil Rights activist Medgar Evers, who was gunned down in front of his family on his own lawn by a lone gun man. The year was 1963 and this lone gun man was thought to be Byron De La Beckwith. Fast forward thirty years, and we are introduced to Bobby DeLaughter (Alec Baldwin), a lawyer who becomes interested in the case when Evers' widow Myrlie (Whoopi Goldberg) appears in the press once more to fight for justice. Taking on her case, Bobby uses all his strength to get Byron De La Beckwith back in court to face the judge. When he does appear, aged yet as arrogant as ever, he is unphased, lacking any empathy for the family who were robbed of a father and, it has to be said, rather proud of his actions - at least when not in court. In the courtroom however, this racist turns on the charm, insisting he is innocent and confident that he will leave a free man. Will justice be served, or will this monster walk free?

As is often the story when it comes to Woods' finest performances, he was not in the director's mind when the film was in pre-production. Hearing about the project, he was fascinated by the subject, and he wondered if there might be part for him somewhere. Not phased by the idea of playing a supporting role, Woods asked to see the script. Time and time again upon reading though, Woods couldn't get the Beckwith role out of his mind. When he went to meet Reiner, who was thrilled to have Woods on board, he told the director that he wanted to play Byron De La Beckwith. Reiner was adamant he wasn't the man for the part, that they were going for an older actor in his 70's. Woods however, was sure he could pull it off, and asked Reiner if he could read for him. James picked up the script and presented himself before Reiner and the casting director. Once Woods read as Byron, Reiner had no choice but to cast him.

And so Woods was cast as the infamous white supremacist. Heavily made up, save the opening scene when he guns down Evers, we are not merely watching James Woods in a role. He eerily becomes Beckwith, embodies him so well to a tee that it's chilling when he first appears in his make up, which to Woods' credit took four hours a day to apply. He changes his whole physicality for the role; his stance, his movements, his way of speaking and, most of all, his actual voice. The tones become aged, with that heavy Southern twang that sounds too authentic to be a mere imitation.

Woods puts in a fearless performance, unconcerned that everyone in the audience is going to hate him for what he's done. He gives Byron a level of arrogant superiority which makes you despise him. Though such a part is one that a true actor would relish, it must have also been a challenge to Woods' morals to embody such a horrible man. (Whoopi Goldberg said he was troubled by his dialogue during filming, and that she had to keep reminding him, "You're not that man!") But he achieves his goal, making Beckwith a believable monster, a morally bankrupt man who believes with all his heart that whites are a superior race.

Woods has several stand out moments, but perhaps the most famous, and the one that surely got him the Oscar nomination, is when he has the interaction with Bobby in the bathroom. Obnoxious to the point that you think the lawyer should smack him in the face, he calls him twisted for "turning on one of his own" and assumes, in all sincerity, that he's going to get away with what he's done. It's as if that as a white man it's his God given right to take out those he considers beneath him. It's a chilling scene and Woods plays it to perfection. Baldwin, confronted by this powerhouse display, can only react. He did refer to Woods in one interview as "the actor as terrorist."

And there was another classic Woods ad lib in the scene, just as he leaves the bathroom, lighting up a cigar. He told me: "One of the great anthems of the civil rights movement was the expression Free At Last, Praise God Almighty I'm Free At Last," Woods explained. "It's Dr King, and it was often said by the great Civil Rights Leaders. That wasn't in the scene. And in one of the takes it just hit me and I said, 'Free At Last.' And the idea of this monster adopting a slogan from the Civil Rights movement, while he is being trialled for the murder of a heroic Civil Rights hero, it is so cringe worthy. And I didn't know where it came from. But it was one of those moments of inspiration which I am very proud of, because it just shows how abominable a person like that is. The act itself is so inhuman that it is detestable, but the sociopathy of a person who would celebrate himself! And that is why I didn't wanna meet him, because he has that kind of ego. And when we were filming, Medgar Evers' children were actually in the jury, they played small parts in the movie. We all became friends. Lovely people, and very helpful to us too. Not only did they talk about what they felt as children - because they were there when their father was killed - but having them in the environment was so inspiring and reminded us how important it was to tell this story. And I love Whoopi Goldberg. She and I had been friends a long time. And I loved Alec, just wonderful to work with. I love those people, I think they are great. Just wonderful actors."

Woods also added in this poignant memory he had on the set: "We had a moment. At that time when we were making the movie, Myrlie Evers, Medgar's widow, was Head of the NAACP. So there I am with all the make up on filming a scene. I mean, the make up people, who were my choice, had done a phenomenal job. I asked Rob to use them. So Rob said to me, 'We're gonna have lunch, we're all gonna be there and we're gonna have Myrlie and her children.' And I believe that one of Dr King's children was also on the set. Anyway, it was a really big lunch. But I forgot about the make up. So I was walking, and as I walked in Myrlie was there and Rob said, 'This is James, he's playing Byron.' And she looks at me and her face just freezes. I said, 'Oh Gosh, Mrs Evers I'm so sorry!' And I remember her daughter Reena going, 'Mom, he's a great guy, he's one of us. Don't worry!' But all through lunch she couldn't get over it. She said, 'You look just like him.' The make up and costume people are great artists."

I tend to notice the details in Woods' performances, and one in particular with Beckwith sticks out. It's this horrible little clearing of the sinuses - not quite a full sniffle, but a small, almost nervous sound he makes, usually when lying or being particularly arrogant. "That was something he did once in some film I saw," Woods said. "I kind of co-opted it and turned it into something, like a signature part of the performance. That's a little actor's thing to do, a way to recognise the character."

Upon the film's release, Woods explained why he so desperately wanted to be a part of the film, and also to play the part of Byron De La Beckwith. It was important to him, after all, to make sure people knew the story and the name of Medgar Evers: "I wasn't the right age or whatever to play Bobby DeLaughter, but the one role I thought I could play was Byron De La Beckwith, as I told you, and I felt like if this story were told, somehow Medgar Evers' memory might be somehow enhanced in a way that was never appreciated so far in history. And when we were making the movie, I was standing in front of the Hinds County courthouse... And a 12-year-old black girl, like 11 or 12 years old, came up to me and asked for my autograph, and said, 'What movie are you making?' And I said, 'We're making a movie about the story of Medgar Evers.' And she looked at me and she said, 'Who's Medgar Evers?' And I thought, Maybe I did the right thing here. Maybe we all did. And I think my passion sort of baited the question she asked at that moment, and I hope when she sees this movie, she'll finally know."

He added that the role was "one of the most challenging parts I've ever encountered in my life. You know, it's like the Olympics degree of difficulty. I mean, this was, you know, a 3.5 off the high board, you know? He has a Southern accent, I don't. He's a racist, I'm clearly not. He's an old man, I'm a young man. His physicality is different from mine. I was going to have to play him young and old on alternate days, so I couldn't, you know, gain weight or lose weight. I had to do it all through pure acting, and it was the greatest acting challenge of my life."

I had read that Woods had been approached to see if he might want to meet Beckwith, and during one of our interviews, I raised this issue. "Well, when we were filming at the courthouse," James recalled, "the real Byron De La Beckwith was being kept at the infirmary part of the jail of the courthouse. He was upstairs and he was watching us film. The real guy! And he was just watching us film out on the street. And I could see him up in the window. There was a corrections officer there, a very lovely black lady - her skin colour being relevant to this story. She said to me, 'Mr Woods, Byron De La Beckwith is in custody here. He'd like to meet you.' So I said, 'Well please tell him I decline the invitation, because he means nothing to me.' She said, 'Oh you're my hero.' I'll never forget that and I said, 'Oh thank you, and you're my hero too.' We ended up being friendly and chatting. And she got it, she understood that I really felt giving him any sense of importance was a morally indigestible stance to take. I couldn't stomach it."

Woods was highly praised for his performance. He was nominated for the Oscar and the Golden Globe, but somehow didn't win. Reviewers complimented him on what was certainly a tour de force, even when they didn't like the picture as a whole. Roger Ebert for instance, who pointed out some faults with the movie itself, found Woods enthralling: "The movie's most convincing character is De La Beckwith, the old racist, who is made by that splendid actor James Woods into a vile, damaged man. Woods goes for broke. De La Beckwith has a shifty, squirmy hatefulness; being a racist is a source of great entertainment to him, and he expresses his ideas with glee. We detest the character from beginning to end, but we react to it..."

Variety went even further with the view that Woods was the film's saving grace. They wrote that its "one unarguable asset is Woods' excellent work as Beckwith, although it could be said that the performance is so good that it effectively undercuts the surrounding movie. As the only really human character on display, the wily old racist, whose irrepressible sense of humour results in some choice courtroom wisecracks, ends up more sympathetic than Reiner and his collaborators might have wished."

One important point came up when discussing this role with James. "When you ask me about the key to playing these evil characters," Woods said, "it is important to remember that they are the heroes of their own lives. And they may justify what they do." This is the way into playing evil in a real, believable manner, rather than as a hands-on-hips, beard stroking mastermind villain. Even though it sounds simple enough when trying to define the craft of playing bad guys, but putting this into action is much more difficult to achieve I am sure. Woods uses his intelligence, his quick wits and his intuition to craft accurate, believable portraits of evil; and, it must be added, in order to play good men too.

Woods also thanked the make up team for their stellar work. "I believe the make up helped me get the Oscar nomination. I really felt like an older man, this lunatic racist. But looking like that made it easier to embrace what he was like. I also had the video footage of him to go on. He ran for office! He was a fucking lunatic. The make up though really helps get you into the correct frame of mind."

Clearly, Reiner and his team put all their passion into this picture, and they definitely made it for the right reasons. But whether you like the film or not, go with its tone or find faults, one thing you cannot deny is the sheer power of Woods' performance. This is acting on another level, one of the bravest, boldest, most fearless and ego-less pieces of work I have ever seen. To play such a morally corrupt man, an evil man in fact, and not flinch away from the most hard truth is one thing, but to go all in the way Woods does as Beckwith is staggering to me. Even today, the performance has lost none of its power. It takes one back to the transformative days of Lon Chaney, where make up was applied to enhance the actor's feeling of the part in order to deliver a more authentic performance. It is valid to liken Woods to Cagney, even James Stewart at times, but there is also Chaney in this most shape shifting of roles, a man who is more horrifying than any horror film you might chance upon.

"I loved doing that movie," he told me, "and the story was one that needed to be told. It was a great and powerful, moving story."

1997: HERCULES, CONTACT AND KICKED IN THE HEAD

After his Oscar nominated turn in Ghosts of Mississippi, and indeed the similarly acclaimed performance in The Summer of Ben Tyler, Woods was cast in what at first seemed to be an uncharacteristic project, Disney's Hercules (1997). One of the best animated films ever made, the witty and smart comedy has Woods on top villainous form as Hades, lord of the underworld. He plots to overthrow Zeus, and the only man to stop him is the mighty Hercules, voiced by Tate Donovan.

The story of Woods' involvement makes for interesting reading. The studio had originally wanted Jack Nicholson for the part, but his demands (10 million dollars plus a 50 percent gross of Hades merchandise) proved too great. John Lithgow was then signed up, but when this casting didn't work out, and the team ran into difficulties with the original concept of Hades, Woods was called in and read for the part. It was, as Woods said, an amicable parting of the ways. A good friend of Lithgow's, James told me that there was nothing wrong with what Lithgow was doing with the role (Woods called him a wonderful man and a very fine actor during our interviews) but that the team were looking for a fresh idea. Impressed by Woods' improvisations, the film-makers were intrigued by what the new Hades could be. Originally a "spooky" character who spoke like a typical English villain (in the John Geilgud/Ralph Richardson classical mode), Woods made him a fast talking Hollywood agent type. For him, Hades was a schmoozer who had to schmooze. "I remember saying, 'What if he were just like some sleazy old time CAA agent.' Like, 'Hey how's it going?' I just took off. All of that stuff was ad-libbed in my audition and they all said, 'We love this, but getting it approved...' And later they came back and said, 'Jeffrey (Katzenberg, Disney head) likes it and said let's go for it.' And we went for it!"

Changing Hades from a lofty voiced English villain to a fast talking James Woods really was a massive leap, but once the team were OK'd and given the go ahead, Woods ran with it. As he worked on his dialogue, much of it ad-libbed, the animators began to mould Hades' physicality to suit Woods and the direction he was going in. He put his all into the role, and it shows from the finished movie. Nik Ranieri, the film's lead animator, said that Woods spoke so fast that one second of animation took two weeks to draw up.

During one of our interviews James gave me a fascinating insight into what it was like being a major part of a Disney movie in the glory years of the 1990's. "This was the way they did Disney movies back then. They didn't really pay the actors. The way they did it was, actors did the voice stuff and created the characters with the directors and the animators. I mean I worked on Hades for two years. You'd come in every month or so and they'd video you as you did the voice to get the way the actors moved. Nik was my animator, who'd just done The Lion King, he was the top, legendary Disney animator. He was doing my character. I had, like, 22 animators because my hair was flaming, and it took 8 animators to just do my hair. Hercules was the last pen and ink Disney movie. It was all drawn by hand, and they had what was called completion artists where they draw it and they close up the gaps. Then they put in the colours. So you do the voice. You don't even do it with the other actors. I didn't meet the other actors until the end. Susan Egen was terrific, just lovely, great. Danny DeVito, all wonderful actors. But you really just work on your own lines. It's strange how they do it, because you are really just working on your own."

One of Woods' personal favourite ad-libs is when Hades' hair blows out. He based the idea on the scene in Saturday Night Fever when John Travolta's father slaps his head and Travolta says, 'Hey watch the hair!' "So I said, 'What if my hair blows out and I'm like, 'Hey my hair!' And they just thought that was hilarious. So it ended up that the hair became a big deal and there were all these animators working on the hair! So all of this ad lib stuff, I can honestly say that half of the dialogue is mine. There is a lot of ad lib in that movie. But in fairness to the writers, it's done that way and again it's a testament to how great the really wonderful Hollywood writers are, and the Disney writers are just fantastic. Because you got to remember, every time you change something or ad lib something, it's just a shit load of animation. But we would come in and have a scene written, you'd get the idea of the scene, and we would do it as written a lot to get a feel of the scene. And then they would welcome us and say, 'OK, come on, do your James Woods thing.' And I would do all this crazy antic stuff. The way Robin Williams did Aladdin, that's the way we did Hades. And Robin - and I say Robin because he was a friend of mine, as he was to a lot of people in the business - the way he did Aladdin gave license to actors who worked that way. And not all actors are comfortable working that way with ad libs, but I was. And it was always a nice surprise for them, you know, with this guy who was always playing heavies, the bad guy in serious movies, and they would be - and I don't want this to sound obnoxious - surprised that I could be as funny as I was, quite frankly."

One thing James did find odd was the fact his character didn't have a song, and also the fact there was never even a suggestion of him having one. "It wasn't like, 'oh you can't sing' or anything, it wasn't one of those things, it just never came up. But one day someone mentioned it and I was like, 'Yeah, how come I never had a song?' I think they wanted him to be just a villain, so they went big villain. I was sort of the villain of the decade then. If you wanted a villain it was me. So they wanted a trademark villain."

Woods had been officially hired at the end of October 1995, and the film made it to theatres two years later. Once released, it received rave reviews and made over 250 million at the box office. Casting Woods had paid off. And from an artistic point of view, it's a triumphant feat of acting. From his first moment on screen ("I'm Hades, lord of the underworld", delivered in a laid back style) it's clear that this is going to be a bad guy like no other. Now, thanks to Woods' wild and exuberant portrayal, Hades stands as one of the greatest Disney villains ever. He gives it his all, bringing Hades to vivid life with sharp humour, sarcasm, cynicism and dark wit. He is intense, hilarious, frightening, highly expressive, multi faceted. For me, it's hard to think of a more memorable Disney bad guy. And credit to Woods, he is still committed to the Hades role to this day. Believing he has a responsibility to kids and Disney fans who expect Hades to sound like James Woods, he has reprised the role for computer games and even Disney World itself. And one cannot forget the Hercules animated TV series, which ran to great success shortly after the movie's release, where once again Woods voiced Hades and won himself an Emmy. "I did the series because my brother's kids were like 8 or something, and I mentioned they were doing the series, and they were like, 'Uncle Jimmy, you gotta do the series! Oh my God, you gotta do it!' And I ended up doing it for three years because the kids wanted me to do it. And I had a great time actually."

At the end of the day Woods is immensely proud of the Hades character, and his love for that role shines through. "It was one of those things, you did the Disney villain, you didn't get paid anything, but to be in the Disney pantheon as a major character is one of the hallmarks of anybody's career. It's like, what are the things you wanna do? One is always to win an Oscar. I mean, I didn't yearn for that so much as a younger actor, but one thing I always wanted to be was a Disney character. And a landmark Disney character. It's pretty great to be one of the biggest villains. And when it came out there were some extreme Christian groups that were, like, Here is a movie with what is basically a satanic character, the ruler of hell. So they had to take me off all the posters (laughs). I was on the early ones but then they kind of worked me off them. Crazy shit."

Hades is widely recognised as one of Disney's greatest bad guys. Cinemablend published a great article on movie-stealing Disney villains, and Hades was at the top of their list. They wrote: "In the 1997 Disney flick James Woods' Hades is the ruler of the underworld and brother to Herc's dad Zeus. As Greek mythology goes, Hades isn't fond of Zeus and Mount Olympus and spends the runtime of the animated film trying to kill his nephew and unleash the Titans. Hades is at his best when he's blowing up at his minions Pain and Panic, especially during the scene when he bursts into flames over them donning Hercules merchandise. Hades is an A-list Disney villain and that's the gospel truth!"

One thing I love about James Woods' career is the sheer variety of the films and performances. The same year he entertained millions of families in Hercules, he was a part of the wild and darkly funny indie comedy from director Matthew Harrison, Kicked in the Head (1997). The film concerns Kevin Corrigan as Redmond, a struggling writer without direction in his dead end life. As we follow him on his various misadventures, we meet his crazy Uncle Sam (Woods on brilliant form) and a sexy stewardess (Linda Fiorentino) who becomes the object of Redmond's affection.

Looking back on the experience of this funny little crazy movie, Woods was enthusiastic. "Yes I remember it very well," he said. "Marty Scorsese was the executive producer on the movie. He helped put the movie together. I go to work with Kevin (Corrigan), who I got to work with again later when I did Dice by the way. And I got to work with Burt Young again! Of course Burt and I had done Once Upon a Time in America together, and I got to machine gun Burt to death in that. That was nice (laughs). So we did Kicked in the Head down in the village. It was just really fun to do. That character was such a New York guy. I loved those guys who had what we called stingy brimmed hats. Those little pork pie hats. I just liked that character. You have to be in New York to know there are so many characters like that, these guys always hanging around at the off-track betting, kind of harmless guys always getting involved in some low level shenanigans. It was one of those movies that you do as an actor and you are absolutely certain nobody's ever gonna see it, but it was fun to do it. I probably did it for scale. It was one of those things; Marty Scorsese has asked if you will do this. It was one of those things. Like, are you kidding? Of course. The director was a nice guy. He and Kevin were good buddies, two guys just trying to make a small film. It was a nice little cast, very nice cast actually."

Sadly overlooked today, this is one of those typically anarchic independent films of the 1990's, which make one slightly nostalgic for that long gone age of filmmaking. Woods is wonderfully feral in this one.

Woods also had a supporting part in Robert Zemeckis' science fiction drama, Contact (1997). A huge budget, much-hyped film upon release, it's vital that at the heart of this expansive production is an intimate tale, about one young woman's love for a lost father and a need to connect, to have contact with something meaningful. In this case, it's Jodie Foster, who plays Dr Eleanor Arroway, a scientist who receives a signal believed to be from another planet. It's the most credible form of evidence of extra terrestrial life, only Eleanor, the very person who discovered the source, has to fight for her place in the mission to make first contact.

Contact is of epic scale, with numerous sets, awe-inspiring visuals, hundreds of extras, and brilliant special effects. Yet it's the cast that really get you involved in the tale. Special effects without a good script and committed actors are just not enough (as is proven by many modern blockbusters), but when the screenplay is tight and the cast the cream of the crop, then it's hard to lose.

Foster is brilliant as Eleanor, and we feel her excitement for the possibilities of what she's stumbled upon, as well as the pain of losing her father (played by David Morse). The mission, as exciting as it is, is filling a void, and Foster makes us genuinely feel for her. She is dedicated, likeable and believable. The supporting cast are just as effective too. Along the way she meets Palmer Joss, played by Matthew McConaughey, who later has a hand in ensuring she is chosen for the mission, and eccentric billionaire SR Hadden (John Hurt), who helps back her endeavours. James Woods is rock-like as Michael Kitz, head of the National Security Council.

When we came to Contact, I pointed out to James that when he did agree to appear in one of the bigger, more mainstream movies, they were always of the highest quality - Contact included. This is a huge film, let us not forget, but it's the actors who ensure the film's success. "Well," Woods began, "Bob Zemeckis had always wanted me to be in one of his movies. I was told that I had been offered Back to the

265

Future, and I know that Bob Hoskins and I both did camera tests for Roger Rabbit. My tests are out there somewhere. But there is an example - and I will be the first to admit when an acting choice is better than I might have been. I actually like Bob Hoskins better than myself for that movie. Firstly, he was a fantastic actor. And I thought he was right for it. And Zemeckis had also talked about me for the part of Lt. Dan in Forrest Gump, but my good friend Gary Sinise did a great job with that. So Bob Zemeckis was always one of my great benefactors in Hollywood, although I never got a chance to work with him until Contact. When he offered it I said, 'I'm taking it! Any part you offer me, I'm taking it!' I think he's a great guy, a phenomenal director, and I wanted to be in one of his movies no matter what! And it was great. I got to work with Jodie and we became lifelong friends. I just LOVE Jodie Foster. She's really funny to work with and brilliant of course. She's just so good. And the funny thing was, I was supposed to be the villain of the piece. The actors were like, 'Oh you're playing the bad guy.' And I was like, 'Well, maybe from the point of view from the character you're playing, but maybe not. We'll see.' Which was fine. The first time I saw Jodie she said, 'Oh, you're the asshole from the government guy!' And she laughed, and I said, 'Good to meet you too, I'm a big fan!' And she said, 'Me too, I'm just teasing.' And we immediately became friends, because she has my sense of humour. That fun ball-breaking as we call it. She's a wonderful person, just really one of my favourite people I've worked with. "

Woods then glowed with enthusiasm when he recalled the rest of the cast. "But just look at the cast! Angela Bassett was great. I loved working with Angela. There was Jodie, Matthew McConoughey. There were so many people in that. I mean, Tom Skerritt. I just love Tom Skerritt. First off, I've seen Alien about a hundred times. I think

266

he is just phenomenal. He is one of those guys who just seems so real. I think Contact had a lot of wonderful actors in it. It had David Morse, John Hurt, who was a wonderful actor. We were doing a scene once in Contact; Angela was in it, Jodie was in it, I was in it, Matthew was in it. We're all moving at the same time in a room and discussing what these signals could mean. And Bob had us rehearse the scene, and we were all so good I have to say (laughs). So we're doing the scene - a really complex scene with a lot of information and a lot of talk. And Bob was setting it up with Don Burgess. And he said, 'You know, there's a possibility that we could do this all in one take with no cutaways.' We all went, 'Yeah!' But he said, 'It's gotta be flawless and quick. I'm gonna shoot 40 or 50 takes to make sure it's flawless.' And that's what we did. I thought, Man, without this cast you just couldn't do this. It was a cast of really smart people, really prepared and just on top of it. We were able to work like a stage company, it was just so great. I said to Bob once, 'You know, this is such a complex movie for a mainstream movie.' And he said, 'Ssshhhh!' I said 'What?' And he said, 'Don't tell anybody but we're doing a 100 million dollar art film.' And the science was such a complex part of it, that its tensions were basically intellectual and political. So imagine any world altering event and the way people would react to it. Had we been contacted by alien beings, if there were actual proof of it, I can't imagine what the politicians would do with that."

And it is Woods in fact who has one of the most important scenes of the film. When Foster is in the pod of the machine that has been designed to help make contact, the signal is lost for a matter of seconds. In that time period, Foster claims to have been beamed to another planet, where she met a being in the form of her late father. When she "returns", her claims are disputed, mocked even by the authorities. It is Woods however, who reveals that though she was gone for only a matter of seconds, the device recorded half an hour of static. It's a subtle finale to a film that refreshingly ends in ambiguity, with Woods' thorough delivery enhancing the moment.

And as I should have suspected, this vital moment was a Woods addition. "When it came to the ending," Woods told me, "that was improvised on my part. And Bob said it finally explained everything, and made it clear that something had happened. It leaves the audience to infer that shenanigans had been covered up. So by doing it that way - and the arrogance of it - made it more like a conspiracy. So every suspicion you had has been confirmed. And Bob really liked that. So a lot of times when you improvise it can be a simple word or an attitude that really defines something in a really different way."

ANOTHER DAY IN PARADISE (1998)

One of the grittiest and most compelling crime movies of recent years (or any for that matter) is Larry Clark's Another Day in Paradise (1998), a hidden gem that harbours all that was good about the liberated world of indie cinema of the 1990's, but featuring none of the superficiality that often ensured movies of that era didn't age so well. Another Day in Paradise though, is a film that is in a league of its own. A mercilessly grimy and occasionally foul exploration of living the life of crime in modern America, it's a film that does not let up, never shies away from showing the truth of the dark underbelly of petty crime, of living day to day, shooting drugs and going after the next big score.

It stars James Woods and Melanie Griffith as two criminals, Mel and Sid, who take a young hedonistic couple under their wings. The sleazy foursome (with Vincent Kartheiser as the boyish Bobbie and Natasha Gregson Wagner as pixie haired junkie Rosie) begin to drive through America, getting into scrapes and pulling off increasingly risky jobs. As more drugs come into the mix, things get out of hand, especially when the crew mess up a particularly ill advised robbery, and ultimately proceedings head towards the tragic.

Another Day in Paradise was filmed through November 1997 to January of 98, with Woods on board as not only star but also one of the producers. His deal had been an advance plus half of the film's revenue. Looking for a great co-star, Woods thought right away of Melanie Griffith. He first had to convince Clark and the Another Day in Paradise team. "Larry thought she looked too pretty," Woods told me. "But when she does that scene where she puts the drug needle in her neck, believe me, I said, 'Does she look a little too pristine for you now Larry?'"

As going through the agents would have proven tricky, especially given the fact there was little money on the cards, Woods instead contacted Griffith directly. Desperately convincing her it was a great role that may even bag her an Oscar nomination, she agreed to take part on one condition; that she be given the same deal as James. Though he could not promise such a deal (naturally, it was impossible), he did split his salary and ownership in half with her, and eventually she agreed to sign up for the part. "You've got to make those kinds of decisions sometimes as an actor and producer," Woods told me, "and if the movie had been a big hit I would have cost myself some money. But I never expected it to be a big commercial hit, but I did expect it to be a critic's darling of a movie. And I liked being a producer; it was something very special to me."

The shoot was a troubled one according to reports, and there were tensions with Clark, who was apparently something of a nightmare during filming. When the shoot ended, it's been said that Clark was too out of his head on substances to finish the edit, and as he had final cut, this presented a problem. Eventually, a finished cut materialised, though Clark's initial 140 minute version, which featured a very graphic sex scene between the two younger actors, was later pulled. In the end, a re-edit was decided upon, resulting in the film which is now available on DVD. Even when it was released though, Clark began insisting that Woods had taken the film from him, when in fact he had saved it (after all, Clark was unfit to oversee a decent cut) and ensured the picture got a release. To Woods' credit, he didn't bite back. "We killed ourselves to allow him to make the film his way and he's saying I ruined his picture," Woods told the LA Times. "He was passed out drunk in the editing room and, as the producer, I could have had him thrown out. But I promised I wouldn't interfere. He got his final cut."

270

Speaking to me about his rift with Clark, Woods was clear form the start: "Look, Larry and I did not get along. You know, I didn't like him; I didn't like him morally, ethically, he was just not my cup of tea. I did a lot on that film that was, quite frankly, like directing. A lot of time he just wasn't there, so I'd say, 'Let's put he camera there and...' Look, I don't wanna get into a battle with Larry Clark, but it was a challenge making that movie. It was down and dirty, I will tell you that!"

In another interview Woods shed more light on his difficulties with Clark: "It's a great source of inspiration when you're making the movie, but at the same time you're working with people who are a little difficult to deal with to say the least. You know, the experience on this picture is crazier than a bag of rocks. It was all very tough in the making. But when all is said and done, and the warfare was engaged and met, we made a great picture and that's all that counts. I think it comes down to the fact that two incredibly strong egos, like Larry and myself, both had a real passion for the film. I won't deny Larry's passion and he won't deny mine. We both put a hell of a lot of blood, sweat, and tears into it, as a special one-of-a-kind document of a way of life that he knows intimately."

Given his freedom, Larry Clark (who made Kids just three years prior to Another Day in Paradise) directs the film with nervy edginess, keeping the viewer up close to the seedy shenanigans throughout. He does not shy away from the grit, that's for sure. The acting is tremendous too; Griffith and Woods are astoundingly good. They had worked together before of course, in 1975's Night Moves, but also in the third part of the 1990 TV movie, Women and Men: Stories of seduction (in a wonderfully put together adaptation of an Ernest Hemingway short story). Here though, we genuinely believe they've had a past together, and that they will go on to have a future,

271

however doomed it may be, after the film is over. When he punches her in the face at the end of the movie, and Bobbie escapes, it seals her fate. They are alone once more, Mel and his woman, and basically stuck together, trapped in this toxic hell that is their reality.

Speaking of the punch, Woods told me that hadn't actually been in the original script. "She had set the kid off and I knew it. So I said to Melanie, 'I gotta have your co-operation on this.' A movie slap, you know when you let a woman slap you and all that, it's OK, but a punch you're not gonna do. Some actresses say, 'If you're gonna slap me, you gotta really slap me.' But I say, 'Oh I dunno.' But some insist on it and you need to talk them out of it. You just don't wanna slap a girl. But I said to her, 'Look, we gotta do this right, we gotta make it look real. We need to choreograph this. I don't want to tell the director. I don't want to tell anybody. Here's where I'm gonna do it. And what I think you should do is, take the punch and not do anything. I want you to really take it like it's real, like a real hard punch, come back, look forward, and just be dead-eyed and don't say a word. You know it's coming, you know he's gonna do it, you know how he's gonna react, he may even kill you. But you're gonna let that kid go free, and you're gonna have to pay the price.' And I wanted to suggest that he wants to kill her, but he punches her and still wants her in his life. She knows she has no other life but him, and this is where we are, this burned out couple at the end of heir tether. And the great tragedy of this dark movie is that they are now chained to each other for the rest of their lives, chained to their crimes. It's actually a very powerful movie. I'm very proud of it."

But this is hyper-Woods at his best, in some ways carrying elements of Casino's Lester Diamond, in mannerisms and dress most of all. But he is a far more competent man and criminal than the pathetic pimp. Mel is different; though a junkie, he has a vision and knows how to carry it through. Afraid of old age, he promises he will drive his car off a cliff when he is sixty. Anything, even death, is better than getting old. This said, as Woods saw the character too, Mel is not a psycho or a sociopath. He's actually OK when things are going well, and is charming, genuinely well meaning. "Mel is a pro, and pros can do a good job if they don't get too involved in things they know are too bad for them," Woods later said in an interview. He is, then, a functioning addict.

Woods has some terrific scenes throughout the picture. Near the beginning he sends Griffith and Wagner into a clothing store to get them both fitted out in new wardrobes. Waiting in the car, Woods sees the sales assistants come out with armfuls of clothes in paper bags. His face says it all. He knows it's going to set him back a few dollars. "Really," he says in all seriousness, "did it cost a lot?" It's darkly funny that, even though he is a serious criminal and quite a dangerous hedonist, he is still concerned about how much the missus is spending on clothes. For that one moment, he is almost the regular domesticated man, cringing at the price of expenses. Immediately though, we remember what he really is and the film carries on.

I raised this scene to James and the memory of it made him chuckle. "Yeah," he said, "because that again is part of the theory that criminals have to live everyday lives. You know, it's like, what are you gonna do when you hold a baby? What will you do when the wife comes home and she's spent too much? I think that was improved, all that stuff. Well, it sounds like me anyway."

A particularly good moment is when Mel and Bobbie arrange a drug deal with two youths in a sleazy motel. Woods is frighteningly intense here, playing with the boys with ease and actually enjoying himself in the process, drawing out two handguns like he's John Wayne before sending the lads on their way. The way he puts the guns away and reclines back on the sofa, resuming small talk with them, is a fine detail that highlights the fact that this is another day at the office... another day in paradise indeed. When the next drug deal goes wrong, and Mel takes a bullet in the shoulder, things begin to change. The reality of the lifestyle hits us in the face. The true ugliness of crime is defined in this one scene alone, and then everything that follows shows the decline. The dream is over, the gloss has worn off.

When we finally see what Woods/Mel is capable of, it's frightening. The major heist, as feared, goes horribly wrong, and Woods ends up killing two people who are in their way. He didn't really have to murder them, but they are disposed of just in case. The way he does slay them, while apologising under his breath, is performed so cold-bloodedly that one gets chills. His subsequent meltdown in the car when fleeing the scene is for me one of his finest moments; it's pure rage and pure panic together in a hysterical mix, a moment of realisation that he's gone too far, he's fucked up bad and it may cost him his life. The desperation comes exploding off the screen.

I brought this scene up to James and he recalled the filming of it: "I have to say, we disagreed on how to frame it. On that one, we ended up shooting all different versions. I did it like twenty times, it was a fucking nightmare. So Larry wanted to come in close and show it, and on that one I think he was right. But then there was a wider shot that I also liked, but the bottom line is you got to get as much coverage as you can on everything."

"What I love about that movie," Woods continued, "is that we all smoke all of the time. And always drinking and always shooting up and everything. Because that's what that was like in the seventies. Larry did a book of his photography of that culture. He was a cutting edge photographer. They are very powerful photographs."

274

I believe that Another Day in Paradise captures drug addiction more authentically than many other films, because it does not sensationalise or make it a thing of true horror. That's not to say it glorifies drugs. On the contrary, the drug pushing is a part of the addict's day, and here it's done in a straight forward way that is so casual it's scary, and perhaps more chilling than if it were hyped up as some fatalistic act with atmospheric music on the soundtrack as the needle goes in. They chat while shooting up, inject it as one might make a cup of coffee. Drugs are all an addict thinks about, and their whole day revolves around them. But as the addicts in Another Day in Paradise can afford their addiction, there is no sense of shaky desperation. They have the money, they have the drugs, and life goes on this way. It is, however, as one sees in the movie, an absolutely exhausting way of life.

Woods also told me about how they got the legendary singer Clarence Carter to appear during the nightclub scene. When he arrived with his wife and lady-agent, it was made clear that Carter required a three room suite, one for himself, one containing his wife, the other for his lady friend, and three sets of keys - but also the requirement that all three rooms were accessible to the other. "He walked it like he talked it," James said with a chuckle. "I loved his music, one of the great soul musicians. And we went out that night for the club sequence, with the I'm Looking For a Fox song. We shot that scene all night. And Clarence Carter got up there and played all night. He even played on the breaks. 'You all want another song?' It was like, 'Fuck yes!' We worked all night at the Ambassador Hotel, where Bobby Kennedy was shot, we used that as a location. We just had a personal Clarence Carter concert all night. Everybody was dancing, even Larry Clark was dancing. We shot some great stuff. That night we improvised a lot of stuff."

Speaking of the film in a 1999 interview, Woods expressed his fondness for the whole venture. "It's not the kind of movie you see very often," he said. "It's always the off-beat movies that I love. Just from an acting and producing point of view, it's so rewarding to be involved with something where you're surprised every day by the kind of work you're doing. You're going to places rarely approached in the usual Hollywood film, which are usually so predetermined in how they're going to look and how they're going to be shot. You might do great work (as an actor) but it's kind of trapped in the predictability of the coverage, a kind of feral thing neutralized by the same old camera angles. I know every shot a director's going to make in a big commercial film. I'm usually way ahead of him. But here, with Another Day in Paradise, with a free-wheeling documentary kind of feel...."

Though the film was not a box office hit, it did attract the kind of critical praise Woods thought it would. And when one considers what else was coming out and getting shoved in our faces in 1998, it's no surprise the film was not a smash success; how could it have been, really, in a year that saw the release of such blockbuster monstrosities as Armageddon and Godzilla? Still, reviewers were impressed.

Roger Ebert wrote: "What brings the movie its special quality is the work of James Woods and Melanie Griffith... A movie like this reminds me of what movie stars are for. Those who we like, we follow. James Woods is almost always interesting and often much more than that."

The Guardian loved the film too, preceding their review with the statement: "James Woods appeared to be mellowing. But Larry Clark's new film Another Day in Paradise sees him returning to his disreputable, antisocial best." Though they were perhaps over simplifying Woods' journey as an actor, they raised some interesting points. "Woods has spent his whole career playing crazy cops, mad criminals, racists, gonzo journalists, driven anti-social and unsociable types, foul-mouthed human time-bombs ready to explode," they continued. "He has no competition for the title of the cinema's least ingratiating leading man. Earlier this year, it seemed as if Woods might be mellowing a little when he played Clint Eastwood's supportive editor in True Crime, but that was only because his humour and buried humanity got a little nearer the surface than usual. In Larry Clark's Another Day in Paradise, which Woods also co-produced, he's at his most low-down, dangerous and volatile."

When I spoke with James about this movie, I got the impression that it was one of his favourites. Even though the experience had its ups and downs, he is clearly proud of the film. "That film felt like we were real criminals, real drug addicts. That movie felt so real, I cannot even tell you."

He praised Melanie Griffith, but also added a funny detail. When he received his star on the Hollywood Walk of Fame later, Griffith and John Carpenter were the two speakers. Griffith had described what it was like to work with Woods: "Working with James Woods is kind of like being pregnant. In the beginning you're amazed you're gonna have this baby or gonna be working with Jimmy Woods. In the middle you're doing it and by the end you can't wait it to be over!"

"I don't know how we got that movie made," Woods said with a laugh, "but somehow we did it. But believe me... Larry is an addict. He has no bones about it, he's been an addict all his life. He got clean, he got back on, he got clean, and he's open about it. You know, I don't know where he is now, what stage he's at now in his life. But he's made movies about it. He's made movies about his life. I don't know man, there are people who have sort of colourful lives, directors or writers, and, you know, they're great. But then there are people who are genuinely from those worlds and they are completely different and look completely different, when you see them on film and when you portray their lives. There is no messing around. I mean, criminals who've written books have an authenticity about their writing that you just can't match. Another Day in Paradise though, was a mosh pit. All we did was fucking argue. I don't know how me and Larry didn't end up beating the shit out of each other. We just did not like each other and we did not get along."

This thread led me and Woods to talking about how the tension between them helped create good art. "But, you know, I have to give him credit that he did pick shots and shape scenes in editing, where I wanted it one way and he wanted it another, and then in the editing he did it my way. I did not go in the editing room, even as a producer because I think that is the director's space. I disagreed with some of the editing and I still do. But whatever happens on the set happens, and you get through it. But when the editing comes down, it's a director's province, especially a writer-director like Larry, who's writing about personal experiences he had. You got to let that be his final say. And sometimes that kind of turbulence leads to great movie making."

Another Day in Paradise is one of the most enthralling crime flicks I have ever seen, and I hope that one day it starts to build up more of an appreciative following.

JOHN CARPENTER'S VAMPIRES (1998)

As good as he is when in supporting mode, whenever Woods gets his chance at a leading role, he dives in head on, and you realise he's also one of the great leading men of the past fifty years. And he is at his charismatic best in John Carpenter's Vampires (1998), a darkly funny and gruesome horror flick from one of the genre's true masters. Woods plays vampire hunter Jack Crow, who tours America with his team of vampire killers clearing the land of fanged scum. Thomas Ian Griffith plays Valek, a powerful vampire who is hoping to get his hands on an ancient cross which will give him extreme power. He appears out of nowhere and wipes out most of Crow's team, and then sets out on his single minded crusade for world domination. It is up to Crow and his right hand man, Tony (Daniel Baldwin), to stop him.

Vampires is a very entertaining film, brilliantly guided by Carpenter and wonderfully played by the top cast. Credit goes to Sheryl Lee as Katrina, a prostitute with a psychic link to Valek after he bites her, but in many ways it's Woods' show, who makes for a perfect anti-hero, jamming stakes into vampiric hearts and coming out with quotable quips. That said, Woods is perhaps most effective here when he is at his bluntest. Never did I dream I would derive so much satisfaction from a man shouting "Fucking die!" while impaling a mutant bloodsucker. But the key to Woods' performance, a movie star tour de force in my view, is the fact he doesn't ham it up. Indeed, the picture is full of the kind of situations which in lesser actors would inspire overplaying. He plays it cool, acting like it's another day at the office, even when harpooning vampires and dragging them into the sunlight where they subsequently explode into flames.

The script itself had been kicking around since the early 1990's, and in its earliest stage was a proposed vehicle for Dolph Lundgren.

When Carpenter read the script and the original book by John Steakley, he saw it as a kind of mutated western. He recalled: "I went into my office and thought, It's going to be set in the American south west and it's a western – Howard Hawks. The story is set up like a western. It's about killers for hire. They're a western cliché. In this movie they're paid to kill vampires."

James Woods and John Carpenter during the filming of Vampires (1998).

He had a view of casting Alec Baldwin as the sidekick, but when Alec said he wasn't available, he pointed Carpenter toward his very capable brother, Daniel. For the role of Crow, Carpenter had toyed with a few actors, among them Bill Paxton and one of his usual go-to guys, Kurt Russell. In the end though, he cast Woods, insistent that he didn't want Crow to be a typical, muscular action movie hero. To Carpenter, Woods was likely to be "as savage as the prey he's after, a guy who's just as menacing as the vampires. James Woods is the kind of guy you'd believe could and would chew off the leg of a vampire."

For Woods, I am sure working with an auteur like Carpenter was a no-brainer. On his Twitter account, Woods described the director as "a cynical gun-slinger with a film vocabulary all his own." He also added that it was maybe the most fun he had ever had on a movie. And it shows, for Woods relishes his role of action hero, a character who should be larger than life but is somehow made grounded and grittily realistic.

Speaking to me directly about working with Carpenter, I asked Woods if he had been an admirer before working with the auteur of horror:

 "Oh yeah! I was always a John Carpenter fan. Look, John Carpenter is one of those guys that if you're a successful actor, a dedicated actor and a career actor, you wanna work with John Carpenter, of course! And then I ended up just loving the guy and having the best time doing that movie. You have to accept that he tells stories - and I say this with ultimate affection and admiration - with a certain corny kind of way that just works wonderfully for his fans, of which I am definitely one."

James continued: "I remember we were doing some scene with Tim Guinee, who plays the padre, and we're in the air, in the midst of the vampire battle. And I'd been dragged and shot at and had arrows thrown at me, and John Carpenter said, 'You know something? I never would have guessed it, but you're actually an action hero. Why haven't you done more of this?' And I said, 'Because no one is as smart as you John. That's why.'"

On this very subject, I raised the point that Woods was such a natural mainstream action hero in Vampires, it really is strange that he hadn't done this type of role before. "The thing is," he said, "you know with this kind of thing you are going to have to ham it up a little in a John Carpenter movie. And when I say ham it up, I don't mean you try to be a bad actor, I don't mean that. I mean you are going to employ clichés and try to make them fun again. I would say to John everyday... You know, I'd have the cigar, the sunglasses, the skinny jeans, the leather jacket and all this stuff. And I would say, 'Remember John, every cliché was a good idea once along time ago. So let's bring it back!' So every day we would do something that was kind of a movie cliché, and try to spruce it up a little bit. I mean, it's really The Wild Bunch, that's what it is. The Wild Bunch with Vampires! And how can you go wrong doing a Sam Peckinpah/John Carpenter combination crusader movie? I mean, it was just so much fun doing a western with modern weapons and a crossbow! I mean, the crossbow they use in The Walking Dead, they got that from us buddy."

Vampires was a decent sized hit at the time, and now has a healthy cult following. Twenty years after its release, many websites and blogs celebrated the anniversary of Carpenter and Woods' collaboration. Nightmare on Film Street wrote in their brilliant piece: "James Woods gives an amazing performance as Jack Crow, emphasized by the freedom he was given with the role. He plays the foul-mouthed, vengeful leader effortlessly. Vampires is still killing it, 20 years later. Though it isn't the most genre defining film of its kind – it doesn't need to be. What is important is that Vampires is fun. It took risks crossing genres and breaking from previously established norms. It brought us vampires that think and act like the superior predators they are instead of just arrogant aristocrats. Twenty years later, Vampires is still an important entry in the ever-growing list of vampire films."

One thing I always loved about Vampires is the way Woods, Baldwin and the others go in and exterminate the vampires as if they are vermin. "Yeah," Woods said, "and we do it like, 'Hey we got another nest, let's get in there and clean it out.' Everyone goes in and does their job. Then the slaughter in the motel room shows that they might not have enough tools against the enemy."

Then James came to one of the film's most famous scenes, and certainly the most extravagant; the one where he blows up the motel upon disposing of all the corpses after the mass slaughter. "They built that entire motel, that was a set. So John said to me, 'You're gonna go in there, you're gonna drop the lighter on to the floor.' So I said, 'OK, so I'm gonna pretend to... And he said, 'No we're gonna see you do it. We have ten cameras and we're gonna blow this whole fucking thing up. No matter what happens, if you don't die in this thing, just keep playing the scene. If you get knocked over, get up. Just keep playing the scene.' So I go, 'So let me get this straight. I'm gonna be in there with all these primed barrels of gasoline?' And there were, like, fifty of them. So that explosion was uncut. You will see cuts in the scene from other cameras, but I was in there with the gasoline. It was primed with explosives. I said, 'What if someone makes a mistake?' He said, 'Then you are gonna die, but we don't make mistakes.' So we did it, no rehearsal. So when I walk out of there, people say, 'Oh you flinched!' And I say, 'OK, I flinched, but just a little, and here's why! I almost got knocked over by the explosion. I was literally knocked forward by the heat wave. They blew the entire place in one take! All at once! I still have nightmares about standing in there, smelling the gasoline and clicking the fucking lighter, dropping it on the floor and walking out. He said, 'We're gonna give you ear plugs, because it's gonna be loud!' Oh My God! And you have to try and look cool too. And I have to say, you know, I thought, 'I'm bad, I'm pretty cool.' But they never stopped the cameras."

Risking your life for a good shot; now that's dedication.

THE VIRGIN SUICIDES (1999)

The following year proved to be one of the most interesting in Woods' career, and he was to appear in four key films of the late 1990's, all supporting roles that were actually more important than they seemed. In each part he displayed his wide range, playing a mix of subtle, condensed men and hyper-Woods firecrackers. In each of the following films however, though all being small roles, it is impossible to imagine each movies without him. This is the art of the supporting player at its finest.

The first was The Virgin Suicides (1999), well and truly one of the greatest films of the 1990's. Sofia Coppola's startling drama tells the mysterious story of one family and the five daughters who, in early seventies suburbia, all take their own lives. Coppola is clear that what is important here is the "unfathomable nature" of the story, and she conjures strange, eerie feelings by tingeing it all with an air of hazy nostalgia.

The girls are brilliantly portrayed by the young actresses, but credit must also go to Kathleen Turner who is brilliant as the mother, and Woods as the mild mannered, decent father. It's a subtle, wonderfully well observed effort, and certainly one of the most unassuming men he has ever played. This is a side of Woods we have rarely seen before. Yes, he had played conventional men, decent fathers, but here he is so mild, so buttoned up, so conservative and utterly without menace. We believe he is the meek dad one hundred percent, and there is nothing unconvincing about his performance. Woods himself saw the man as a "lost soul" living with a domineering wife. He is, at the end of the day, a rather curious man too, a quiet fellow with his own odd little hobbies and interests.

Coppola holds the whole thing together, revealing herself to be a master of mood and atmosphere while overseeing this disturbing but compelling study of the mysteries of youth. The music, by Air, also contributes to the film's enigmatic mystery, but ultimately it feels like a tragedy, but the kind of tragedy it seems that no one could have stopped from happening, especially not the father Woods plays.

Speaking to Charlie Rose just as the film was to be released, Woods said "The Virgin Suicides is a really lovely little picture that was from a wonderful book that Sofia Coppola had adapted and directed, and it was for me a great experience, playing a very different kind of character. And I really thought it brought up a kind of important subject, in an odd sort of way -- I mean, a truly lovely, artistic sort of way. And it brought up the issue of teenage suicide, but not in a typical kind of, 'Eat your vegetables, they're good for you,' you know, but, 'Let's examine this horrible issue kind of way, but in an almost nostalgic view of what the 70's were really like, if you lived out in the suburbs,' and so on. And then without defining why, you know, these five beautiful young girls end up finally, you know, doing the horrible thing that many teenagers still do, which is killing themselves. And it's a pretty compelling film."

Sofia Coppola said that Woods was one of the first people to sign up for the film, and showed his loyal support early on. "He has this loveable side that you don't see in movies. I didn't know him, at all, but I had seen him speaking at some thing and he had this funny, charismatic side. Then he read the script and I starting talking to him, and he really got it. He was like, 'Look, I want to help you get this movie made, whatever I can do.'"

Woods mentioned to me that he thought Sofia fought for him in the movie in a similar way her father had with Al Pacino in The Godfather; that she saw something in him that was right for this character. Woods himself said he was always more of a firebrand, an energetic type, so he asked Sofia why she thought he was right for the unassuming father. "Because I think you're a great actor," she replied - which is a good answer, and just what an actor needs to hear from his director.

It's a fact that without Woods the film wouldn't have got financed, but Woods wasn't just in this for a favour. He genuinely loved the script and really wanted to be a part of it. His agent told him that if he did this film they would fire him as a client. Woods did not back down though, for he believed so strongly in the script. He told me: "I knew she was gonna be a great director. She was chasing me around town and she'd show up at restaurants. Finally I said, 'I'm doing it.' And I was gonna be doing The General's Daughter and my wonderful friend, Mace Neufeld, who was the producer of that movie, said, 'The films overlap, you can't do that movie.' I called him and said, 'Look, I really wanna do this little film.' And he said, 'Listen, let me see what I can do.' And he convinced Paramount to change the schedule, which cost them almost $100,000, to give me the opportunity to make The Virgin Suicides. Now that's a producer. And he stayed my friend for life because of that. No one could ever say a bad word about that wonderful man to me."

Woods spoke to me at length about life on the set of The Virgin Suicides: "We did an improvisation. Sofia said, 'We're gonna sit around today in the house, and we are gonna interact as a family, improvise all day.' So Kathleen was doing her thing, the busy body with her daughters, controlling them. I mean, she was truly brilliant in that part, I don't think people realise how good she was. I thought she was brilliant, just fantastic. So I just decided to sleep through the whole thing (the improvisation). I put my head back and went to sleep. And Kathleen said, 'What the hell are you doing?' I said, 'I'm doing what the character would do. He's so happy to be in his chair with his family around him, he's got the sound down, he's watching the baseball game and he falls asleep. So he falls asleep to the symphony of cackling women. I'm not saying this, but the character would feel this way.' Then of course we found a way to get him into the mix. If we set him up that way and his first daughter commits suicide, all of a sudden it's incredibly powerful."

James and I also discussed the famous scene when, after the first daughter's death, the family turn up at the cemetery, where the workers are on strike (I must note, I found it was always the scene that moved me the most). "So we turn up at the cemetery," Woods told me, "and they are blocking people at the cemetery, because of the strike... You know, that great scene when he gets out of the car. There was actually a scene of dialogue, where he explains, 'My daughter committed suicide' and so on. And Sofia said, 'What would you think if I had the camera in the car, we see them out there, we see you get out of the car, we see you talking to them, they take a long pause, listen, and then turn and open the gates.' And I said, 'So, not cover it outside and forget the whole scene?' And she goes, 'Yeah.' I said, 'I think it's brilliant.' Now you don't often get actors who say, 'You know, cut all my lines from it.' I said to her, 'There is nothing you can write - and she's a wonderful, Academy Award winning writer - but there is nothing you could write that will be as powerful as what people can see in our hearts as they watch that scene.' I mean, we know what happened, we don't need to hear it."

Woods elaborated further on his experience with Sofia: "So we had a scene where we cut all the lines, then I had a scene where I had no lines, the one in the basement with the boys and the little boy who has Down's Syndrome. It's the night of the first suicide. So Sofia said, 'What could you be doing here?' I said, 'You know, he's got these model planes'. How about I start talking to the boys about these planes and how to do them?' You know, and they all leave one at a time because they are so bored. She said, 'Great idea!' So now I do something where I improvised an entire scene and have lines that I didn't have in the script. So that's the process when you work with a wonderful director, especially an auteur like Sofia, who I just think is brilliant. I just loved working with her and we laughed all the time. When we finished filming she gave me an award. It had a little metal base with a can of ham on it. All the girls were there and they all applauded, and I got my ham. You know, being a ham is being a big show off actor, so it was really funny. To this day I laugh at that."

Oliver Stone, Cameron Diaz and James Woods during the making of
Any Given Sunday (1999). Photo courtesy of James Woods.

ANY GIVEN SUNDAY (1999)

Then, for the third time, he was directed once again by Oliver Stone in the engaging American football drama, Any Given Sunday (1999). Woods found himself in an all star cast, which included Al Pacino, Cameron Diaz and Jamie Foxx. This character-driven film takes us inside the running of a fictional team, the Miami Sharks, but is more of an exploration into the corruptive nature of the sports industry.

Stone actually combined two scripts to make Any Given Sunday, one an adaptation from Robert Juizenga's book, the other a screenplay by John Logan. Stone saw parallels with his battles in Hollywood with the ones had on the field and behind the scenes of the sporting world. Speaking to Entertainment, he recalled: "In the 90's, Hollywood was becoming more and more corporate, and so was football; sports just became a giant and almost ridiculously out-sized industry. The salaries are enormously inflated and lose meaning for most people. I felt like football is not just about now, there's a tradition; people play for money, but there's something else going on."

He also recalled, predictably enough, that the sport establishment did not welcome his warts and all exposé with open arms. "The NFL was very nasty. They hated the script. They tried to kill the deal by telling players not to be involved. We barely got the stadiums. [Cowboys owner] Jerry Jones helped by telling them to f— off and giving us Texas Stadium. It was a fight all the way. And then when the film came out, the NFL went out of its way to completely black ball us. There was no coverage from the sports shows. It was not fun to fight them, it's like fighting the Pentagon."

Stone, by then already a film-making legend, had gone through various stylistic shifts since Salvador and really evolved as a dramatist and cinematic force. In his political epics, namely JFK and Nixon, the mood was fast cutting, multi-layered and often dazzling. In this and his previous film, U Turn, he opted for shaky, often extreme close shots, to heighten the viewer's disorientation. Any Given Sunday, a complex film in its construction and presentation, is handled with expertise by Stone. The match sequences are breathtaking, while the action away from the field is just as enthralling. Stone's directorial guidance aside, the cast are great. Pacino is Tony D'Amato, the head coach of the Sharks who is so committed to the team that his private life has suffered for it; Cameron Diaz is the owner of the team having inherited it from her late father; and James Woods is Dr Mandrake, the team's physician, a juicy role he really gets his teeth into.

His first appearance during the opening game tells you everything you need to know about Mandrake. When one of the players is genuinely injured, writhing in agony on the ground, Woods bends down and tells him he can get up now, because they've gone to a commercial. In another scene we see he's a player with the women. After flirting with a particular cheerleader earlier in the picture, he is later seen leaving the stadium with a woman who is apparently his steady girlfriend, arm in arm with her. "Who's Courtney?" she asks him. "How should I know who Courtney is?" he replies. "You gonna start this shit already?" This one line defines him, a man who Woods saw as a "rock star medic".

Yet his best scene is when - spoiler alert - he is let go by Tony for his unethical methods. Woods and Pacino go face to face, their conviction and fire utterly electric. Woods, a man who'd faced De Niro in his prime, here proves that he belongs up there with the recognised greats. His speech defines the film in fact. "Who am I," he says, "to defy men their dreams?" He says they are warriors, gladiators, a rousing speech captured by the media's cameras. When he tells Courtney to come with him, she refuses. "OK," he says, "you stay here and get fucked by 12 Neanderthals." His exit from the film is fabulous and explosive, and for me is one of the movie's most poignant sequences.

Woods told me in one of our interviews that this (the Neanderthal line) was another ad-lib: as I should have guessed, as it's been a favourite Woods quote of mine since I first saw the film twenty or so years ago. James said that Oliver immediately howled with laughter after he uttered the line. "Oliver!" Woods cried, thinking the take was ruined. Thankfully, they managed to erase the sound of Stone's raucous laughter and Woods' ad-lib remained intact.

Once again, Woods had room to breathe in his role and was given the opportunity to improvise. He later said: "A lot of what we did was improvisational. I said to Oliver, Hey, every time you cut away to me on the sideline, have me flirting with one of the cheerleaders... I have never in my life laughed that much. I mean, if you could imagine this group of guys, the shit that L.T. would give to Jim Brown, in a fun way. Dennis Quaid and I would be crying laughing. You hardly ever are privy to two of the greatest athletes that ever lived, just shucking and jiving each other all fucking day, every day."

The original cut of Any Given Sunday was much longer, and sadly some of the scenes that hit the cutting room floor featured Woods. One of these I do believe really should have stayed in the picture; it features Woods and Modine, tuxedoed and taking a stroll together. They go through their opposing views of the sport, Woods the no-nonsense doctor who prefers to let the guys get on with what they do, Modine being more hands-on and concerned about the physical and psychological effects the game has on them. Woods has the great lines here: "They have four years to make their fortunes and that's it.

293

It's a short life but it's a glorious one. As long as you don't mess with their minds!" The clashes that erupt between the pair later, when Modine replaces Woods, would have made more sense had this scene made the final cut. It's a shame it was snipped for other reasons too, because Woods acts it with real gusto. "This is a spectacle of warriors!" he shouts with passion.

"I really enjoyed working with Jimmy on Any Given Sunday," Oliver Stone told me. "He brought such a different note to the character of the doctor. Watching him with Al Pacino was a delight. Jimmy was a true star and a half. He was the best back up you'd ever want for a leading man. I mean, it was a very scripted movie, but on the scene when he was fired, when him and Al are shouting at each other... No one shouts like Jimmy. But I think he came up with some humdingers." I reminded Oliver of the Neanderthal line, which made him chuckle. "Oh yes, get anally fucked! Yes, he is very good on the insults. Him and Cameron Diaz had a great relationship with each other too, joking around. But he is a great ad libber. A great actor and a great friend."

Any Given Sunday was a critical and box office success and hasn't aged a bit in the twenty odd years since its release. Like much of Stone's work, it uncovers a rotten truth about a world where profit is king, and people, in this case muscle bound modern day gladiators, are used as pawns for the games of the filthy rich.

THE GENERAL'S DAUGHTER (1999)

In that same year, James also had a key role in Simon West's slick, masterful thriller, The General's Daughter. The movie stars John Travolta as Paul Brenner, an undercover Chief Warrant Officer who, after wiping out a scheme by an underground freedom fighter (for which he adopts a nifty Southern accent which he abruptly drops once no longer undercover), finds himself in the midst of a grisly murder; that of Elisabeth Campbell, the commanding general's daughter. Alongside Madeline Stowe (a rape specialist and ex-girlfriend), Brenner begins to investigate the killing and hopes to get to the bottom of a case which takes him closer to the higher ranks than he might have thought.

Travolta puts in a sturdy effort, as brilliant as ever as Brenner, while he is aided by a top supporting cast; James Cromwell is excellent as the general, while Timothy Hutton and Stowe are also strong. But it's Woods who has the most curious part here. He is Colonel Moore, a close friend of Elisabeth and, for a short time at least, a key suspect in the murder case. As written, the Moore part may have been more straight forward. He is a man who comes across as strange, someone definitely keeping a secret. His caginess could be interpreted as guilt, and proof that he is the man behind the murder. But the truth is (spoiler alert) Moore is gay, and if one is picking up on odd behaviour, it's in the fact he is concealing his sexuality.

For Woods, doing the part was a certainty. Firstly, he had known Travolta for years; in the seventies they had done a table reading of a play and also appeared together in an episode of Welcome Back, Kotter. Twenty odd years later, in comes the script for The General's Daughter which will reunite him with Travolta. "So I was offered the part and I thought it was great," Woods told me. "A terrific script. And he's gay, this guy, but not overtly gay. And you have to remember, this is before gay characters were that prominent in movies. So the reveal that the character was gay in the military, and he was a big officer and so on, was a unique aspect to the story. And he was pegged to be perhaps the villain. But I didn't want to play him as this sneering, leering villain. Instead I played him very contained. And I grew up in a military family. That military bearing and look was very important to me. And we got that down."

One of the film's best scenes is when Travolta's character comes into Moore's office, with the thought in his mind that the man before him may be the killer. James told me: "We did my close up first, my side of it. I said I wanted to just shoot it. So what you see in the movie when I'm sitting with John at that desk, that was the first time I'd ever said those words aloud. We did the whole scene the whole way through with two cameras. So everything you see there on my side was the first time I had said those words. Just like the opening night of a play. And John said, 'Ooh, I haven't learned these lines. I think we'll come back and do my side tomorrow (laughs). You kinda knocked that out of the park!' And John has a great sense of humour. He's a very funny guy. I love John Travolta."

One of my personal favourite moments in The General's Daughter is when Moore has been locked up in the prison and is awaiting questioning. Travolta comes to see him and the pair have a strange conversation through the bars. Woods, ever one to do something outside the ordinary, performs a strange gesture, moving his fingers across the bars before turning away. There is something so curious and odd about the way he does this, that the act alone moves Moore from being a murder suspect into an enigmatic man we are learning more about with every passing minute, but know we will never learn the full truth about. I mentioned the hand gestures to James. "Funny you should say that," Woods said. "Mace Neufeld loved when I dragged my fingers across the bars. He said, 'I just loved when you did that!' It was just one of those little things that comes to you. When you're working with a great director and a great actor - and John Travolta is a great actor. He can really get into a character. He's wonderful to work with, very inspirational. But he said he loved when I did that (the hands across the bars). There was just something eerie about the character. And it's a little pre-cursor too... The way gay men use their hands; just for some reason it just seems to be more of a signature way, the way they move their hands. It's the physical mannerism an actor will use without trying to be a cliché. You know, it's embarrassing that a person would use all that stuff, unless you are creating a flamboyant character in a comedy. But to do this, it was just a way of expressing that this person had a kind of complex life. It's different to playing, say, a deer hunter in Pennsylvania. Some guys out in the woods."

I also brought up the kitchen scene, where Moore is making his way around the work tops, mixing pots and pans. "One thing I loved is that they had a wooden counter top. And I did that thing where I throw the knife into the cutting top at the end. Because whenever there's a scene when a guy has a knife, I said this to Simon, 'I have a knife and I'm a potential suspect. Let's let this knife be a character in the scene.' Not over the top, but just have the audience think, Ooh I don't like the fact this guy has a big sharp knife. You don't make it threatening. But when I threw it down it was a little bit like, the gauntlet is down. These little gestures are sometimes just inspired, I can't explain it. You get into the character, and you do things that *you* wouldn't do. I actually have some very collectible knives, and I would never throw them down like that because it would hurt the tip. But this character might do it and you just take a chance, because it just says something in the scene. I knew it would also be a great punctuation to the scene, and Simon loved it. He was very attentive to detail. And we did this just before vinyl came back again, and we did a lot of shots of my character, close up, wiping the records. All of that stuff. The fastidiousness said something about this character. And not because he's gay, of course, but you use cinematic language to create a character and many characters will come to life because there are flags that are part of cinema lexicon, and you try to mute it as much as you can so it's not a caricature or insulting to a group of people. I never wanted to do anything that was a cliché. And with this character, it wasn't so much that he was gay, it's that he had a secretive life. To be an officer in the military, living alone without a wife, an ex-wife, any of that, it was a tough spot for a man to be in, in that situation. In those days, it was a situation where he could have been court marshalled. It was a secret life that was a potential jeopardy for this character in that story. I don't want anyone to get the wrong idea. It was an important part of the story that he had a secret, and the secret makes him look like a suspect, but in fact it's a double layered red herring. Very cleverly written."

TRUE CRIME (1999)

He then took on a role in Clint Eastwood's underrated True Crime. Clint plays a journalist who hopes to bring to light some evidence which will prove a man's innocence who is destined to be executed on death row. This measured and carefully paced picture, a ticking time bomb of a drama that mostly takes place in a 24 hour period leading to the execution, has aged very well. Eastwood, a master of his craft, takes a mature tone with the material as director and is great in his role as the recovering alcoholic ready to step up. But some of the best moments are filled out by the splendid supporting cast, which includes Denis Leary and James Woods as Alan Mann, Eastwood's editor-in-chief.

Woods is pure vital energy in this small but important role, wired up at all times as he makes his way back and forth through the busy office. He's fast talking, funny and full of quips, put downs and witticisms. He works against Eastwood's more laid back style beautifully and they enjoy some genuinely fantastic moments together.

Woods' involvement with the film came about in a rather unusual way. When I asked Woods if it felt surreal or odd having the iconic Eastwood face directing him from behind a camera, his response was surprising. Eastwood and Woods had been friends for a while before the film was even written, and had played golf together for a long time. One day after golf Woods jokingly asked him why he hadn't put him in one of his movies yet. "By the way, you know I'm an actor right?" he joked. "I had noticed," Eastwood responded, before adding that, in fact, he had a role for him in his forthcoming project. A few weeks later, the script for True Crime arrived with Woods' agent. He would finally work with his old friend.

"So by the time we got on set," Woods recalled, "it was kind of unique for me, because it was like, Oh, here I am with my buddy and we're suddenly making movies. I am really comfortable on movie sets, so it was like, Yeah, it's like going to work another day!"

As Woods is so effective in True Crime, delivering the quip-filled dialogue in a speedy and efficient manner, it's hard to imagine anyone else in the role. Eastwood, to his credit, obviously knew Woods had what it took to bring this man to the screen, and the sharp script by Larry Gross, Paul Brickman and Stephen Schiff is ideal for Woods' intelligent delivery.

On the subject of Clint Eastwood, James was full of compliments during our conversations. "Clint is so economical as a filmmaker. But every time I watch a simple narrative movie by Clint, I get to the end and I realise, Oh my God, this movie's a treatise on capital punishment! Or, this movie's a treatise on race. But Clint is a very shy guy. He doesn't like talking about movies. He makes them and he never expects them to be awarded. I mean, when he gets accolades, he is genuinely shocked. I have never seen anyone with such a reserved ego when it comes to being lauded and being an icon. Believe me, if you refer to him as an icon (laughs), I don't think he'd ever wanna spend time with you. But he understands that a lot of his characters have become iconic. I mean, if someone ever says, 'Make my day' to him, he just hates it."

When we came to talking about True Crime specifically, Woods found the ambiguity of the ending rather interesting. "I saw the movie and thought, Oh my God, is the ending fantasy or real? Did the guy die or does he not die? It's done in a very subtle way, the way he did that ending, where you just don't know. He leaves it up to the audience to decide whether the wrong man was executed, and whether execution is ever a good idea."

300

Woods has a brilliant scene with Eastwood where, without breath it seems, they verbally spar together and let off a stream of wonderfully penned dialogue, often overlapping the ends of each other's sentences. On the subject of this memorable sequence, James had some interesting memories. "I had heard he worked economically. He often does one take, and if you mess up that's it. So you get really tuned into the fact that this is it! I gotta get it right. So he said, 'You know that scene we have in the office? You wanna give this scene a little try?' And we started the scene, we did the whole scene. He said, 'Great, I loved that. Slate that.' And we were done! And you think, 'Holy shit, did we just film an entire three page scene?' And it was great because he started on my end. That was the first time I'd said those words. We didn't rehearse. Boom! He was amazing. In the scene, we talk really fast over each other. Usually you have to rehearse that, because it's like a tennis match. But we got it! We got it without ever rehearsing it. And I don't know how we did it! It was really fun to be working with a friend, as technically proficient professionals and also as actors just having fun. I'd never thought of acting with Clint. It was such a pleasure to work this way. I'm a theatre actor! In theatre you never get another take. You gotta go out there and do it. So I was very comfortable working this way, being a one take actor. On the other hand, I had forgotten how much I instinctively loved Clint as an actor. And I don't mean as a movie star. I mean, as Dirty Harry he is just fabulous. He's a star, so iconic. But man, I voted for him to win for Million Dollar Baby. He was brilliant in Million Dollar Baby. Brilliant."

The 1990's were a varied and exciting time for Woods, and he proved his range in a variety of productions; low budget comedies, stage adaptations, slick thrillers, action pictures, heavy dramas, animated adventures and everything in between. Most importantly of all though, despite huge successes, his feet remained on the ground. He has stated time and time again how well paid he is for what he does, something he loves so much he'd do it for free (the latter fact, as he joked to me, is a secret he's kept all through his career). Financial stability meant he was more able to choose projects that inspired him, not for the money but for the script and the part. "But how much fuckin' money do you need?" he said in one interview. "I mean, I don't need money. I have a beautiful home. A nice car. I can take care of my family and myself and my dog. I'm fine. I don't need $20 million a picture. I'll do Another Day in Paradise any time over a billion dollars to be in Godzilla. I want a secure life but I'm paid well enough."

As the 20th century ended, and cinematic trends and tastes shifted heavily towards popcorn entertainment, Woods would move on with the times, evolving as an actor in a climate that was becoming watered down, and didn't always suit such an alive, liberated actor. He would often lose faith in the industry, become disillusioned with what he was offered, but he remained realistic, picky with what roles he took on, and stayed level-headed through it all.

INTO THE NEW MILLENNIUM
2000 - 2002

By the year 2000, James Woods was already a film legend and a cultural icon, known as one of cinema's most reliable character actors. He had been a part of undeniable masterpieces (Once Upon a Time in America), made more than his fair share of classics (Videodrome, Salvador) and won various awards for his formidable acting skills. In the new millennium though, an era when pop culture reigned supreme, he would become iconic in an all new way. Thanks to his ongoing voice role as himself in Seth MacFarlane's Family Guy, plus appearances in hit TV shows and yet more important films, he became a kind of world of his own. James Woods - his name meaning something much bigger than your everyday actor. He became legendary, notorious to some, larger than life, quotable, a kind of reference point; even, god forbid, in this internet age, a "meme" and a "GIF". Yet he remained, despite all this, and with the changing taste of the new millennium, committed to his craft, a man insistent on delivering the best performance he could, whatever he was cast in. He also continued to push boundaries and challenge himself, as well as his viewers.

One of his first credits of the new millennium, and also one of the most impressive, was the acclaimed TV film, Dirty Pictures (2000). Marking, after Citizen Cohn, the second time Woods had worked with director Frank Pierson, it's based on the true story of a 1989 exhibition of Robert Mapplethorpe's controversial photography at the Contemporary Arts Center. Woods is Dennis Barrie, the owner of the gallery, who finds himself in hot water over the content of the images. Many protest against the exhibition, given the collection includes homosexual masochism and, most controversially of all, even nude children. But Barrie (a married family man himself) thinks that freedom of expression and the right to come to our own conclusions overrides any potential moral damage the pictures will have on the public. His passion comes at a cost however and he is indicted in court for obscenity charges. A media circus ensues and the trial is at the centre of a national dilemma about censorship and free will.

In an interview at the time of the broadcast, Woods said that he told Showtime he would only do the role if the actual pictures were allowed to be used. This in itself was an act of extreme integrity, a stipulation that could charge up a whole debate about whether what one person deems shocking (and others, of course, do not) should be displayed for artistic or historical reasons. The film itself then, a highly engaging drama that is beautifully acted and written, is almost like a microcosm of the entire concept of censorship, and where the cut off line between art and obscenity, pointless gratuity and artistic merit, can be drawn. Obviously, for Dirty Pictures to succeed, we simply had to see those pictures. And whether we like them or not, view them as immoral of artistic, smutty porn or enlightening mastery of the medium, the whole film would have been weaker without them being presented. But the film does not tell us who to agree with. No, it presents the story as it happened, as fact; and also - very interestingly I must say - intersperses the drama with talking head interviews with various cultural figures who discuss censorship, the value of controversial art and the Mapplethorpe exhibition specifically. (Gore Vidal was a personal favourite of these interludes.) The whole film offers up theories, though thankfully does not force us towards a "right" view on the matter, even if we can quite easily come up with our conclusion of where we stand on such graphic imagery.

Woods, in a Golden Globe nominated performance (he also won a Satellite gong for Best Actor), holds the film together. His portrayal of Barrie is straight forward. He is a man who loves his job and cares about what he's doing. In parallel to his work life is the fact he also loves his family, and the abuse they start to suffer, all because of the exhibition, reminds us of the consequences of when we put our necks out for something we believe in. Woods does not turn Barrie into a fist-shaking spokesman, but simply a liberal, free thinking progressive person (progressive as it once was, not as it might be interpreted today) who isn't afraid to stand by his convictions. It's a brilliant effort and he's the film's back bone.

Speaking to Charlie Rose in 2000, Woods opened up about how the Mapplethorpe pictures, and similar artists in general, brought about conflicting feelings in him: "I have to say, I by and large, personally, am so offended by most of these pictures, so I kind of wanted to do the film because I am - obviously, as an entertainer and as a citizen, you know, such a defender of the 1st Amendment and so abhorred the idea of censorship. But I must say, my patience with certain artists was tried to the limit with this particular film. So I'm in it, but I find myself as challenged and as perplexed and provoked and troubled by it as I think anybody would be. Censorship can almost not in any way be fettered because if it's unfettered, then we get to see, what every artist is thinking and there won't be that slippery slope. And it is a very compelling argument because once you start, it gets worse and worse and worse. And then, all of a sudden, you have committees deciding what can be said and what can't be said, and it is very dangerous. So I firmly believe in that."

To the New York Times, James was clear what his views were on the photos themselves: "You can say all you want and be politically correct and so on. I don't see the artistic merit of one man bent over with his forearm inserted up another man's anus. What is the artistry in that shot?"

When we came to Dirty Pictures in our chats, Woods had warm memories about the experience. "It was written by Ilene Claken, who is just a wonderful person. We got along great. Frank Pierson directed it. He was really one of my greatest benefactors. I loved Frank. Just a great guy. We had done Citizen Cohn. If Frank hadn't died we would have done another twenty films together. He was a great writer and director and he found his niche in television. And it was also great for Showtime, because they won the Best Picture Golden Globe. Showtime and I actually had a great connection. But Dirty Pictures was interesting because this was a huge censorship issue. I mean, I'm a fanatic about censorship because I've been censored, especially on Twitter. It's ironic that I did an award winning film about censorship, and then the same so called-liberals who believe that censorship is one of the great sins, then went out and promptly censored me."

We did end up talking about Dirty Pictures again during the interviews, naturally of course, with it being such a fascinating film that still strikes up debates and serious questions. "I was not a Mapplethorpe enthusiast as a lot of Hollywood was," James told me. "I mean, it was beautifully done photography and everything... I mean it's none of my business what people do in their bedroom, I just don't care. But when children are involved, obviously, we all agree on that. But the other stuff, whatever they do, fine. And I agree that should not be censored. Should children be allowed to see Mapplethorpe's pictures? I think it's a very troublesome issue of censorship that should have been addressed. And I have to tell you, me and Ilene talked about all this stuff, and I said, 'You know, there's this picture of a girl and you can see... you know, it's an unfortunate picture. It's a nude child!' So she said, 'I think these are issues that will be argued a lot.' And it was one of the things she liked about the project and the screenplay, and that I was troubled by it in the performance and as a person. I told her I was troubled by it. I am against censorship but I am vehemently on the side of those who want to protect children from paedophilia or grooming. It is, like, no! There is no discussion. So this was all very difficult subject matter and I liked the fact it was disturbing. It was a disturbing movie actually. I love that people have strong feelings for and against that movie. I had no comfortable sense of resolution on my opinion of that movie. There were parts that disturbed me and there were parts that I truly championed. It was a very troublesome movie for me to make, and I have to tell you that I had a very hard time with it."

Elsewhere in the early 2000's, Woods was lending his voice to animated pictures. A popular Woods voice role (though not as well celebrated as his iconic Hades) came in the wonderful Recess: School's Out (2001). Based on the classic 90s Disney series, this feature length edition features the regular Principal Prickly (voiced by Dabney Coleman) and his evil genius friend Phillium Benedict (Woods on brilliant form), who plan on getting rid of summer vacation. It's up to the kids, as ever, to put a stop to their fiendish scheme. This often overlooked Disney gem is great fun and thankfully is just as entertaining for adults as it is for the kids. Woods is brilliant as the devilish doctor, certainly at his most intense. He isn't as fast talking and wise cracking as Hades, for this character is evil in a more stern way, but he is a formidable bad guy and Woods handles the role with class.

He also lent his voice talents to Final Fantasy: The Spirits Within (2001), a beautifully animated feature based on the video game series. Again, he was relishing the role of the bad guy, in this case General Hein, who in a post-apocalyptic earth, plagued by terrifying creatures known as Phantoms, wishes to use a powerful cannon to rid the earth of the beasts, but in the process damage the planet's eco-system. A genuinely entertaining film, with life-like animation lending much to the intriguing plot, Final Fantasy: Spirits Within was monstrously budgeted at nearly 150 million dollars. It received solid reviews from some quarters at the time, and twenty years since its release the film has become more popular. Woods aside, there are the voices of other fine performers to enjoy; such as Steve Buscemi, Alec Baldwin and Donald Sutherland.

"It was a big deal, that movie," Woods told me, "and the idea was that for the first time ever we were gonna have animation that was going to make it possible to have characters be generated and look like people. We used to speculate on the set, like, 'If we can do this now, in 10, 20, 30 years from now, will Tom Cruise sell the rights to his face? Will Julia Roberts sell the rights to her look?' We really thought about it. It was like, Will they not need actors at all soon? I remember one thing that was said: they will always need actors, because they could really re-create faces, but the one thing that was so complex were the nuances of emotion in the human voice. But they are getting closer and closer now, obviously. But what actors can do is they can use subtle variations of emotion in the voice and that is something they couldn't do at the time. But the film was great to work on because we not only did the voices, we were on camera and they wanted to watch our movements as we spoke. And I played General Hein. So it would be one thing to talk the way I would talk, but I would have to stand the way a general might stand. The digital animators needed to see how an actor would interpret that character, so I had to behave very differently in front of the microphone. We were standing up, and I was literally almost acting out as if I was in the scene as an actor doing it. It was really amazing the first time we saw the characters come to life and look real."

Woods went from one big movie to another, this one more outrageous it has to be said. The Scary Movie franchise has been one of the most popular comedy sagas in film history. Crammed full of crude but genuinely funny gags, movie spoofs and celeb cameos, when at their best they are shamelessly entertaining fare. After the success of the 1999 original, a sequel was put together pretty quickly. Scary Movie 2 (2001), directed by Keenan Ivory Wayans, is in my view much sharper than the first film. There are some great turns here; Shawn and Marlon Wayans, Tim Curry, and a brilliant Chris Elliott. But perhaps the most famous guest appearance is from James Woods as the hilariously named Father McFeely, a priest who enters Hell House to help exorcise a possessed teenager. I remember the first time I saw it as a teenager, howling with laughter at Woods' knack of nailing physical comedy. Just watch the opening scene and it's full of little comedic gems; when he tries to bolt out of the room when he first sees the demon child for instance; when he ends up flirting with the girl before mounting her; and, of course, the vomit fight before his infamous demonic shit. It's one of the funniest opening ten minutes to any comedy I can think of. Not for the easily offended of course, or anyone repulsed by coarse humour, but for those who can stomach it, it's bloody good fun. It's also the broadest comedy Woods has ever done, and he's a natural with the material.

"That was one of my absolute favourite experiences," James told me. "What had happened was, Marlon Brando was cast in the role and he dropped out. So I had never worked for the Weinsteins, and this was for Harvey's brother Bob who had Dimension Films. They called my agent and they said, 'We have to have this movie out on the July 4th weekend, no matter what. We're gonna shoot it. We know Jimmy Woods is able to shoot really fast, really quick and that he's very professional. We need him to replace Marlon Brando. We will pay him an astonishing amount of money and he's got to show up tomorrow and do exactly what we need him to do.' So I said, 'Sure, I'll do it.' So we jump in, we do it. They had an editor sitting to one side as we shot. They had video playback so they could edit it as well. And then we started improvising and ad-libbing too. I mean, it was hilarious. Hilarious. One of the funniest moments is when I come in and I see the demon for the first time. Keenan, the director, said, 'We should have a response from you here.' So I said, 'OK, why don't you just shoot it. I have some ideas but I don't wanna ruin it for you.' So I come in, see the demon, the camera is rolling and I say 'Fuck this!' Honestly, Keenan literally fell on the floor laughing. Oh my God, it was so funny!

On the famous shitting scene, Woods recalled: "But by the way, they said, 'If you don't wanna do any of this, don't worry.' I said, 'Are you kidding? This bit is a spoof of the Amityville Horror. Of course I'll do it. It's funny!' I mean, if you're gonna do a Scary Movie version, you just got to be willing to do all the craziest stuff that they do in those movies. You can't be all, 'Oh I don't feel comfortable doing this. It might be the death of my career.' If you're gonna do it, just have fun and do it! So we did it. And I loved that movie. So many people love all that opening of the movie. I think that sequence for the first eight minutes of the film is just hilarious. I loved it. I mean, you got to have all this pea soup and all this shit in your face, but you sign up for it, and you got to be a sport about it and you just got to do it."

There were two other notable films from 2001 which featured Woods in varied roles; the first was in Race to Space, a pleasant family drama set in the sixties. Woods is Dr Huber, a NASA scientist who, having lost his wife, moves to Cape Canaveral with his 12 year old son, Billy (played by Alex D Linz). Through his father, Billy ends up helping train the chimps that are going to be sent to space by NASA. He befriends one in particular, Mac, who is then selected to become the first American into outer space (remember, this is the time of the space race with the Russians). Only then does Billy realise what possible danger his new friend is going to find himself in.

Race to Space is a film well worth re-investigating, especially if you have kids. The characters are warm, the acting is good and the plot moves at a healthy and careful pace, giving plenty of time for Billy's relationship with both Mac and his stiff father to become something you are invested in. Nicely directed by Sean McNamara, it's another film which reminds us of Woods' range. There is no volatility at all here, and he is utterly convincing as the NASA scientist.

When I raised this film in one of our chats, genuine warmth came into James' voice, but he also seemed surprised I had brought it up. "Oh, Race to Space," he enthusiastically began. "You know, it's funny you should mention that movie. I loved that little movie! It was low budget, just a little story, but I just - you know, the kid being bullied about being German so close after the war, and the father being cold and everything. But that scene on the beach, I just loved that scene with that little boy. He was so great that kid. I just loved that little boy, he was so cute. He really had an emotional range, he was very talented. It's a little gem, that movie."

He then shared more memories of the film with me. "My brother was in that movie by the way, he played one of the technicians. And we were filming in the little bunker right near the launch pad of

311

where Gus Grisham and his two fellow astronauts (Robert B. Chaffee and Ed White) died, during the malfunction of the take off. So we filmed in all the real places. It was so exciting making that movie. My brother and I were invited by Dan Goldin to watch a shuttle launch. And we were like three miles away from it, and I was up in the bench watching. And I said, 'Boy it must be exciting being down there watching closer.' And Dan Goldin said, 'You're the closest person on earth to this launch right now. No one can be within three miles, because you can't believe the blast. This is the closest we can get.' When you count to three and it takes off, and you get to three, BOOM, you're almost knocked off your feet. Even from three miles away. To watch that thing take off from the face of the earth is astonishing. It's so bright. It lights up the whole world. So it was a wonderful experience working on that movie. I just loved working on that movie."

He was then even further from his tough guy image in the underrated, Riding in Cars with Boys (2001). Directed by the great Penny Marshall, it is adapted from Beverly Donofrio's memoir. Drew Barrymore is Bev, and the story begins in 1961, when she is still a young girl and being played by young actress Mika Boorem. Bev is living with her mother (Lorraine Bracco) and father Leonard (Woods), a police officer, and thinking of dating boys. But Leonard is adamant she should get the other sex out of her mind and focus on her work. The opening scene featuring Woods involves him and his young daughter going to buy a Christmas tree. He asks her what she wants for the big day from Old Saint Nick, and she says a bra, which will attract the attention of a boy she likes. Crushed, he lights up a cigarette and tells her it's a no. His quiet disappointment here is very well observed. Just by the sudden weight in his eyes, he seems to sum up how every dad feels when it's clear that their baby has turned a corner and is growing up too fast.

After this scene we go to 1986, where Bev is just about to see the publication of her memoir, the very book this film is based on. She looks back retrospectively on her life and we then end up in 1965, where Bev and her friends (one of whom is Brittany Murphy) go through the typical trials and tribulations of teenage social life. Pretty soon however, after meeting the "wrong" boy, Ray (brilliantly played by Steve Zahn), she realises she is pregnant, and her life takes a turn she never thought it would, especially so early. The film eventually takes us right back to the mid 1980's, where she's spending time with her son before the book is launched, and they are on their way to meet Ray, so he can sign the release form before publication.

What I like about Riding in Cars with Boys is how it is not totally typical of its era or genre. Though it does have the softer edge of Marshall's work, it does not over sensationalise or go down too many tired and familiar paths, and occasionally knocks you back with the more serious themes. We go the whole way with Bev and are engaged in her story (thanks to the writing and Barrymore's confident performance), but it's so straight forward and to the point that we are spared the eye rolling moments of predictability. For Woods too, it's a great opportunity to be a normal guy, in this case on the right side of the law as opposed to the other. As in Race to Space, he is a very convincing father, though here a very different one. He is an honest man, a hard worker who wants the best for his family. He is a caring, committed man, and it's a touching performance at times. (It should also be noted that this was the second time he had played Barrymore's father, after Cat's Eye in 1985.)

When I spoke about this film with James, he came up with some interesting points about films like Riding in Cars with Boys, where

313

young female stars were given meatier roles, parts with an arc of their own. "Now I'm gonna sound like a big liberal here," he began before going on a fascinating train of thought, "but I think the women's liberation has been very good in the industry in a lot of ways. It enriched the experience for everybody, but one way in particular is that beautiful young women, in this case Drew Barrymore in Riding in Cars with Boys, in earlier times might have played the femme fatale, the girlfriend or the wife waiting for the husband to come back - all of which are great characters and issues - but they now get to explore other issues. Not only power. For example, Riding in Cars with Boys, this young woman who could have easily been cast as the gorgeous young girlfriend, those parts, are also now getting to explore something very important to women - the relationship with their fathers when they are coming of age, and when they make all the mistakes that teenage girls and boys make. But there is a particular relationship between young girls, girls becoming women, and their fathers. It stamps their understanding of what a man should be and how men should treat them and so on. And that was something we were able to explore and make movies about, which wasn't something we were able to do before, because women were, like, stereotypes, studio ideas of what women's roles should be. And you can feel it when you're working with young women, they get an opportunity to explore this dimension. I think there was a lot greater depth in those stories after the women's movement enriched screen-writing for women."

There are a few scenes and little touches that make Woods' father a realistic and relatable one. There's a great moment when Bev, knowing she is pregnant, is building up the courage to throw herself down the stairs. As she comically does so, tumbling down a few steps with little impact, her parents watch comedy on TV. Woods, laid

314

down with his head on his wife's lap, is in hysterics. There is something very clever about this, and the way Bracco strokes his hair and kisses his forehead lovingly. He's a decent family man who likes to spend time with his loved ones after a hard day at work.

Another key scene is when he reads Bev's note about her pregnancy. He begins to tear up, and we feel his upset. Woods tells her he just wanted to be a hard working dad, to hold his head high, to raise a good family. "But you ruined your life and you broke my heart," he says, and it gets right to your stomach. You feel it, but only because Woods plays it realistically, not as if it's a "film moment", an ideal opportunity for a big emotional scene. Woods keeps it natural and that is what makes his Leonard such an open and likeable character.

The same can be said for the afore-mentioned final scene, in which he and his daughter, driving in the car as they did at the start of the film when going out to buy a Christmas tree, quietly sing "their" song together, All I Have to Do Is Dream by The Everly Brothers. It's a genuinely touching moment in a film that isn't afraid to be hard at times, but soft when it needs it the most.

On the father and daughter relationship between he and Drew in Marshall's film, he said: "It's a very complex relationship. And it doesn't end with angels singing and orchestras playing, it's just the two of us singing Dream, in a quiet, sweet way. And I have had a million women come up to me and say, 'Oh I cried at the end of that movie, because it was like me and my dad. We didn't get along and then all of a sudden I saw that moment...' It's wonderful. It inspired a lot of women to have that kind of relationship with their father, or hoped or wished they had."

One great little cameo was in an episode of the short lived Clerks animated series (2002), where the hapless shop workers from the hit Kevin Smith movie, here in cartoon form, see themselves in the middle of an outbreak after letting an infected ape into the town. Woods plays one of the team brought in to deal wit this ebola-like disease and gives his role real gusto. It's a minor credit, but for a true hidden gem and proof that he was game for anything that interested him.

Woods got the chance to make his directorial debut in 2002 with the short film, Falling in Love with Pongo Panga. Produced by SKYY Vodka, this brief little gem focuses on a film shoot involving a demanding and bitchy star, being carried around by ass licking aides and having assistants run around for her. Genuinely funny and sharply acted (Jodi Lyn O'Keefe is particularly strong as the spoilt celeb), I would have loved to have seen this fleshed out into a longer feature. As it is though, it's short and sweet... well, not sweet, but pretty savage actually.

John Ottman, the film's editor, wrote of his experience: "It's an understatement that James is an enthusiastic film-maker! And his debut reflected his energy. In about 2 days they were to shoot a 7-minute, helter-skelter comedic romp. I was quite astounded that, when I got the footage, they actually made it though the shoot and got most everything." He added that James was often "joking that everyone would assume his debut to be some fucked up morbid violent affair." You can find the film in its entirety on Vimeo.

Woods returned to animation in 2002 with House of Mouse, where he reprised the role of Hades. A year earlier he had stepped back into the shoes of the underworld lord in Mickey's House of Villains and the Mickeypalooza special. It was, after all, a part he relished playing. Providing voice work obviously appealed to Woods. An expressive actor in every way, he is ideal for the animated movie or TV series. Though he often uses his hands to put across emotion and feeling, it's the Woods voice that is perhaps his most prominent trademark.

He was also the voice of Gloomius Maximus in Rolie Polie Olie: The Great Defender of Fun (2002), another dead-on vocal performance. "When I did that it was for five year old kids," he told me about this rather obscure movie. "I played this pirate who it turns out is mean because no one ever sang Happy Birthday to him. You've got to do it so five year old kids can relate to it. So they hired me and I said, 'Look, can I just do this my own way?' So I did this over the top, bad cockney accent (laughs). So many people tell me their kids loved me in the Rolie Polie Olie movie. It was my version of the Pirates of the Caribbean before Johnny Depp did it. It was just completely self indulgent. It was really fun to do."

It could be said that Woods really stretched himself in the early part of the 21st century, choosing roles that were totally different from the ones the public at large knew him for. The mobsters, psychos, hit men and cop killers gave way to scientists, gallery owners, even cops. There was much lighter fare too in this era. He voiced the evil falcon in the charming Stuart Little 2 (2002), the sequel to the 1999 hit about a talking mouse, voiced by his old Hard Way co-star Michael J Fox. "Oh yeah, that was a sweet little movie," James recalled. "I loved doing that. It's funny 'cos I'll meet kids and I'll do the voice, and they'll go 'Argh!' It's really funny."

In his next film role, he was not a lawbreaker, though he did personify a fatal flaw in the US health system. John Q (2002) is one of those extremely enjoyable and enthralling thrillers of the late 90s/early 2000's that we just don't seem to see any more. Starring Denzel Washington as a father whose son suddenly needs vital heart surgery or he will die, it becomes a hostage situation when John takes a gun into the hospital and demands the surgeons act fast. He hasn't the money to pay, but he does have a gun!

Suspenseful, with heavy drama and much tension, it's excellently directed by Nick Cassavetes, has a tight and sharp script by James Keams, and, just as importantly, is superbly played. Washington is the film's heart (no pun intended), his anger, frustration and undiluted emotion powering the film forward in every respect. Much of the supporting cast, though representing types to a certain degree, prop up the film around him, and it is certainly one of the meatiest secondary casts I can think of. The two strongest players, for me, are Anne Heche as Rebecca Payne, a hospital administrator who borders on heartless for the first part of the picture, and James Woods as Dr Turner, the cardiologist who hammers the reality down John's throat from the get go, points out the unfair injustices of the health system (without the money, you're buggered), but eventually aids him in his singled minded pursuit to save the life of his son.

Some critics criticised the obviousness of the message, that the health system in America is just plain unfair, but for such a point to be made it has to be as sharp and pointed as the surgeon's scalpel. John Q is both highly entertaining and thought provoking, even if the thoughts are not had during the picture, but once it's finished (after all, it's too engaging a movie to allow distracted sessions of pondering).

James remembered this film with fondness, and in our chats we discussed the various themes explored within it, primarily the idea that his character embodied the kind of predicament every surgeon faces every day. "Firstly," he told me, "Nick Cassavettes' daughter had had heart surgery. So this was very personal to him. He had very definitive positions about medicine at that time, and he was pretty intransient about it. I love Nick, and he's a buddy of mine. A very creative guy. I said, 'Nick, you know, the doctors don't feel that way. Doctors in my experience can be very dedicated to their jobs. And what you find you don't like about them may be what helps them survive.' I'll never forget this thing a doctor once said to me. I thought it was very relevant to this. Doctors can be very cold blooded about decisions they have to make sometimes. And this doctor said to me, 'If they don't do that, they can't do their job. They can't get emotionally involved with a patient to a point they are going to make mistakes. They have to just approach this as a bio-mechanical device they are trying to fix. If they stray away from that, they are going to go off the rails. It's going to affect their judgement and it's going to break their spirit.' So my character, he's sitting there - it's an 800,000 dollar operation and the guy can't afford it. He's not the first guy he's had to tell that the person he loves is gonna die. 'We don't have a warehouse full of viable hearts. We have to wait for someone to be killed in an accident. Without a viable heart for your beloved child, basically we can't do anything. And you can't afford it anyway.' It's a horrible situation..."

On the experience of working with Denzel, Woods said: "Denzel is such a brilliant actor. When we did that scene with him and Kimberley Elise, when I'm sitting with her and they're both sobbing as I'm delivering the bad news. And I thought, first of all, Shit, these guys are so damn good! It just hit me! Denzel can just turn on the water. It's hard to cry, but Denzel is just sitting there and tears are running down his face. She's hysterical. And I'm thinking, This is a big emotional story. In the same way that doctors have to be cold blooded to some degree to be good doctors, to be objective in their work - especially a surgeon - you have to do this as an actor as well. I improvised a scene that was about the things that doctors have to do. And Nick let me run with it, he said, 'Just do your thing.' They cut a lot of it out, of course. A lot of what made that movie powerful is the pressure that's on people who are hostages, and the pressure on the person who is taking hostages. A catastrophic situation. There was a lot of emotion involved in that movie, I have to say. All of my stuff was basically with Denzel and I really like him a lot. I admire him as an actor. He's just phenomenal."

Talking about Denzel then got James into realising something about his career. "I mean, when I think of some of the actors I worked with: Anthony Hopkins, Bob De Niro, Jodie Foster, Denzel Washington... you start to take it for granted. And you think of these people and you think, Jesus Christ. There were so many actors, and I just took it for granted. I mean, Meryl Streep! And you don't think anything of it. But I think what happens is, when you're working with them, you're not thinking about it. We just start doing all the mechanical stuff you do. We just do the acting process, you just do it without thinking about it. I mean, there are those actors that I really wish I had gotten to work with. Kind of my favourite actor of all time is Jack Nicholson. I love Jack Nicholson. He's the all American guy. I really wanted to work with him. But I'm glad I got to work with the guys I did; Joe Pesci, Bob De Niro, Sigourney Weaver. So many actors I love. I could go on and on. It's like, Wow!"

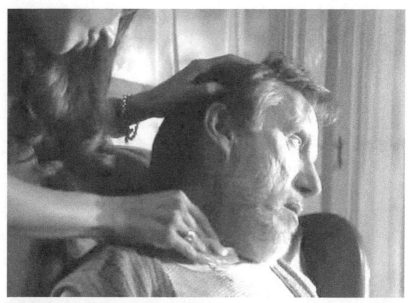

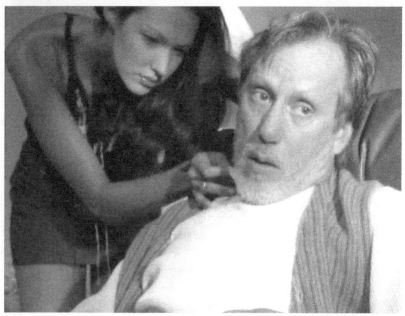

James Woods as Pops in This Girl's Life (2003).

2003: THIS GIRL'S LIFE, NORTHFORK AND RUDY

This section covers three of Woods' films from the year 2003. Grouping together films that were made close to each other makes sense not only for chronological reasons, but also in understanding the sheer range he has as a performer. In this one year alone for instance, he played a suited 1950's evacuator, a father with Parkinson's disease, and one of the most famous Mayors in New York history. Now if that isn't an example of range, then please tell me what is!

One of Woods' biggest challenges was to come in Ash's blackly comedic drama, This Girl's Life. The film focuses on Juliette Marquis as a young woman who works as a porn star on an internet reality show. We follow her in her daily life, seeing the problems she is faced with everyday. Woods plays her father, who is suffering from Parkinson's, and he's absolutely brilliant. Referred to only as Pops throughout, he becomes the man so much that one often forgets it's even Woods. With great subtlety, he gets everything right; the shakes, the mannerisms, the frustration. But he also gives the character depth beneath these tics. He is funny too, telling silly jokes to his daughter and her friends, and trying to remain positive, despite still being heartbroken that his wife died years earlier. Unaware that his daughter is a porn star, he believes (or chooses to believe perhaps) she is a vet. "Did the animals misbehave today?" he asks as she helps dress him one day. His work here puts a lump in your throat, and he's so effective that you even feel it in your stomach. Pops is one of my favourite of all of Woods' characters.

I asked James if he had done any research into Parkinson's for the film: "Yes I did quite a bit actually. It was a really odd movie. The lead, Juliette, I had never see her do anything, before but she was wonderful. The other actors were terrific. There were some real people, real women who were in that world; they played some of the minor parts and they were excellent. And I did the research on that affliction. I got nominated for an Emmy after this for an episode of ER. But for this I had done work on Parkinson's. My dear friend, Michael J Fox, had Parkinson's, so I did do a lot of research, just wanting to know what they felt. I asked my doctor too. You always ask what the affects might be, like for instance when I researched Schizophrenia, one of the affects is tardive dyskinesia, which makes them sound mentally challenged because they slur their words. With Parkinson's, you have to be very careful that it doesn't look like you're doing anything that could be seen as disrespectful. Some of the physical behaviour is actually quite extreme and you just don't wanna look like you're mocking a person's liability or disability. The good news is that now, these people who are affected by it have the medication to help suppress the affects. But back then when we did the movie, not so much. In terms of performance, we were fortunate enough that people sometimes barely exhibit it and other times there are spells and breakouts of high dysfunctional activity.

"So I was able to do the character with the breaks on quite a bit and at times have these little eruptions. When we'd shoot it with Ash, I'd say, 'Let me do it a little strong, you know, a strong presentation of the physical aspect, and then we'll do a more suppressed version. And then in the editing you can decide which is more relevant for each scene.' But it's hard to watch that stuff and you have to be very careful not to overdo it. Or if you are overdoing it in a valid way, you have to make sure you see very little of it. We all know what's gonna go on, but we wanna see enough and make it authentic. So those are very hard parts to play, honestly."

Juliette Marquis and James Woods in This Girl's Life (2003).

James also told me the film has a rather well known fan: "But the irony was that I bumped into Quentin Tarantino at Book Soup. We had a long history because he had offered me Reservoir Dogs and my agent at the time turned it down. They had a bigger offer on another movie for me that they wanted me to do, so they didn't tell me about this one that was a low money offer. I felt bad about it. That was the back story to us. Anyway, so I bumped into him in Book Soup years later, and he said, 'I saw this movie, This Girl's Life!' And he loved that movie and loved that performance. 'Oh that's my favourite performance!' And I thought, that's odd. Of all the things I've done... But I think he liked the kind of raw, improvisational nature of it. I was out on the end of the gangplank. It's what I have always tried to do with my career, take risks that are kind of strange; strange characters, difficult movies. If it means that every now and then I get blasted by some guy living in his mom's basement, for taking a chance one time, so be it. I've had success with people appreciating that I'm taking some risks in dealing with these kinds of characters."

Woods was given room to ad lib throughout the shoot, and one scene that was wholly improvised was the one when he tells all his daughter's friends the dirty joke. "That joke," he told me, "was one that Buddy Hackett used to tell in his routine in Vegas in the 1970s. No one had heard it in years. He also told it to me once when we were playing golf, an incredibly funny, dirty joke. So I thought it would be great and so inappropriate that he's telling it to her friends. That made it even odder and funnier. It was in keeping with the whole strange environment that Ash - who I liked very much - wanted to create."

Reviews of the film were positive, and even those not won over by the picture as a whole were glowing about Woods. Roger Ebert, who was niggled by what he saw as flaws (incorrectly in my view), wrote that Woods' performance was so good it was almost too good for the film itself; a compliment for Woods, yes, but also a misjudgement on the film. Reel.com wrote of Woods: "Though he's never been the sort of performer to lose himself in a role, that's exactly what Woods does here; stepping into the shoes of a seriously disabled man, the actor delivers an utterly convincing, heart wrenching performance that's unlike anything he's done before."

There was another under-appreciated film released the same year. Mark and Michael Polish's Northfork (2003) is a sharp, arty drama set in a small town that is in the middle of a mass evacuation. The film focuses on various town folk who refuse to leave, including Nick Nolte as Father Harlan. Among the wonderful cast are James Woods and Mark Polish as Walter O'Brien and son, two men attempting to clear everyone out of Northfork.

On how he got to be involved with this most curious of films, Woods told me that the Polish Brothers had come up to him at a party and said they wanted him to read their script. He took a look, skimmed over it, said it was interesting, but said, "No, I don't think so." The brothers told Woods the reason they wanted him was because they intended Northfork to be a direct homage to Once Upon a Time in America. They wanted to open the film with an extreme close up on Woods, similar to the end close up on De Niro in Leone's masterpiece. "It's a homage," they said, "we have to have you! We think you are the greatest actor alive." Still, Woods said no. "A year later," James told me, "I bump into them at another party. I said, 'Hey guys, what about that movie you were doing?' And they said, 'We're waiting for you.' I said, 'What are you talking about?' They said, 'We're not gonna make it without you. We will only make it with you.' I said, 'Are you kidding?' And they said, 'No, we told your agent that. We will never make the movie without you.' So I said, 'Fuck it, I guess I gotta do it.' And I did it. I was thrilled that I did it."

When asked what attracted him to Northfork by Salon (the only question they asked about the film, I might add), Woods explained: "I thought it was a very bold subject, this whole idea of the transition from life to death or how to make life more meaningful while you're living it in the face of death. Secondly, I thought it would be exquisitely presented. I spent a lot of time with the boys (the Polish brothers). We talked about using the gray scale in colour. I thought that was really going to be powerful, to make essentially a black-and-white movie but on colour stock. Everything was painted gray, the ketchup bottle, the flag, everything. I love the humour in it. And I just thought that they are real artists."

Northfork is very much an art film, in that the stylised visuals, though consciously applied, not only enhance the picture but characterise it too. Over stylisation can often lead to a hollow experience, but Northfork is a film enriched by the conceptual colourisation. As Woods noted to me, it is full of symbolism, and wings are a recurring image throughout. The acting, often muted and in fitting with the mood and shades of the cinematography, is also particularly strong, though understated too. Woods gives his part a firm but subtle quietness, and the whole cast seem to be at one with the atmosphere.

Woods was also executive producer on Northfork, a film he truly believed in. It wasn't a matter of money. "A lot of it had to do with the creation of the film," he said. "I was able to lean on people for favours and things to help out because their budget was so low. It was half of what John Travolta's perk package is on a film. Our whole budget was half of what his staff makes on a film. Everybody was so utterly dedicated to the film. Because you have to remember, we work in an environment where your options are to do, you know, Batman 10, so when you get to do a movie that's a really great film like this, people really step up to the plate and enjoy it."

Speaking to me, Woods said that Northfork is "one of the greatest lost films ever made. It's a real filmmaker's movie. It's so strange; Daryll Hannah playing a little role and so on. Everybody wanted to work with the Polish brothers."

That said, the low budget ensured the shoot would not be a smooth one, as Woods told me: "You know that scene under the Dam? We were 330 feet below that Dam, with a trillion tons of water pushing against it. There was no way out. If that thing cracked, you were buried alive. We went down there, and Graham (Beckel) said, 'I'm gonna lose it!' So we did it, we got back up and they said they had a hair in the gate and we had to re-shoot the whole scene. We had to go back down that fucking ladder. I mean, you hear the water going

328

over you... And by the way, I will never be able to say how cold it was there. We were four hours from the nearest airport, and it was November up in the tundra of Northern Montana. One day, we were in the middle of nowhere with the camera, and out of nowhere, two jeeps come up. There was a helicopter, and the jeeps had fifty calibre machine guns mounted on them. We were going, 'What the fuck?' We raised our hands. They said, 'Turn that camera off and turn around!' We said, 'Uh, which way?' They said, 'Away from us!' We didn't realise we were 300 yards from a nuclear missile silo. They were not happy about that."

Proving that 2003 was a stand out year for him, Woods then took on Rudy: The Rudy Giuliani Story, an acclaimed TV movie directed by Robert Dornehlm that has recently garnered renewed interest. Woods is terrific as the former New York Mayor in this well made dramatisation, which charts his rise to power from the 1980's onwards. It's nicely directed by Dornhelm and is very straight to the point, while the 9/11 sequences are particularly good. As it focuses on his strong leadership in that era, and does not obviously extend to more recent events, the film is a straight forward depiction of a man in the centre of a storm, who finds himself in the glowing light of the world's spotlight during the most catastrophic event of recent times.

But it has to be said that the main reason to watch this is for Woods, on top Emmy nominated form. The underrated Penelope Ann Miller is also particularly good too, but for me this is a prime example of the power Woods can harbour when put into the centre of things in a role he can sink his teeth into. He is staggeringly good, so under Rudy's skin that we forget at times that we aren't watching the real guy. Not that he's his doppelganger of course (though the hair and make up did a great job), but more that he embodies the man in the heat of his rise and in the trying era of the Twin Towers devastation.

There are some great Woodsian moments too. Though it is included to highlight Rudy's refusal to suffer fools or those who didn't wish to put in their all, the scene where he shouts in the ear of the man who's been unwise enough to fall asleep during a meeting is hilarious. It's a mini Woods classic.

"Rudy is interesting," Woods told me, "because Robert Dornhelm who directed it is from Transylvania, believe it or not. He and I ended loving each other. Every night he would make dinner, and he was like a world class chef too. So my brother Mike was in the film, he played my driver in it. So he said, 'Would you and Mike like to come over for dinner?' So we said, 'Sure.' And he cooked for us every night. We had so much fun. But the thing is he's a Communist. He'd say, 'My father was in the Communist party, I am a Communist and I believe in Communism' And he is very adamant about it. And I said, 'You and I could not have more divergent opinions about Rudy Giuliani.' At the time I mean. The Rudy at the time saved his city. He was a very heroic guy to me. None of the stuff now, I mean the guy then. The stuff now I have no idea about. But at the time he broke the mafia in New York and he saved New York after 9/11. He was an inspiration to everyone in America at that time. And I had to argue about every frame with Robert, and to Robert's credit he listened to me. We ended up having a good synthesis between my point of view and his point of view, and we came up with something... He wanted to do a hit piece on Rudy and I wanted to do a heroic piece on Rudy, so we ended up with something that had a mix of both. And to his credit he listened and to my credit I listened. We stayed friends because he was willing to be open to my opinion, and he changed things because he started agreeing with my point of view, which I appreciated. They were gonna do a hit piece on Rudy and I saved it, that's what that was."

330

Whatever you might think of the real Rudy, no one could really deny the strength of Woods' effort, which won him a Best Actor gong at the Satellite Awards. He said before the airing of the movie, that he intended to play Rudy "warts and all." That he most certainly does, but he captures most of all the man's drive and determination. Speaking upon the film's release, Woods commented on the hair-do: "I've immortalized the comb-over. He'll never escape it. Luckily the story only goes through 2001, so we didn't have to deal with the new slicked-back look."

If someone had been living under a rock for the past fifty years and really didn't know who James Woods was, and you wanted to demonstrate that he is one of America's most versatile actors, the year 2003 is a good year to demonstrate to them that said versatility.

Woods during the filming of 2005's Pretty Persuasion.
Photo taken by Chris Jepsen.

"ANOTHER BAD GUY IN A SUIT"
2004 - 2008

In an A and E biography on Woods, James himself said that in the early to mid 2000's he began to tire of what work he was being offered, and was losing some of the passion he had once had for the acting world. "Another bad guy in a suit," is how he summed up many of the roles coming his way, and for a man with so much range, appearing as another villain must have been tiring for him. Just as he grew disillusioned however, he began to appear in work that allowed him to demonstrate his extraordinary skill and versatility.

There was more voice work firstly, in 2004's The Easter Egg Adventure. In this charming kid's tale, he voices one of the villainous Takits in EggTown, the place where every Easter egg is made and prepared for the big day. On Egg Day, the Takits plan to steal all the goodies, but they are watched over by Good Gracious Grasshopper. An entertaining, light and brilliantly voiced picture, with very unique and appealing animation, this is ideal if you have little children - and pretty fun for the grown ups too!

Then we come to one of the great unsung oddities in Woods' career, Pretty Persuasion (2005). Directed by Marcos Siega and scripted by Skander Halim, it stars Evan Rachel Wood as a high school student who, with two friends, accuses her teacher of sexual harassment. Genuinely funny with a sharp script, the cast are especially brilliant here; Wood nails the narcissistic sociopath schoolgirl who will do anything to achieve fame, even accusing an innocent man; Jane Krakowski is excellent as a sassy reporter covering the case; and James Woods is hilarious as Evan's foul mouthed, bigoted father, and he gets all the best lines too. A sharp satire on fame and infamy, and what separates the two in these modern, cynical times of ours.

"That script was unbelievable," Woods told me. "It was such a great script. You know the guy (the father) is this ridiculous, racist, anti-Semite, sexist. He's just everybody's nightmare! He's so over the top that I thought it would be great to play. Evan Rachel Wood was wonderful in her part. All the actors were wonderful; Jamie King (as James' wife); everybody. They were all fabulous. It's really a sort of under-appreciated gem. But it was a very funny character, self indulgent and so narcissistic. I don't get to do a lot of comedy and it was just balls out black comedy, which was very appealing to me. And I loved the director, Marcos Siega. In fact I hired him several times when I was producing and got him as an episodic director on my series, Shark. I think he did three or four episodes. And I have to say, that part was very, very tightly written. It's such black comedy, it's horrible. It was out of the park insane, that movie, but very shrewd and clever in the way it was written. So I didn't have to improvise at all on that one. It was really right on the money all the time."

Speaking of the finale where Woods really lets rip into his daughter, he told me that you often have to be careful with such a strong scene. "Obviously she knew what she was signing up for," he said, "and I don't think that movie could be made now in the middle of all the insanity of the woke cancel culture that goes on now. But she was an absolute trouper. I said to her, 'You know, I'm gonna have to say some really unfortunate and ugly things in the scene.' And she said, 'Yes of course, it's in the script!' And then we did it and it worked out great. But it was all so dark, every scene, it's a dark, powerful, satirical, real cinematic treatise on narcissism and the lure of celebrity, fame, power and money, all of which are tied together."

Reviews at the time were not so kind, because many critics felt there was no one to side with. Roger Ebert wrote: "Pretty Persuasion is the kind of teenage movie where James Woods can play the heroine's dad and not be the worst person in the story. He comes close, but then everyone comes close, except for the innocent bystanders."

Woods on acidic form in Pretty Persuasion (2005).

I genuinely believe, when all is said and done, that it comes down to taste. The humour in Pretty Persuasion is very black, and if you can't stomach that, then this film - which deals with important issues within the comedy - is not for you. Me? I love it.

Woods has always been good at nailing a good cameo, as seen in F. Gary Gray's Be Cool (2005), the sharp sequel to Get Shorty (1995). In the opening of the picture, Woods is Tommy Athens, a friend of John Travolta's character, Chili. Tommy's a fun loving music business veteran who wants Chili to write a film about his life. He isn't in the movie much but the brief part is notable and actually sets things rolling. Chili is going through a transition. The former criminal

335

turned screenwriter feels he's sold out by writing a sequel, hilariously titled Get Lost. Tommy says the films are good, but Chilli's thinking of leaving town. "Why would you wanna leave all this?" Woods says, pointing at a group of young women. Woods' role is an intriguing one and he is genuinely funny in it, but he is snubbed out by the Russian mob. Still, even without Woods (who would have been an interesting addition to the film had he hung in there) Be Cool is great fun. He had originally been lined up to play Harvey Keitel's role, but had to pull out due to surgery. Once recovered, they urged him to make a brief appearance, and he made room for the cameo.

Woods provided another neat cameo in Season 3 of Entourage (the Aquamom episode, which aired in 2006), when he makes an appearance as himself, in high charged Woods mode, demanding free tickets for a movie premiere. He is at his most intense and funny, terrifying the Entourage guys with a typically Woodsian rage-rant.

He put in a voice cameo in the overlooked animated series, Odd Job Jack (2005), and in Ark (2005), another animated adventure, this time from John Woo's Digital Rim studio. After what was deemed the commercial failure of Final Fantasy: The Spirits Within (also featuring Woods, funnily enough), Ark was developed as another attempt to combine state of the art computer animation with high-octane thrills. Woods provides the heavy duty character of Jallak, General of the Army who rule over the Storrians. Not as well known as the Final Fantasy film, but in some ways very similar, it is rather entertaining and has a good plot. The main reason to watch though, or in this case listen, is for the voice work, with Woods on particularly good form throughout.

In 2005, Woods appeared in an episode of ER, in the season 12 episode, Body and Soul, an appearance which is often looked back on as one of the show's finest guest spots. He plays Dr Lennox, a professor suffering from ALS. He first comes into ER after being found at the ice rink in his electronic wheelchair and is brought in for supervision. Telling the story of his illness and its development through memories of the staff and his carer, Woods' character begins the episode wanting to give up on life. He does, thankfully, come round to being more positive at the end, thanks to his former student, Abby, played by Maura Tierney.

First off, the episode is brilliantly written by Joe Sachs and creator Michael Crichton, and directed with ER's usual professionalism by Paul McCrane. But Woods is fabulous and on another level all together, capturing the horrors of his debilitating disease and also the strength of the human spirit. Rightly so, he received an Emmy nomination for his work, though I cannot for the life of me think of a reason why he didn't win it. For me, it is one of the most moving and affecting performances I have ever seen, either on TV or the big screen. I have said this a few times throughout this study of Woods' work, but my admiration hit a new peak with this.

I had seen the episode years ago, but re-watching recently, I was moved to the point I was slightly overwhelmed. What Woods does here is extraordinary. First off, he is utterly convincing when catatonic and only able to move his eyes. But the flashbacks are just as breathtaking. As we go back to 2004, he can still speak, but he slurs and knows he will soon lose the ability to even grunt. Further back, we see him at a gala dinner, suddenly choking and finding it hard to breathe. When he is in the ER ward later that night, he becomes overwhelmed and cries uncontrollably, one of his episodes of emotional incontinence. Rewind further, and we learn why Abby is so adamant that they do all they can for him. In 1999, she was his student, just about to quit. We are treated to one of Lennox's passionate classes, where he jumps around, picks up students on his back and displays his passion for his work. When Abby says she wants to leave the college, he subtly says he is having none of it and offers to tutor her one-on-one outside class. She has him to thank for her career. At the end, she takes to the ice rink and glides away as the credits appear. It's a tribute to Lennox.

Woods does not go for over dramatic flourishes, nor does the episode itself resort to stirring music and emotional pulls of the heart strings. In fact it is very blunt and to the point. When they operate to put in the tracheotomy, the blood oozes from his throat in a gory fashion. It is rather graphic in fact, but it fits the tone of the episode. This is a warts and all depiction of ALS, and Woods is flawless from beginning to end.

"Well," James began when we came to ER in our chats, "what's interesting about it is... I really wasn't ready to work yet. My brother had just passed away unexpectedly, and I was dysfunctional, just destroyed because I was so close to him. God rest his soul. But they called me up and they said, 'Listen, every year we do our Emmy episode, like an episode that's really special. It's written by the creators usually. It's always a kind of powerful guest episode.' So I said, 'Let me take a look at it.' And I looked at it and I was like, Oh my God. It was called Body and Soul and it was about ALS. And I got to meet all the ALS patients. They walked me in and they had a circle of people who had ALS. To my left was a person with no symptoms, and it went around ten people until it was at a person in a wheelchair who couldn't talk. You know, blowing into a straw basically to get movement. And the way they described it was that ALS in its worst incarnation is basically you're a soul in a corpse. You can't move anything but your eyes. Each person in that group could see where they were heading. They would say that if you have ALS, you got to start training for the wheelchair that has the straw now because by the time you learn how to do it you're gonna be at this stage. So it was like this horror show, and to this day I still appreciate these people giving me their time and experience. That really helped.

"And the script was great. And most of all, the star Maura Tierney, who played Abby. Most of my stuff was mainly with her. It was my connection to her character, and she was just great to work with, just great. We felt a real kinship working. And Paul McCrane, who was an actor on ER who then became a director, did a fantastic job. But to act and go through the experience of what that guy was going through, I just remember thinking that if I was ever diagnosed with this disease, I would literally pull the trigger. I'm not kidding. I mean there are some horrible diseases. ALS is just absolutely a bitter and horrible disease to experience. A brutal disease. Just brutal. And I have to tell you, I was so affected by that experience that it has stayed with me ever since. It was a very unsettling experience. It was a happy experience working with the people of course, they were just great. The ER set ran like a Rolex watch, it was perfect. But also the actors are very committed to those parts. They knew they were in a legendary, great series, and rightly so. It really got into the science and the deeper psychological, ethical issues of the day. I was very vulnerable at the time too, and it just broke my heart doing that thing. Maura and I had a great connection when we did it. It was like a father-daughter relationship, it had that kind of power."

When I brought up how powerful I found that performance to James, I raised the point that a lot of work is being done in his eyes. They carry a weight, a sadness, and a certain acceptance. "Funny you should mention that," James said. "I appreciate you saying that. One of the things Paul and I spoke about was the fact I couldn't do my usual James Woods type of thing where I am in control of my ability to wield language like a weapon or a tool. I said, 'I'm hamstrung in the area that I am most effective, as both a character and an actor.' He said, 'That's why it's a great choice, because we will have a flashback and we'll see how fantastic and on top of it you were before the ALS.' So I had to act with my eyes a lot; my eyes, my heart and my soul. That was a challenge that made it interesting. I mean it was written by Joe Sachs and Michael Crichton! Come on!"

Woods then turned to the action genre in Andy Chengs' End Game (2006), which stars Cuba Gooding Jr. as Alex, the US president's bodyguard. When the big man at the White House is assassinated, journalist Kate (Angie Harmon) begins to look into the killing. She meets Alex, who is especially guilt ridden, as the bullet passed through his hand and went into the president's torso. With Alex's help, she finds information on a shifty character named Baldwin, who traces them to the murky and untrustworthy Vaughan Stevens, played by James Woods.

Woods' character is actually there at the beginning when the deed is done, working as part of the president's security team. Though we might suspect he was involved in some way from the first moment he comes on screen (also during a scene when he tells Alex not to feel guilty and closes the door on him in a most suspect manner), the story is engaging and keeps us guessing. The all star cast, which also features Burt Reynolds, are great too and do wonders with roles which could have easily been flat. Though not seen as the greatest action thriller of recent times, it is a film which keeps you engaged to the end. Woods, of course, is deviously brilliant.

Though Woods' film and TV credits are the best example of his abilities, you cannot omit his contributions to video games either. Two of the best are Grand Theft Auto: San Andreas (2004) and Scarface: The World is Yours (2006). In the latter, Woods is George Sheffield, who was played in the flesh by Michael Alldredge in the

1983 Brian De Palma picture. In the hit video game, Woods' role is brief but he gives it a healthy amount of sleazy vigour. In San Andreas, he voices the character of Mike Toreno, who has gone down in pop culture as an alternative icon. For example, when one goes online, Toreno is in there with Hades, Lester Diamond, Jack Crow and his role in Family Guy as a Woods reference point. Indeed, it's rather odd that a relatively minor credit in Woods' rich career should become not only one of his trademarks, but something that generations to follow will be enjoying, seeing as "retro" games (calling this retro, to a guy my age, just makes me feel old) have long lasting appeal.

"When I did those video games," Woods told me, "I tended to do the exact opposite of what I did when trying to create a character. In San Andreas, you have to impart the character they want by the tone of your voice. If you're playing the villain you have a certain timber to your voice, so it's like, here's the bad guy! But if you're a character where you're not quite sure where and who he is, you have to be a little more up for grabs in the player's mind. You're playing a double agent. So they give you the tone they want, and they don't want you going out into the world telling people about the plot, when they want the player to solve the story. But it's fun, just a different kind of discipline for me, very regimented and devoted to the vision of the game's creators. There is so much programming involved, so anything you do and say then becomes ten times more complex for them to construct. So it's a completely different discipline; and a good one too. It's a good exercise for me as an actor."

There was more voice work in the big budget Sony Animated picture, Surf's Up (2007). In a cast that includes the vocal skills of Jeff Bridges as a famous surfing penguin, Woods is excellent as Reggie, a bad tempered otter who manages Tank the Shredder, a rival of the

341

film's surfing hero, Cody (voiced by Shia LaBeouf). Though primarily a spoof of well known surfing documentaries, Surf's Up is more successful as a straight forward family comedy, which, like the best of them, will please adults as much as kids. For the grown ups, much of the joy is had in hearing Woods and Bridges tear it up, having some guilt-free fun in this light and breezy treat. It received an Academy Award nomination for Best Animated Feature and was a sizeable box office earner, though not on the ludicrous scales of Disney and Dreamworks.

Woods in An American Carol, holding up Malone's latest script, Fascist America.

One really unusual and intriguing film was David Zucker's Big Fat Important Movie (2008), also known as An American Carol. This sharp, straight to the point satire boasts an outstanding cast of players, including James Woods, Kelsey Grammer and Dennis Hopper. Written and directed by Zucker, the comedy genius behind Airplane! and the Naked Gun films, An American Carol is immediately unique in modern comedy as it's a satire from the more conservative angle.

Here, Kevin Farley is a spoof of left-wing filmmaker Michael Moore, Michael Malone, who wants to put to bed the Fourth of July celebrations while he brings out his new film, Die You American Pigs and planning a new one, Fascist America. In a Dickensian turn, the filmmaker is visited by three ghosts. The first is Kelsey Grammer as General Patton, who shows an alternative America if the Civil War had never been fought. Jon Voight turns up as George Washington, and Trace Adkins is the angel of death. James Woods appears as Todd Grosslight, Malone's wily agent, in a lively and genuinely funny cameo.

I must say firstly that it is refreshing to see a satire from a less left leaning perspective, here poking fun at a far leftist ideology that could easily be perceived by some to be an anti-American and self hating. Hollywood is famously left wing, so it was somewhat brave of Zucker to come out with such a savage spoof of what some might see as over the top, anti-patriotic beliefs. The fact that An American Carol is so rare an outing though, and was greeted with hostile reviews, explains why more non-left-leaning filmmakers are less likely to stick their necks out. This aside, it's genuinely thought provoking and, most important of all, funny too.

SHARK (2006 - 2008)

James Woods has always shone in his TV work, but from 2006 to 2008 he was given the opportunity to really illustrate his power on the small screen, with his own hit show, Shark, created by Ian Biederman. For the two seasons it aired, Shark was one of the most exciting shows on TV. It starred Woods as Sebastian Stark, an LA defence attorney who has fallen out of love with the justice system when a wife beater he gets off ends up killing her. After a break from the courtroom, Shark makes a reversal and becomes a prosecuting attorney, devoting his life to putting the bad guys away, rather than saving them jail terms. He assembles a crack team of assistants and aides, underlings who he is, at first, rather heavy and harsh with (after all, they have to prove themselves to Shark before he shows too much respect). As the show progresses though, they begin to understand Shark's methods, and ease into his way of getting things down.

One of the things I really like about Shark is the Woods character. While other legal dramas will have their hero's whole life being their work, it isn't the case with Shark. Yes he is dedicated to the job (and then some), but he is also a father, raising his teenage daughter alone who has opted to live with him. Their relationship is strained at first, but they grow closer. He is an understanding father, and she in turn begins to see another side to him as the series progresses. It is interesting that the daughter believes his job was the reason her parents split up, all because the mother repeatedly told her so. It's later revealed though, that she was having an affair. Still, Shark is not petty. He says it was one mistake, and basically can see that when someone is not getting attention they may stray. In this regard, Shark is much more multi faceted than the more flat, cardboard lawyers of movies and TV. And he becomes a better father as the show progresses, even as he struggles watching the little girl he once knew growing into a young woman.

"What gave it real spirit," Woods told me, "is the relationship between him and the daughter, who he thought he was gonna lose and thought was gonna go live with the mother when she was about to re-marry. Danielle Pannabaker was just fantastic as the daughter. We had such a rapport. And we had a different director each week, and we'd say, 'Where are you thinking about putting the camera? Just shoot this, watch!' And we would literally without rehearsal shoot a scene, she and I, because we just knew! She'd come in and know how to stand. She'd put her head on my shoulder because she was feeling sad about something to do with her mother. These great touches that we had... You know, we were two people who were wary of each other because we had been estranged, but we were discovering each other as a father and a daughter. She was very good, just a brilliant actress, I thought."

As an added detail, James told me that they were going to replace Danielle at the end of Season One. "I said, 'Are you on crack? She's the best thing about this show! Look, I took this series because I didn't wanna do a procedural cop/lawyer show. There's a million of them. I'm not disrespecting them; they have tremendous, well deserved audiences, but I didn't wanna do that kind of show. I wanted a more human element being involved, and having this complex relationship with the estranged daughter, trying to understand her, it makes the show.' And I insisted, I said, 'If she goes, the series is over.' I threatened to quit. I was very adamant about it. Not that I was throwing my weight around, but it did help to be the star of the show. If you are ever going to use that kind of political currency, that kind of weight - I mean, it's Shark, you can't get rid of Shark, that's the show, that's it! So, I was aware of that, and didn't tend to throw my weight around. But this one time I felt it was fundamentally damaging to the show in the way I had always envisioned it and on the basis I accepted it, it would have been destroyed. So I wasn't going to allow that to happen."

On the law side, Shark feels 100% authentic, and that's because time and care was invested in ensuring each episode had a plausible plot. As James told me: "Well we had Bob Shapiro, who's a friend of mine and a great, great lawyer, who was our main technical adviser. But we had other lawyers. Of all the writers - and we had a big writer's room - a couple of those people were also lawyers as well as writers. And they would look everything up, and they'd call specialists on things, so they did tremendous amounts of research to get it right. And the creator, Ian, he was very clever about making those stories come to life based on legal technicalities that were inventive. And again, we'd push the limits of the law for the sake of telling the story. Ian said, 'I always write for you, for your tone,' so he was very clever in that way. There was once a New Yorker article where they quoted four great lines I had, and Ian laughed and said, 'well, they quote four of my best lines and you ad-libbed three of them.' Well, OK (Laughs). But I didn't ad lib that much because he wrote so well and there was so much tense legal stuff that you had to keep it alive and keep a sense of urgency and drama to it. You couldn't just be making wise cracks in the middle of this complex legal stuff. "

Shark was hugely popular during its run, and reviewers praised Woods' performance throughout. New York Times memorably wrote: "Shark, a new drama on CBS, has it the other way around: the lead prosecutor in Los Angeles's high-profile crime unit earned his predatory nickname by being ruthless, glib and sleazy. Naturally he is played by James Woods. There aren't that many living actors who can tap into the joys of villainy. Kevin Spacey is one, and certainly

James Spader has had great moments. Mr Woods, however, has been doing it longer, in a career that spans The Onion Field and the voice of Hades in Hercules. He is fearless, as demonstrated by his recent self-parodying cameo on Entourage. As Sebastian Stark, a high-priced trial lawyer who switches sides, Mr. Woods has found a television role that suits his gift and runs away with it. And that could be one reason Spike Lee chose to direct the pilot episode. In full harangue Mr Woods is a pleasure to watch: he wheedles, bullies and whiplashes his words better than almost anyone. But Stark's egotism and passion for winning are undercut by fatherhood: he is a loving, self-absorbed dad who can't remember birthdays or grades and is pained by his failures. In those rare family moments when Stark is still, silent and at a loss for words, he is even more eloquent."

Though a dad facing daily predicaments (his daughter's growing interest in starting a sex life) in the office and the courtroom he is every bit a crusader for justice. Like True Believer's Eddie Dodd (without the slightly crusty counter-cultural left-over air) his commitment is tireless. Shark is one of Woods' most memorable characters and it's a shame we weren't treated to more episodes. That said, the two seasons we have are a goldmine.

FAMILY GUY: 2005 - 2016

You can't explore James Woods' career on TV and film without mentioning his recurring role as himself in Seth MacFarlane's massively popular Family Guy. He appeared in 8 episodes between 2005 and 2016, as himself of course, and his first outing was in Season Four's Peter's Got Woods episode. The plot involves Woods coming to town when Peter Griffin informs him they are changing the name of their local school from James Woods High School to Martin Luther King High School. Unexpectedly, Woods welcomes the idea and says so at the town meeting. Once the matter is settled (it remains James Woods High), rather than leaving straight for Hollywood, James sticks around and becomes Peter's pal. But after a while, Peter gets sick of him. They hilariously have a movie night, enjoying a screening of Videodrome. "Is there nudity in it?" asks Peter. "Yes, I get naked," replies Woods. In the end, Griffin hatches a plan to get rid of Woods. He lays down a trail of candy, which leads him to a box trap, making him ready for shipping out of town and into a mass storage facility, rather like the one we see at the end of Raiders of the Lost Ark. But this is not the last Peter sees of James Woods. The episode is full of great gags, brilliant Woods ad-libs and a catchy-as-hell song. Once you've heard the "I've Got James Woods" ditty you will never get it out of your head.

When I asked James about his experiences on Family Guy, his voice lit up: "Me and Seth became pretty cool friends. But it was interesting how I got into the Family Guy thing. Ben Stiller was doing a table read - I mean, I think Ben Stiller is a genius, I just love his stuff. So he had this thing he was doing called Confederate Land, a very funny idea, just ridiculous, about a Confederate Amusement Park. Really funny. But he invited me, Nick Nolte and a bunch of actors to do this table read. One of the guys came up to me afterwards and he said, 'Hi my name's Danny Smith. We play at Meadowbrook Golf Course in Rhode Island.' It's a really rugged, low key country golf club. I used to go with my late brother Michael. I loved my brother so much. We were so close. We were famous for being close. But sadly I lost him, God rest his soul. But we used to go there, and Danny Smith said, 'I know you and your brother play at Meadowbrook.' I said, 'Yeah we play there all the time!' he said, 'Yeah we have our Family Guy reunion there every year!' So I said, 'Oh, you're from Family Guy? I should sue you guys for using my name for the high school.' Of course I was kidding, but I said, 'I won't sue you if you write me an episode.' Again, kidding. And he said, 'Oh my God, would you do it if we wrote you an episode?' I said, 'Yeah!' We swapped number and that was that. And I thought that was the end of it. Three weeks later I get a call and they said, 'Well, we got your episode!' 'Of what?' 'Family Guy! Come on in!' So I went in. I read the episode and it was the "Ooh Piece of Candy" episode. It was fabulous, the star of the episode! I was like, 'Oh my God this is wonderful!' So I went in, did it all with Seth. It was the first one of the season and it was a smash hit. To this day I've had people say "Ooh Piece of Candy" to me a million times."

James then told me that when it comes to the Piece of Candy joke (unless you've been living under a rock, you will get this reference) he often felt like Margret Dumont in the Marx Brothers movies. Margret famously didn't understand the Marx Brother's humour, Groucho's lines in particular. "I remember saying to my brother, 'I'm the Margret Dumont of Family Guy! What is so funny about the piece of candy episode?' And he said' Jimmy, are you fucking kidding me? You're going up the stairs saying the same thing a thousand times and they store you away! It's beyond funny!' And the funny thing is, Seth told me to keeping saying 'Ooh, Piece of Candy.' And I said, 'Seth, why not just have me say it once or twice and then repeat it?' But he said there was something funny about it being almost exactly the same every time. So I just did it. And I never understood what was so funny about it. I swear, to this day I think, Well I guess it's funny (laughs). I mean, I got what was so funny about the rest of it. But for some reason, that joke... I mean, afterwards I would be on movie sets, and I'd look on the floor and I'd see a piece of candy, then I'd see more and more, and then there'd be a box there with a string. The whole crew would be laughing. Crews were always trying to trap me on sets. I was doing a movie once and there was all these M and Ms on a desk and I was like, 'What the fuck?' And there was a little tiny box at the end. It was so funny. I had a blast doing Family Guy!"

For me the best episode is And Then There Were None, where many of the show's recurring characters are invited to a mansion for a dinner by a mysterious figure... who happens to be James Woods. Hilarious from start to finish, it has extra value for me personally because it brings to mind Woods as Secretary Bailey, inviting Noodles to his mansion at the end of Once Upon a Time in America. One cannot help but laugh when, after taking longer than expected in the bathroom, Woods apologises for the delay, because he was distracted by, and enjoying, the sight of his own penis.

352

SCREEN HIGHLIGHTS:
2010 - 2013

When you look through the decades and see the shifts in tastes and approach to filmmaking, it's arguable that there has never been a more drastic shift than in the past decade or so. It seems that the further we got into the new millennium, the more Superhero movies began to dominate the box office. Here are films that cost hundreds of millions to make, and which aren't considered successful unless they take a billion in ticket sales. Gone are the days when Hollywood could take a risk on a quirky thriller, an intense character study, or a dark drama. If the protagonists aren't dressed in spandex, showing off well defined pecs and abs, or running around shooting lasers in space operas, then Hollywood aren't interested.

James Woods, an actor who stands for creative freedom and emerged during the New Hollywood boom, was lucky enough to be in the peak of his fame while the indie film market was having major influence on the mainstream, when serious or provocative themes could be explored even within the constraints of a commercial blockbuster. At the height of this mentality, films such as Ghosts of Mississippi and Casino were box office competition. In just a short few years though, the monstrous blockbuster mentality seemed to push anything else out of the way. In the New Hollywood years and the decades that followed, the film industry was always very much a business, only it didn't shove this fact in the viewer's faces. While a sly side eye was kept on commerciality, films were still very much an art form. Now, the movie business is primarily that, a business, and everyone knows it. Where once a film might have been judged on its reviews and accolades, or God forbid its artistic merit, now it's the box office takings. A man like Woods, known for his spontaneity, his sheer aliveness, his vitality, wasn't ideal for this shift.

Though James has dallied with blockbusters, his priorities lie in attempting to define what it is to be human. "I've never really done many blockbusters, actually," he said in one interview. "I wouldn't know how to do them. I couldn't hop around in Spider-Man in, like, a little Spandex outfit. I mean, I enjoy going to those movies. I'm really glad they're making them, because it makes it possible to make other movies and it makes this business healthy. But I don't know how good I'd be in them... If you're the more mature, accomplished, middle-aged, white, heterosexual male in that equation, you're usually going to be the villain because that's how those things are set up. And to hop around in a little mask and tights, I can just find better things to do with my time."

For the next few years Woods did work in some interesting projects. But work must have looked trivial to him while there were real things affecting his life, like the loss of his beloved mother. Asked by TV Guide why he hadn't worked as much in recent times, Woods was honest as usual: "I went through a hard period. My mother was dying for four years and I kind of quit working to take care of her. I kind of never wanted to work again. The wind was out of my sails. It was a very hard time, watching someone you love suffer like that. I just loved her so much, and it was a very big loss for me."

At the start of the decade though, he did find some parts that piqued his curious interest and sharp intellect. Unexpectedly, he took on the voice role of Owlman in the animated feature, Justice League: Crisis on Two Earths (2010). This enthralling cartoon, which features Batman, Superman and many major DC heroes, focuses on a parallel earth where the heroes and villains have reversed their roles. Woods provides the genius villainy as Owlman, a role he seems to have relished and seen much to admire in when he was sent the script. Here he is playing a calmly psychotic existentialist, who insists that nothing really matters, even the destruction of all the alternate earths, which he plans on getting rid of by ensuring the prime earth is destroyed first. A subtle performance, Woods never even raises his voice in this one and is controlled all the way through. His part, and the film itself, is intelligently written and structured. Though he was a voice actor in a mainstream piece of entertainment, Woods saw a lot of content in Owlman which freed his imagination. He was, in Woods' eyes, very much a villain with a twist.

Speaking to Major Spoilers when the straight-to-DVD film came out, Woods said that "Owlman is a very, very modern character. He's really the doppelganger of Batman." He was drawn to his intelligence, the fact he was "a thinker... Owlman is a very calculating, dangerous individual because of his extraordinary brain power. And at the same time, it causes him to have incredibly dark, existential reservations about his acts. He's very self-destructive and self-loathing. The whole future of the multiverse may be in his hands in our story. You know, this process of creating a comic brought to life is very interesting, especially a sophisticated comic like this story. I had a thought of his being a very sardonic, almost charmingly sarcastic character."

What is great about Woods, and what enhances the power of his voice roles in particular, is that he looks at the role individually, removed from the rest of the plot and action. Clearly, as he did with Hades and his other finer voice parts, Woods examined Owlman as if he were a psychotherapist analysing traits of a warped mind. Woods had fun working him out, defining his less savoury characteristics. A man forever fascinated with human behaviour and the choices we make everyday, the key to Woods' most villainous portrayals being so successful is actually quite simple - though only because he makes them so. By not going over into clichés, he explores their contradictions, their twisted psyches, and resists from resorting to familiarities like evil laughter, the devilish voice and the comic book fiendishness, even when literally dealing with an actual comic book character! He takes such parts on as he might a physical role. Owlman is no different then, from Cleve of Best Seller, or Max of Once upon a Time in America. Like them, he faces predicaments and harbours dark motives that drive his behaviour.

Woods also saw Owlman (and other voice roles of course) as a chance to express with his voice alone, and to work collaboratively with the animators. "It's a wonderful character to work on because you have to do certain things with your voice," he said. "I'm a very passionate, animated actor. There are people like William Hurt, a wonderful Academy Award-winning actor, who are great at being very spare in the use of their voice. I am a guy who's a little more dynamic, so for me to repress myself, it leads to a kind of different character than I usually get to do. It's a lot of fun for me to play something that's not innately or instinctively what I would do. And then the great collaboration comes from these wonderful artists, including the director, the producer, the writer. Everybody has an artistic vision of how things should be and, when you work together, you come up with some confluence of ideas that creates a unique character. I really think we came up with something nice."

In live action roles he was just as effective as ever. The 2011 remake of Straw Dogs, directed by Rod Lurie, moves the action from the obscure English countryside to Mississippi, following a Hollywood screenwriter (James Marsden) and his wife (Kate Bosworth) moving back to her home town where they fail to fit in with the locals. James Marsden is just as effective as Dustin Hoffman was in Peckinpah's classic, while Bosworth puts her own stamp on the Susan George role.

356

Woods is fabulous and slightly frightening as Tom Heddon, coach of the local football team whose daughter falls victim (albeit accidentally) to Jeremy Niles, an intellectually disabled young man who's a little too heavy with his hands. The film's finale takes place at the couple's farmhouse as Tom and the boys (two of whom rape Bosworth earlier in the film) attempt to break in and retrieve Jeremy so they can act out their own unique form of justice.

Straw Dogs is an effective updating of the original and is, in some ways, a much better film. The acting, perhaps, is sharper, and the script makes events unfold in a clearer manner. The violence too has even more of an impact and, once again, we find ourselves quietly celebrating - with some guilt I might add - the timid writer's vengeful spree. I must add too that I can't think of an actor who would have played the part of Heddon as effectively as Woods. He is first seen in the bar after having too many drinks (shades of Curse of the Starving Class in these scenes) and gets the chance to really flesh out his part. His final sequence, too, is unforgettable.

Again though, Woods did not wish to make him an all out monster. To make his Heddon less cartoonish, he had certain suggestions for Lurie. "And of course this thing is done in broad strokes," he said upon the movie's release. "It's entertainment on one level, so of course my character's kinda drunk and tough and kind of a clichéd Southern red-neck character... and I said to Rod, it'd be interesting if he was a guy who was successful as a coach. He wanted me to flirt with one of the waitresses once and I said, I don't want to do that. I think this was a guy who was really happily married. Strong guy, tough guy—the kinda guy that if you came from LA or West Hollywood, would probably think was a bad guy because he was accomplished and very firm in his beliefs and he didn't agree with yours. I said it might be more interesting if the guy had been a good guy and maybe he got fired because he made some kind of comment that's no longer politically correct and called a kid a name that now is unfashionable, so of course he got fired for exercising his right of free speech, even if it's distasteful."

As Straw Dogs had transferred itself from England's Cornish outback to the South of the United States, the picture might easily have resorted to an overtly broad depiction of certain attitudes in that part of the country. By refusing to resort to predictable images of social types, Woods makes Heddon a more believable character. After all, in some ways, his motives are justified. Let's not forget, the man's daughter is actually murdered. So his anger is not irrational in itself, even if it all gets out of hand due to raised tempers and mis-understandings.

"In the original Peckinpah version," Woods told me, "my character was just another one of the tough guys. I said to Rod, who's a smart guy, I said, 'He's a tough guy, the coach, he has a lot of problems, but his motivation is to find his daughter, the one decent, good thing in his life. And he loses his mind over her being strangled. What part of that does someone not get?' Look, they are the villains, you end up as the villain. But again, you need to ask yourself, what is the character's quest? And this character's quest is very simple; where is my daughter? And the character's journey is, how do I avenge my daughter? So that's it."

That said, Woods knew his script and his character, and was aware that, though similar to earlier psychotic characters in his career, the only way to go was with highly charged anger. "I think one of the challenges of this character was to play a cliché," he said in a 2011 interview. "Not only in the perception of the environment, but a cliché in what I've done in my life. I don't want to do too many more snarling bad guys, but this guy was the epitome of that. And I was like, I think I'm going to jump in feet first and do what I've done before. There are no shadings in this movie. There are no subtleties in this movie. One thing about this movie is that it's balls out, right in your face. And I thought if I'm going to do this, play a snarling southern football drunk, angry violent man then that's what I'm going to play."

Producer Marc Frydman is the man who came up with the idea of remaking Straw Dogs. A long time fan of Woods, Marc told me he first saw him in The Onion Field, which he viewed at the cinema when he was still a teenager living in Paris. "My friend called me and he said he'd seen a movie called The Onion Field. He told me I had to see it. It played in a small cinema in Paris. I stayed until midnight and kept watching the movie again and again, because of Jimmy. I couldn't believe how good he was. And then I saw Salvador and I wondered, How can a human being be such an amazing actor? With Jimmy, you forget you are in a movie."

Decades later, and with Straw Dogs in production, James Woods' name came up in casting possibilities. "We didn't think we could get him," Marc told me. "I had never met him in real life before we shot Straw Dogs. So when I met him for the movie I told him I was a fan, and that my jaw was dropping. I couldn't believe it. A lot of the modern actors are great, but my memory of Jimmy went back to when I was like 18, so it was like, Wow! Rod Lurie directed it, we ran it by the studio at the time, we approached Jimmy, and he said yes, much to our surprise. It was great!"

Even though Marc has worked with massive stars on numerous movies, he admits that at first he was intimidated and slightly overwhelmed about working with James Woods. But pretty soon, as work got under way, his nerves eased. He saw that Woods was a force of nature on the set. "Jimmy improvised a lot," Marc told me. "Jimmy has an acute sense of what a movie is. Sometimes in improv, you don't know where to cut, and you've got to have a sense of timing. Jimmy has that, but maybe he enjoys it a bit too much. He did improvs that we kept in. There's a scene at the bar when he tells a joke, and we kept that. He was a complete pro. Just great. He brings electricity to a set"

Much to Marc's surprise, he and Jimmy stayed friends after production was over. They nearly worked together again on a project or two, but nothing ever panned out according to plan. For Marc though, being friends with a man he idolised on the screen as a teenager is something that still amazes him.

Woods told me that he liked Rod Lurie a lot, and added that they would tease each other's political views. He is, according to Woods, "a crazy left wing liberal, uber uber ultra liberal" (he says this with tongue half in cheek and with a certain amount of affection), and he saw the seize on the house during the finale as a metaphor for George Bush invading Iraq. Woods, understandably so, was slightly puzzled by this idea. "I didn't think anyone would get that connection. Rod is a great filmmaker, but I don't always think it's a good idea when you go in with a political agenda. It's the curse of death for a movie."

One of the finest recent works to feature Woods is Too Big to Fail (2011), the TV adaptation of Andrew Ross Sorkin's book, scripted by Peter Gould and directed by Curtis Hanson. Beginning during the 2008 financial breakdown, William Hurt is US Treasury Secretary Paulson, while Paul Giamatti is Chairman of the Federal Reserve System. Woods is on fine form as CEO of Lehman Brothers, Dick Fuld, who sees his organisation fail against all odds. The all star cast also includes Bill Pullman, Matthew Modine and Billy Crudup. But this is no "spot the faces" piece of novel television. It's an intelligently written, superbly structured and wonderfully played out chronicle of one of modern history's most turbulent eras. Heavily recognised at the Emmys and other organisations, Too Big to Fail also attracted highly positive reviews. It is, for my money, one of the strongest pieces of TV in the 21st century.

As Woods was playing another real life person, he had to approach the part with care, though he did not have to change his usual approach when taking on a character. Speaking to Charlie Rose, who asked what he tried to capture about Fuld, Woods once again opted for a multi dimensional portrayal. This was no straight forward bad guy. He was a man who'd been powerful for so long he had become complacent, in denial that his position could ever be threatened. "When I was approached to play it, I got the phone call. I had read the book. I was aware of the complexity of this story. I just did not understand how dangerous this situation was. And so when they came to me and said this is the story, I thought it really is like a thriller. As I read it and did my research I thought there is a distinction between a person who suffers from hubris and a person who does something criminal. Bernie Madoff is a criminal. As I looked, I said this guy (Fuld) wasn't a bad guy. He was a guy who thought he could fix anything. Let's put up the sandbags and the river is rising and the levees are breaking, but we can do something. This can't happen to us."

To New York Magazine he described Fuld as a man who "simply did not see this coming. He was Nero fiddling as Rome was burning." To Piers Morgan, Woods drew comparisons between big business and the movie world. They had a similar curve of success he said, the "as good as your last movie - as good as your last earnings quarter" mentality. Woods gives it a certain Shakespearean quality, this powerful man seeing it all crumble beneath him. He lends the film some genuine weight.

Speaking to me about this experience, Woods recalled an incident involving his old friend and contemporary William Hurt. "There was a scene where my character had to vote to basically destroy the company that I had built up, and I was fighting for my shareholders and my colleagues, and to cast this vote would be the end of everything. So Curtis Hanson said, 'I'm gonna come in on you, so take your time to make this decision.' And I'm not kidding, I took like 45 seconds. And they kept it, it was weird. It was a huge moment. But there was no music, no fancy camera work, beautifully shot though. And Bill Hurt came up to me a week later - he must have seen the dailies or something - and he said, 'That moment was a paragon of the greatest acting I've ever seen.' And I was like, 'My God! What?' He said, 'I was so impressed.' So first of all I was honoured that he would say it. He went out of his way to make me feel good about it. And I felt very good about that moment. But what was great was, there was no dancing around it. It was just a flat out embrace of a fellow artist. It made me feel great."

An interesting addition to Woods' more recent credits is Coma (2012), an acclaimed two part miniseries produced by Ridley Scott. Created by Robin Cook and directed by Mikael Saloman, the 4 hour tale focuses on medical student Susan Wheeler (Lauren Ambrose), who learns that an unusual amount of surgeries in the Peach Tree Memorial Hospital are ending up in comas. Dr Bellows (Steven Pasquale) is seeing Agnetta Lindquist (Geena Davis), the Head of Psychiatry, who may or may not be happy about Wheeler's snooping into the bizarre rise in comas. She learns these patients are being sent to the Jeferson Institute, a murky organisation run by Emerson (Ellen Burstyn), who has a strange maternal relationship with her sleeping "babies". Woods comes into the plot as Dr Stark, who aids Wheeler and Bellow in their investigations.

Coma is a superbly acted, sharply shot and engaging drama which aired in two 2-hour slots on the A and E channel in 2013. Had Coma been slightly shortened and made into a motion picture instead, I feel it would have made a bigger impact. That way, at least, it might have been made more widely available and enjoyed a longer life. Sadly Coma has already slipped out of many people's memories, despite the formidable list of names on the cast. This is a shame, because it's a consistently engaging piece of television. It genuinely keeps you guessing who's behind the mystery of the sleeping patients. (It made its way to the UK in a three hour cut, which aired on Channel 5.)

He was then part of the solid supporting cast in Officer Down (2013), a crime thriller from director Brian A. Miller. The movie stars Stephen Dorff as a cop with a dark past which comes back to haunt him as he investigates a series of female targeted attacks. A solid character study within an engaging thriller plot, Dorff puts in a strong effort, while Woods is sturdy as ever as Captain Verona.

When this film came up during our discussions, I raised the point that Verona rears his head early on in the film, and then fades out so much for most of the picture that we almost forget about him. When he does re-appear, only then do we realise how important he is to the eventual unfolding of the plot. Woods agreed. "Funny you should say that," he said. "When I read that script I thought, What am I doing here? Why would I do this? But then I saw the cast. I like Stephen Dorff - he actually played my son in In Love and War. A wonderful guy. I love him as an actor and really I like him personally. But in that movie I didn't even realise where my character was going until the end, and then it was like, Oh I see how he folds into this. I get it! I

363

mean, we had a cool cast in that movie. I don't think they had enough money to do it right, and it never got any kind of release or anything, but I don't think that it's a bad movie at all! It's a smaller movie but I loved working with Stephen Lang again. Dom (Purcell) I had worked with on Straw Dogs, and it was him that wanted me to get involved and work with the director. So I said, OK, and I just gave it a shot, you know? I thought I'll do it, I'll see what happens. And it actually wasn't bad."

There was a small bit part in Jobs (2013), the biopic of Apple mastermind Steve Jobs, where Woods played Jack Dudman. And he put in a memorable appearance in the acclaimed TV film, Mary and Martha (2013), a wonderful movie that for me is a particular stand out. Based on true events, it stars Hilary Swank as Mary, a mother who loses her son to malaria. At the start of the picture she takes him to Africa, a kind of time-out from school, where he was struggling and being bullied by two class mates. Though he comes to life in Africa, and thrives in the pure, earthy environment, away from his Minecraft and iPod, he tragically catches the disease and goes downhill fast. Mary goes back to the US for the funeral, but feels the pull to Africa. She returns, this time alone, and makes a connection with a British mother, Martha (played by Brenda Blethyn), who also lost her son to the disease. Her boy, Ben, was 24 and teaching children when he contracted the disease. Together, these two women, who aren't ready to stop being mums, commit themselves to spreading awareness of this awful disease which takes the lives of hundreds of thousands of children each year.

Mary and Martha is very moving and affecting for various reasons. It succeeds most because of the fine acting, with Swank and Blethyn utterly brilliant as the two very different mothers who bond over their shared tragedy. James Woods is Mary's politician father, a cold, distant man who always put his job before his family. His first appearance is at the boy's funeral, where he comes into the church and quietly sits at the back. At his daughter's home during the muted after-service, he stands on the balcony, detached as ever and says he forgot how beautiful her home was. "That's because you've only come here twice," is her harsh reply.

Later in the film, he comes out of his shell, when he agrees to help Mary with a speech she plans to make at a Congressional subcommittee meeting. He is fabulous in the scene where he says he will do all he can and pull all his favours. He lists off all the US casualties of war, deaths from other terrible tragedies and incidents. Yet even when putting all these deaths together from 1967 to present day, they do not compare with how many African children die of malaria every year. There are tears in his eyes but Woods plays it with subtlety, pulls himself back, resulting in a moment much more moving than had it been played by another actor. This is one of my favourite Woods scenes, because it's totally sincere. The way his eyes well up is a master class of emotive expression, and in making us feel the moment.

After she and Martha triumph at the meeting (where they pass around images of dozens of African children, now all dead from malaria), Woods comes towards his daughter with pride all over his face, holding out his hand to express his love. Given the man is built up as a glacial ice block (Mary says that she never remembers him on family holidays, on a beach or even out of a suit) this moment is quietly powerful. Woods plays it so well that you can't picture any other actor in the role.

Written by Richard Curtis, and directed by Phillip Noyce, Mary and Martha is a great little film which never goes down familiar roads and always keeps its reins on. Though the grief is captured more effectively than any film of recent times I can think of, it does so with restraint. It received positive reviews when first aired and given it deals with a very important issue, while also entertaining the viewer, this is essential fare. It also offers yet another dimension to Woods' abilities.

"Now the director, Phillip, and I were mutual friends," Woods told me. "We didn't really have a close friendship but we had met and spent some nice times together with Mace Neufeld, the producer. They'd done some movies together. So Phillip asked me to do this. Philip's wife, Vuyo Dyasi, is actually African. So this was a very personal thing for him. It takes place in Africa obviously, is based on true events. And I remember the big scene when she's testifying before congress. Phillip used all these pictures of all these children, which he used as prop pictures for children that had died of malaria. So Phillip would get everyone gathered, and he said, 'These are the children. I'm going to show you the pictures. But the real pictures we're using are of children who did die in Africa, but of AIDS, because we don't have the pictures of the children who died of malaria.' But he said, 'Every picture of every child I am showing you has died.' So he took it very personally and was very devoted to the story. I did it because I really wanted to work with Phillip. I really admired him as a director and person, he is such a quality guy. And of course to work with Hilary and Brenda Blethyn, and especially Hilary because my scenes were really with her. I was very happy to do a role I might not ordinarily do in terms of its impact. And it was nice to play a guy who was very restrained and at a loss and does this one gesture that's within his abilities for his daughter. And Hilary Swank is fantastic, she's just great. I was very happy to work with her. She was everything I hoped she'd be. So full of passion. And Brenda Blethyn is a fantastic actress, as you know. I wish I could have done more with her. But she was delightful, as you would expect."

He was back in political action mode for Roland Emmerich's huge budgeted White House Down (2013). Starring Channing Tatum as a man who is attempting to save the president and his own daughter from a terrorist threat inside the White House, once again Woods provides the villainy, but it's villainy with the kind of twist that only Woods could provide. He plays Martin Walker, the Special Agent in Charge who double crosses the president in an act of revenge and leads the anarchic attack with a view of blowing up as much as he can. Martin's plan has a root though; he blames the president for the death of his marine son during a botched attack in Iran. Though the plot and action often feels close to what we have seen before, Emmerich keeps it exciting, and the cast elevate it above other thrillers of this breed. Jamie Foxx is solid, but Woods steals the whole thing with a complex portrayal of a good man gone bad, but one who believes his plan is good and true. Critic Marsha McCreadie called it a "bravura performance" and I think she was dead-on.

Woods later revealed that he had been offered parts in two previous Emmerich films, including Independence Day (how great he would have been in that!) but had been unavailable at the time. "As soon as he offered me White House Down," James told me, "I said, 'Yes! Yes! Yes! I'll take it' He later offered me Stonewall too, but we ended up doing White House Down." Woods was glad he finally got to work with Emmerich, who he called in one interview, "the nicest guy. So attentive. Roland's a very powerful director, he's on top of his stuff. So we finally got to work together and I said, in a way, I'm glad. Because when you do a role with somebody, sometimes you don't get to do another one. And this role... it's the Charlotte Russe, boys. The creme de la creme."

Speaking to me about the film, Woods said that he had been unhappy with the part as written, thinking it rather clichéd in parts, even though he greatly admired the work of the screenwriter, James Vanderbilt. It was arranged that all three should go out and discuss how to make Woods' part more believable and multi faceted.

"We went out to dinner and I said, 'Obviously he's got a brain tumour and he wants to blow up the whole world. But rather than making him the mad scientist, why not put at the basis of all this a point of view that is highly commendable, respectable and its only vice is that people with the other point of view will disagree with it. But that he has a great validity about his point of view. So let's discount what he ends up doing... and not because he just wants to avenge his son who lost his life, because after all he does say he'd be able to accept the loss of his son as part of a great fight for this great nation. But for him to be sacrificed and then betrayed with a deal by a politician which makes his sacrifice worthless.' And Roland said, 'That's great, let's have it.' You know, he's got a point, but he went too far. It's an action movie, an adventure movie, and I am definitely playing the villain who goes too far. And obviously it's a Roland Emmerich, high octane action movie, basically, but with a political undertone that you can crank up and make work. So it was fun. And there are directors even in that realm who will work with you to make it more believable, even in an action popcorn movie."

That said, there are still moments of Woods magic. Midway through a massive battle scene, Woods goes off to one side and picks up a plate and fork, and starts to eat some cake, very casually I might add, as if he's a dad at a kid's birthday party. He even offers some to his machine gun-toting accomplice. "I actually did throw that in there yeah," Woods said with a chuckle. "I always try to put those things in because I think the quirkiness of it enriches the character for the audience. Gary Oldman does that very well. A lot of them people have that ability to ad lib and crackle the edges."

Though not an acting credit, it would be foolish to ignore Futurescape (2013) in a James Woods retrospective. This fascinating 6 part series, white aired in 2013, explores several concepts which will undoubtedly change our society in the years to come. With each episode focusing on a different theme - telepathy for instance, and robotic technology - the show is consistently engaging. Refreshingly, Futurescape stays away from the often ludicrous theories of many modern science shows, most mercifully of all, extra terrestrial life, a phenomenon that gets way too much air time on TV. The points are put forward simply despite the complexities of the subjects discussed, and Woods is a fabulous host, which comes as no surprise of course. After all, anyone who saw his presenting work on the Discovery Channel's Moments in Time documentaries, in particular Valley Forge: The Crucible, knows he is a welcoming, even comforting host who puts across the information in a concise and appealing manner. He is also playful, and it's great the way they were able to insert him into everyday situations, providing ironic commentary and subtle cynicism.

When the show aired in 2013, Woods spoke to the Hollywood Reporter all about it. He said he was at a point where he only took roles that were "extraordinarily special", and having enjoyed the Moments in Time series, had an urge to be a part of something similar. For Woods, the show wasn't about what man could create; it focused on the moral implications and one vital question: just because we can, does it mean we should?

"There's that awful, dreadful moment when you realize what you can do with science, where this fresh sort of creature emerges from the chrysalis and you don't know whether it's going to be something evil or great," Woods reflected. "Every sea change in the history of humankind has always been fraught with peril and embedded with promise. That's the premise of the show. It's possible that extraordinary advances in technology and science could help the human race move toward curing the most heinous of diseases and limit the ability to age, to live longer and more gracefully. By the same token, if these potential advances are not managed, we very well could be in worse shape."

RAY DONOVAN (2013)

Woods then had a part in the brilliant Ray Donovan series, created by Ann Biderman. In this truly excellent hit TV show (one of the most watched in recent years), the fantastic Liev Schreiber stars as law firm fixer Ray Donovan. Through Season One, aired in 2013, James Woods has a recurring part as Sully, a nasty veteran hit man (who is one of the FBI's most wanted men and hiding out in obscurity) hired by Donovan to take out his troublesome father, played by the fabulous Jon Voight. Woods is terrifying and fittingly cold as Sully, and he has some brilliant scenes and quotable dialogue in his seven episodes.

"Ann, who has been a great friend of mine for years, wrote something for me years earlier," James told me when we came to discussing Ray Donovan. "And I was the bad guy in it, but I was trying to get away from the bad guy parts. I met her and thought she was a fantastic writer. We never made that movie but we stayed friends." Woods then told me some hilarious stories involving him and Ann, which highlighted their wonderful friendship. Later, Ann told James she wanted him to play Whitey Bulger in Ray Donovan. He asked to see the script, and she informed him there was no script. Woods was confident however that whatever she wrote he would like, though he was adamant that he didn't want to be in the whole thing and asked to be killed off at the end of Season One. "But you might wanna come back!" Ann protested. "No whining," Woods said, "I gotta be killed. And if you shoot me, there's no trying to convince me to come back. I want you to shoot me in the centre of the forehead!" She was true to her word.

Anyone who's seen the first series won't forget the line "I always hated your fucking mother!" and surely won't be able to get out of their mind the awful act he is committing while saying it - killing his girlfriend. When I brought this scene up during our chat, we both laughed at the sheer blackness of it, that while he is killing her he's not above putting down his mother in law. Again, it's a Woodsian moment of realness, the fact that even a psycho like Sully wants to vent on his wife's mother. "I had just had surgery before that scene," James added, "but I did it anyway, and tore the stitches. But it's an art." But it is also one of the most chilling scenes I've ever seen, and the way he looks at her, with the dog leash in his hand, and the manner in which she looks back, tells us everything we need to know. We know what's coming.

"Ann was like, 'I should have kept you in for another couple of seasons.' And actually," James told me, "maybe I should have done a couple of seasons. It was such a great character, but I didn't know where we'd have gone from there. But I loved that character and had the best time. That was another great cast too. Jon Voight talked me into becoming actor all those years ago. So the first time I got to ever work with Jon Voight in all the years I've known him, after all the kindness, the first was on Ray Donovan. I said to Ann, 'You got to write a scene between me and Jon, and it's got to be a championship scene, because we've been wanting to work together for fifty years, and he's the reason I became an actor.' And you know what? She did t, and it was a great scene. I love that scene when we kill Rosanna Arquette."

When asked how he mastered Sully's Boston accent, Woods told TV Guide: "Well, I'd like to say that I'm a genius, but I grew up in Rhode Island, so I was nearby. To be honest with you, I struggled with it, and I was surprised because I went to MIT, which is in Boston. It's like when people say to do a Southern accent, the accents vary town to town in Mississippi. So we had a very adept and extremely talented accent coach, and she stayed on us all the time. I worked very hard on it, as did everybody else. It's harder on the guest stars — I was a guest star even though I was in almost every episode — because the contractual cast, they live that accent. We're dropping in and trying to get it right. It was a bit of a struggle, but it's what I do for a living. And I've had some success. But the irony was, it was almost harder for me because I grew up near the accent but not with it. My accent was just off. It's harder to do an accent that's similar."

One nice touch with this performance is the raspy voice. "You know, Ann came to me and said, 'What's with the rasp?' I said, 'Look, the guy's spent a long time living in a hotel room and not talking because the bitch is screaming every ten seconds, she's yapping. He doesn't talk.' This is the voice of a man who hasn't talked aloud for ten years."

On the subject of Sully leaving the show, I suggested it would have been a silly idea for such a wanted man to be seen swanning around in public. "Exactly," Woods told me. "The FBI's Most Wanted in the world, it's not like he's gonna be walking around without his girlfriend with no cash and no place to go. I mean, come on! It would be absurd for him to be out on the lamb, and they'd catch him in a day."

Ray Donovan is a truly brilliant series, and even though I totally agree with his reasons for wishing to have Sully written out, it's a shame Woods' part didn't last and go into the second season. But James added a little detail that put a sadly ironic twist on the whole Ray Donovan phenomenon. "Ann hates Hollywood," he said, "she just hates the people, everything. And in a twist, they ended up firing her from her own show. She was devastated, she was destroyed and she never recovered. They stole from her. It was horrible what they did to her."

Most people agree though that the first season was undeniably brilliant. The Guardian, in their original 2013 review, found it compelling and singled out Woods' remarkable characterisation: "That creeping sense of unease is assisted by a strong support cast – while James Woods has brought his usual slithering menace to the part of Whitey Bulger-style gangster Sully. When the show takes a chance with its material, forgets about emulating past shows and concentrates instead on letting its outstanding cast play off each other, then glimpses of another, more coherent drama shine through."

JAMESY BOY (2014)

There is another important film role to explore, the overlooked Jamesy Boy (2014), written and directed by Trevor White. Telling the true life story of convicted criminal James Burns (the real Burns acted as co-producer), the picture introduces us to the juvenile delinquent of the title struggling with life after building up a sketchy record. His mother (played by Mary Louise Parker) wants him to do well and attempts to get him enrolled in college. Though his wishes to go straight are sincere, he quickly drifts back into crime when he meets what for him are the "right" people, though they are very much the wrong ones. He ends up in the slammer and we are shown, unflinchingly, the harsh truth and daily difficulties of prison life. The film goes back and forth from his days in incarceration to the outside world, exploring the mistakes he made to end up behind bars.

Spencer Lofranco is strong as James, but for me it's the supporting cast that impressed the most. Ving Rhames is good as Conrad, a quiet, reflective, but tough inmate of the prison who encourages Jamesy Boy to write to block out the harsh reality of life ("It don't matter what about or if it's any good" he tells him), while Woods is especially great as Lt. Falton, the tough official who doesn't go soft on the prisoners to say the least.

His first appearance is classic Woods. After a yard fight between two inmates is broken up, we see his feet first, and then the camera pans up to reveal the formidable Falton. He basically hands them their balls, is unflinching with his words and ensures they know who's in charge. "You like it here, I like it here," he says, smiling. The smile disappears however when he continues. "The difference is I like it here 'cos this is my yard. You like it here 'cos it's an opportunity to suck dick!"

When I brought this scene up in a chat with James, he told me it was an ad lib. "I just let rip on that scene," he recalled with a laugh. "I did all that, but Jamesy Boy is a good example of this... A lot of the best writers are willing to let actors who have a gift for improvisation - they are willing to let them give it a shot. But it can be dangerous. In the old days you were burning up film, which is different now everything is digital. But you have to be careful it doesn't turn into an exercise of self indulgence."

The film is full of such moments and Woods is one of the film's strongest forces to keep the whole thing feeling alive. And he has another excellent scene. It begins with him quietly eating his lunch in his office (some kind of toasted sandwich by the looks of it, which he looks to be enjoying) when there is a knock on his door. He does the classic Woodsian eye roll and lets in Jamesy Boy, who is there to "tell" him to separate one of the more sensitive inmates from the others, because he knows his days are numbered. Woods/Falton gets angry. "Watch your tone," he shouts, before reminding him that in comparison to the 30,000 inmates, there are only 3,000 staff, who all come to work to face assholes like him everyday, terrified out of their wits. This scene reminds us we should not just consider the harsh environment behind the bars, but more importantly what the guards have to endure in their day to day working lives. (A thought not encouraged in most prison movies, which often make the guards out to be villains.) Aside from what the scene tells us, it's brilliantly played too. The way Woods lurches forward, shouting in his face, is close to frightening, highlighting how Falton feels about the lawbreaker and how he genuinely cares for his own men.

Speaking on the set of the film, a relaxed and happy Woods said: "I've been surrounded by a lot of first timers, but you would never know it. If I hadn't been told I'd have thought I'd gone to cinema heaven. They are very accomplished, very inspired young people. Spencer is great in the lead role; Trevor, the director, is very focused which I like about him. He reminds me of another young director I worked with, someone people didn't think would turn out to be so dazzling... a young Sofia Coppola. I knew she was going to a great one. He has that kind of promise. He has an ability to be decisive about what he wants but also open to ideas."

Trevor himself, speaking during filming, said of Woods that "as an actor he makes really interesting choices. He likes to be bold." Trevor said that James would always give him a take of what was written, but was also flexible too. "If we nail it," Trevor continued, "perfect. Then I just let him roam with stuff. And when James Woods roams, seriously, pure brilliance is created." Trevor also observed that he found Falton the character as they filmed, which suggests that Woods really was free to express himself, to improvise, to expand the parameters of the character. It shows, because Woods' Falton is a spontaneous firecracker and the picture's most authentic inclusion.

Speaking to me about such improvisation, Woods said that before all else he has a conversation with the director. "The first thing I am going to do is the script as written, and the performance as directed. Tell me how you want it and I'll do it. But then give me a shot at tearing it up." Performances like the one he gives in Jamesy Boy are a combination of these two approaches; one servicing the director, the other letting loose and experimenting.

White directs beautifully and depicts the gritty events in an up front, fearless manner, while the grey cinematography also enhances the dark gloominess of James' story. While it explores the harsh truth of surviving in the jungle-like atmosphere of prison without hesitance, it also sums up the challenges that come *after* the jail sentence.

James Woods and Andrew Dice Clay during the making of the TV series, Dice (2017). Photo by Sara Miller.

RECENT WORK

In the past few years, the usually selective Woods has become even more careful with his choices. In the recent half-decade, there have actually been few credits, but the reasons for this are valid once you look closer.

To go alongside his sizeable sub-filmography of voice roles, he did have another voice part, this time in Bling (2016), a nice kid's flick directed by Kyung Ho Lee and Wonjae Lee. But he had the most fun with American's most loveable and hard-edged outlaw comic. In 2017 he appeared as himself in two episodes of Andrew Dice Clay's underrated and hilarious sitcom, Dice. The best of the two episodes is The Twelve, in which Dice is cast in a crappy musical alongside Woods, which both men know is doomed. Dice begins to suspect that Woods can't sing, and confronts him about this fact, which prompts Woods into delivering a hilarious monologue about his legendary reputation. He is also involved in the episode's big twist, but I will not spoil the end in case any readers haven't seen it. For me, it's one of the funniest guest spots in TV history, and "Get some fucking sleeves" is one of the best closing lines ever.

"We had so much fun," James told me. "If you ever saw the outtakes, you would literally piss yourself. I'm in the bathroom and I'm singing, and I come out and I don't wash my hands and I just slap him on the face. It's so fucking funny, but there wasn't room for all of it. I wish it could have been an hour episode rather than just half an hour. I love Dice, I've known him for years. And when David Nevins, the Head of Showtime, asked me to do it, I said, 'I'd love to!' I'd done Ray Donovan for Showtime, so I knew David well and was happy to do that for him. And I just had a blast!"

379

He then did some voice work for various Justice League Action episodes (as well as a few special shorts of the same series), taking on the role of Lex Luthor, and giving it some real gusto. In his hands (or vocal chords), Luthor is sarcastic, biting, and sharp as can be. He is clearly having a great time too. In one episode, when being his usual Luthor-villainous self, the Justice League arrive to foil hi schemes. "Oh," Lex says, "I thought they would have sent someone more... challenging." Woods is so good as Luthor that it's hard to imagine anyone else playing him.

Recently Woods also reprised his Hades part for a new Kingdom of Hearts video game, but the Dice cameo, for the time being at least, is the last time we've been treated to seeing Woods in action. This is no simple case of a man retreating from the spotlight. Like me, Woods believes film has changed. As Martin Scorsese said, a lot of these new movies are not cinema, they are more like roller coasters, theme parks. For Woods, TV is the place where the decent stuff is being made. "These cable shows are so tempting because they are exactly what my career was based on when it used to be movies," he told TV Guide. "We have videogames masquerading as movies now. I say to my friends, Tell me the plot of any one of these big movies. Who do you care about? Nobody. I can't tell you the plot of any of these movies."

And since the superhero genre took over the film industry, what room is there for an actor like Woods, a man who works on intuition and spontaneity? "I just never got into the superhero thing," he told me. "Putting on tights was just never my idea of a good time." He then added, jokingly, "But I guess I'm wrong because I didn't become a billionaire. When people asked me, do I wanna do a movie like Salvador or The Onion Field, I'd say, yes of course. People say I'm a movie star, but I'm not, I'm a character actor who got opportunities in the independent movie scene. People say I could have made a ton of money, bought a house in London, a house in Malibu, had my own private plane. I don't want a fucking plane. I don't even like to fly." Undeniably, Woods played the game his own way and now, looking back, is perfectly happy that he did so. There's not a dud in his filmography, not a single thing he did for money alone. He did them all for the part, for the script. And it shows.

Though his legions of admirers miss his presence on the screen, that presence which was so strangely comforting even when at its most villainous, it's just a plain hard fact that the movies Woods liked to be a part of just aren't being made anymore. The roles that do come his way, and the scripts that arrive on his door step, just don't interest him. Where are the Once Upon a Time in Americas? Where are the Videodromes? Where are the Salvadors?

Speaking to me more specifically about this issue in 2021, Woods opened up about his decision to step back from movies. He took me back to the day in the mid sixties that he first wanted to be an actor. "You have to remember," James said, "that I had the scholarship at MIT and I only had half a semester to go. I called my mom and said, 'Mom, I hope you are sitting down. I've decided to leave school and become an actor, and I just wanted to get your blessing.' And I am not kidding you, there was a long pause. And then she said to me, 'I made two big decisions in my life at your age. One was to marry your father when I was 19. He was back from the war and severely wounded. I will have to care for him until he's back on his feet. And two years later I had you, and they were the best two decisions I made in my life. I made those decisions with my heart! I want to ask you two things. Are you making this decision with your heart?' I said, 'Yes I am.' And she said, 'Can you promise me that if you succeed or not - and I am not asking you to succeed - but whether you do or not, will you promise me you will give me your very best everyday of your life?' And I have never broken that promise. So when people say, 'Why aren't you working now?' I think, 'If you knew this story, you'd know why I'm not working.' There is no way I can keep that promise in today's industry. It's a lot of commercial fodder, just fodder."

But this is not the end of the story. James Woods may just reappear if the part is right, if the project is good enough, but it's got to be pretty special and unique to be worth his time. If this really was going to be the end of Woods' illustrious acting career, he can be confident and sure that he never sold out, never chased the big bucks or accepted any old part for a pay check. His integrity remains intact, his commitment to giving the best performance possible, to offering us a truth far greater than 99 percent of actors could hope for. He's worked with so many great filmmakers - Martin Scorsese and Oliver Stone, John Carpenter and Harold Becker, Elia Kazan and Robert Zemeckis, David Cronenberg and Rob Reiner, Sergio Leone and Clint Eastwood - and gave more heartfelt, compelling and enthralling performances than any actor I can think of. Going through his work as I have these past months (and the many years before I wrote this book), I can say in all honesty that I haven't come across a filmography like it, one that is so multi-faceted, so exciting, so consistently engaging. If there is more on the horizon, I welcome it with enthusiastic anticipation, for whatever might come next, we are guaranteed it's going to be special.

"But I think of Gene Hackman," Woods said. "He went to New Mexico, he now plays golf, he flies his gliders, you know? He's done a great job with his career, and he quit while he was ahead. It's like, I'm proud of the last few things I did. It's several years ago now, but I was doing stuff like Too Big to Fail, White House Down and Ray Donovan.

382

That little cameo in Dice of course. I did that for the fun. But I was on a nice little roll there."

There is also a sense of satisfaction with his career. Woods is a man who is content that he gave it his all, made good choices and stayed true to himself. In one of our last interviews for this book, he said to me: "I always remember the time someone asked me, 'If you could have anybody else's career, someone else's career in the film business, whose would you prefer to have?' I didn't hesitate for a second and I said, 'Mine.' I mean, I wouldn't swap my film career for anybody's. Have I had big commercial hits? Not on a regular basis, to be on a level of the top box office guys. I certainly got awards and nominated for awards, but all in all I always did movies that I felt I would be proud of. By and large I thought I did the best I could and that each film would be 'about something', if you know what I mean. A lot of these films, I think, could still be made today. Had they not been made then, so many of my movies could be made today. They are subject matters that people would still be interested in. I like to think my films had a resonance and that resonance has held up. I'm proud that my filmography seems to be standing the test of time."

I feel a perfect place to end the book is with something rather poignant that James said to me. During our interviews he would often go back to the wisdom his mother had shared with him. To this day, his love for her shines through, and I believe that lady, who sounded like a remarkable person, still influences and guides him in his life. "I once said to my mom, 'You know, sometimes I feel so unlucky. I work my ass off yet I feel unlucky. Do you see yourself as a lucky person or an unlucky person?' And she said, 'You know, I learned this in life: The harder I work, the luckier I get.' And it's one of my great quotes. By and large, I think if you work hard more good things happen than bad things, even though bad things still do happen. But I feel that I worked hard, sometimes had some luck, but most of all I had and still have some tremendous blessings. But the other great quote of my mother's is actually on the back of her gravestone. If I ever was upset about something, she'd say, 'Honey, life is a precious coin, and you can only spend it once.' And that's so true. You can only spend it once. And right now, the spending is good..."

Jimmy Woods and his mother, 1995.

Photo by James Woods. A long closed cinema, 2020.

Oliver Stone and James Woods.

JAMES WOODS
FULL LIST OF ACTING CREDITS

2019 Kingdom Hearts III (Video Game)

2016-2017 Justice League Action (TV Series)

2017 Justice League Action Shorts (TV Series)

2017 Dice (TV Series)

2005-2016 Family Guy (TV Series)

2016 Bling

2014 Kingdom Hearts HD 2.5 Remix (Video Game)

2014 Jamesy Boy

2013 Ray Donovan (TV Series)

2013 White House Down

2013 Mary and Martha (TV Movie)

2013 Jobs

2012 Sorcerers of the Magic Kingdom (Video Game)

2012 Coma (TV Mini-Series)

2011 Straw Dogs

2011 Too Big to Fail (TV Movie)

2010 Kingdom Hearts Re: coded (Video Game)

2010 Justice League: Crisis on Two Earths (Video)

2010 Kingdom Hearts: Birth by Sleep (Video Game)

2009 iCarly (TV Series))

2008 An American Carol

2006-2008 Shark (TV Series)

2007 Surf's Up

2007 Kingdom Hearts II: Final Mix+ (Video Game)

2006 Scarface: The World Is Yours (Video Game)

2006 Entourage (TV Series)

2006 End Game

2006 ER (TV Series)

2005 Odd Job Jack (TV Series)

2005 Kingdom Hearts II (Video Game)

2005 Ark

2005 Be Cool

2005 Pretty Persuasion

2004 Grand Theft Auto: San Andreas (Video Game)

2004 The Easter Egg Adventure

2003 This Girl's Life

2003 Rudy: The Rudy Giuliani Story (TV Movie)

2003 Northfork

2002 Robbie the Reindeer in Legend of the Lost Tribe (TV Movie)

2001-2002 House of Mouse (TV Series)

2002 Rolie Polie Olie: The Great Defender of Fun (Video)

2002 Stuart Little 2

2002 Kingdom Hearts (Video Game)

2002 John Q

2001 Mickey's House of Villains (Video)

2001 Race to Space

2001 Riding in Cars with Boys

2001 Scary Movie 2

2001 Final Fantasy: The Spirits Within

2001 Clerks (TV Series)

2001 Recess: School's Out

2000 Dirty Pictures (TV Movie)

1999 Hooves of Fire (TV Movie)

1999 Play It to the Bone

1999 Any Given Sunday

1999 Hercules: Zero to Hero (Video)

1999 The General's Daughter

1999 The Virgin Suicides

1999 True Crime

1998-1999 Hercules (TV Series)

1998 Another Day in Paradise

1998 Disney's Hades Challenge (Video Game)

1998 Vampires

1998 Of Light and Darkness (Video Game)

1997 Hercules (Video Game)

1997 Disney's Animated Storybook: Hercules (Video Game)

1997 Contact

1997 Hercules

1997 Kicked in the Head

1996 Ghosts of Mississippi

1996 The Summer of Ben Tyler (TV Movie)

1995 Nixon

1995 Killer: A Journal of Murder

1995 Indictment: The McMartin Trial (TV Movie)

1995 Casino

1995 For Better or Worse

1994 The Specialist

1994 Curse of the Starving Class

1994 Next Door (TV Movie)

1994 The Getaway

1994 The Simpsons (TV Series)

1994 Jane's House (TV Movie)

1993 Fallen Angels (TV Series)

1993 Dream On (TV Series)

1992 Chaplin

1992 Citizen Cohn (TV Movie)

1992 Diggstown

1992 Straight Talk

1991 The Boys (TV Movie)

1991 The Hard Way

1990 Women and Men: Stories of Seduction (TV Movie)

1989 Immediate Family

1989 My Name Is Bill W. (TV Movie)

1989 True Believer

1988 The Boost

1988 Cop

1987 Best Seller

1987 In Love and War (TV Movie)

1986 Promise (TV Movie)

1986 Salvador

1985 Badge of the Assassin (TV Movie)

1985 Joshua Then and Now

1985 Cat's Eye

1984 Once Upon a Time in America

1984 Against All Odds

1983 Videodrome

1982 Split Image

1982 Fast-Walking

1981 Eyewitness

1980 The Black Marble

1979-1980 Young Maverick (TV Series)

1979 The Onion Field

1979 ...And Your Name Is Jonah (TV Movie)

1979 The Incredible Journey of Doctor Meg Laurel (TV Movie)

1978 The Gift of Love (TV Movie)

1978 The Billion Dollar Bubble (TV Movie)

1978 Holocaust (TV Mini-Series)

1977 The Choirboys

1977 Family (TV Series)

1976 Raid on Entebbe (TV Movie)

1976 Police Story (TV Series)

1976 The Disappearance of Aimee (TV Movie)

1976 Barnaby Jones (TV Series)

1976 Alex & the Gypsy

1976 Bert D'Angelo/Superstar (TV Series)

1975 F. Scott Fitzgerald in Hollywood (TV Movie)

1975 Foster & Laurie (TV Movie)

1975 The Rookies (TV Series)

1975 The Streets of San Francisco (TV Series)

1975 Welcome Back, Kotter (TV Series)

1975 Distance

1975 Night Moves

1974 The Gambler

1974 The Rockford Files (TV Series)

1974 Kojak (TV Series)

1973 The Way We Were

1972 A Great American Tragedy (TV Movie)

1972 Footsteps (TV Movie)

1972 Hickey & Boggs

1972 The Visitors

1971 All the Way Home (TV Movie)

392

References and Acknowledgements

First and foremost, I wish to thank James Woods, who has been truly amazing to me through the writing of the book. For an actor I admire so greatly to be so enthusiastic and open is not only a huge honour, but also very moving. I cannot thank him enough for sharing his memories and thoughts with me. Our chats became a highlight of my week for months. It has been a wonderful experience.

Special thanks to Oliver Stone, Marc Frydman, Harold Becker and Tim Metcalfe for speaking to me on the phone, Jim Belushi for doing the Q and A about Salvador, Joe Wambaugh who told me about The Onion Field, Sharon Stone for her thoughts on Casino and The Specialist, Debbie Harry for her recollections of Videodrome, and to Dolly Parton for sharing her memories of working with James on Straight Talk. Additional thanks to Sara Miller, Susan Becker, Ash Baron-Cohen, Borivoje Vukadinovic, Marcel Pariseau, Cassandra Jaskulski, and Zoe Wilder. Also thanks to my partner Linzi for helping with research and feedback, and my dad Andy. Also thanks to Lily, my daughter, who became an expert at recognising James Woods on the TV, and asking me, "Why does James Woods always do the voice of the baddies in the films I watch?"

Magazines and websites referred to;

Den of Geek
Roger Ebert.com
Variety
New York Times
LA Times
Revue Magazine

Charlie Rose.com
Cigar Aficionado
TV Guide
Time Out
Metro
New Yorker
New York Magazine
The Face
Empire Magazine
Total Film
Hollywood Reporter
Salon.com
Reel.com

Books;

Chasing the Light, Oliver Stone
Oliver Stone, Stephen Lavington
Film Voices, Gerald Duchovnay
Caught in the Act, Don Shewey
Classic Film Series: Once Upon a Time in America, Chris Wade
The Garner Files, James Garner
The Films of Robert De Niro, Douglas Brode
Cronenberg on Cronenberg, David Cronenberg and Chris Rodley
The Films of Sergio Leone, Robert C Cumbow

Radio, TV interviews, Documentaries and Podcasts etc;

Fresh Air Radio Interviews with James Woods
Howard Stern's Various Interviews with James Woods

A and E Biography: James Woods
Saturday Morning Rewind: Interview with James Woods
Johnny Carson's Various Interviews with James Woods
Charlie Rose's Various Interviews with James Woods

Picture Credits

I want to thank James Woods and Sara Miller for sending me some great pictures for inclusion in the book. Photos were also licensed from Shutterstock and Dreamstime. Special thanks also to Ash Baron-Cohen and Borivoje Vukadinovic for allowing me to use images from This Girl's Life. Cover image courtesy of Photofest. Additional photos were taken by Glenn Francis, Alan Light, Larry Kang, and Chris Jepsem, licensed through Commons. If any copyright holders have been left out I apologise and will correct omissions in future editions of the book.

ABOUT CHRIS WADE

Chris Wade is a UK based writer, filmmaker and musician. As well as running the acclaimed music project Dodson and Fogg, he has written books on Federico Fellini, Marlene Dietrich, Pablo Picasso, Marcello Mastroianni, Bob Dylan and many others. He has also released audiobooks of his comedic fiction, such as Cutey and the Sofaguard, narrated by Rik Mayall. He records music with Nigel Planer, and runs a cult movie magazine called Scenes. For his varied projects he has interviewed such people as Catherine Deneuve, Stephen Frears, Henry Jaglom and Bertrand Blier. His art films include The Apple Picker (winner of Best Film at Sydney World Film Festival), and he has made documentaries on such figures as Charlie Chaplin, Ken Russell, Orson Welles and George Melly, which have been shown on TV, had theatrical screenings, and are available on various streaming services as well as on DVD.

More info at his website: wisdomtwinsbooks.weebly.com

CPSIA information can be obtained
at www.ICGtesting.com
Printed in the USA
BVHW040030140322
631363BV00021B/367

9 781458 379337